ACROBAT handbook

Adobe ACROBAT Handbook

Kenneth D. Grant

W. David Schwaderer

FIRST EDITION

International Standard Book Number: 0-672-30393-0

Library of Congress Catalog Card Number: 93-85104

96 95 94 93 4 3 2 1

Interpretation of the printing code: the rightmost double-digit number is the year of the book's printing; the rightmost single-digit, the number of the book's printing. For example, a printing code of 93-1 shows that the first printing of the book occurred in 1993.

Composed in AGaramond and MCPdigital by Prentice Hall Computer Publishing

Printed in the United States of America

Trademarks

Publisher
Richard K. Swadley

Associate Publisher
Jordan Gold

Acquisitions Manager
Stacy Hiquet

Senior Editor
Tad Ringo

Development Editor
Dean Miller

Editorial Coordinator
Bill Whitmer

Editorial Assistants
Sharon Cox
Molly Carmody

Technical Reviewer
Nabeel Al-Shamma

Marketing Manager
Greg Wiegand

Cover Designer
Michele Laseau

Director of Production and Manufacturing
Jeff Valler

Imprint Manager
Kelli Widdifield

Manufacturing Coordinator
Barry Pruett

Book Designer
Michele Laseau

Production Analyst
Mary Beth Wakefield

Proofreading/Indexing Coordinator
Joelynn Gifford

Graphics Image Specialists
Dennis Sheehan
Sue VandeWalle
Tim Montgomery
Teresa Forrester

Production
Lisa Daugherty
Carla Hall
Linda Koopman
Wendy Ott
Juli Pavey
Linda Quigley
Michelle Self
Barbara Webster

Indexer
Jeanne Clark
Craig Small

Dedications

To my father, James Pickens Grant.

—Ken Grant

To Mother, Father, Gregory, Melissa, Charley, Katie, Sweetheart, and the indomitable spirit of hope and optimism, Mr. Carrot. Mookie, we miss you.

—Dave Schwaderer

Overview

Part V Appendices

Contents

Foreword

by John E. Warnock
CEO, Adobe Systems Incorporated

Since Johannas Gutenberg's invention of moveable type in 1450, the business world has continually increased its use of paper to communicate visual material. Today, that growth rate continues such that demand will easily outstrip supply in a very few years. We use paper at a phenomenal rate, consuming trees and energy, and producing millions of cubic yards of waste in the process. The entire cycle of paper production, use, and disposal is straining the economic, environmental, and business infrastructure to a point of collapse.

Even if this growth rate is somehow constrained, the sheer volume of material that confronts us on a daily basis is overwhelming. Ninety-nine percent of the information—at least the information I get—goes into the circular file. I daily receive newspapers, magazines, catalogues, promotional pieces, forms, and all other manner of printed communications that I can't possibly store, because I quickly run out of space and I don't have an efficient way to retrieve it. There is no way that I can read it all because there is too much of it to carry around.

The current desktop computer systems offer the best solution to this problem. These computers are being equipped with more and more powerful processors and even larger memory capacities. Corporations are interconnecting these workstations with local and wide area networks, allowing the easy exchange of files. The future promise of a national digital highway will only enhance this capability.

What data, though, should these systems exchange? Current computer and networking systems offer only the crudest of mail capabilities, leaving users with plain text as the least common denominator. Users have different computers, use different operating systems, and produce documents with different programs. A user working on a Macintosh using Microsoft Word cannot exchange a document with a user working on a PC using Adobe Illustrator.

The technology of Adobe Acrobat solves this long-standing problem. Acrobat provides a cross-program, cross-platform solution. It provides a family of tools that enables users to use their current workstations—be they PC-, Macintosh-, or UNIX-based—to create documents for consumption by any other of these workstations. Users continue to use whatever programs they have been using. The important thing to understand is that user work habits don't have to change to use this new technology. And although Acrobat documents are designed for consumption, the textual information is not lost; it can be searched or copied into other documents, and the documents can also be printed, if need be.

Although Acrobat is simple enough for anyone to use, many people want a deeper understanding of a product. The *Adobe Acrobat Handbook* and its accompanying Acrobat files provide a clear and concise reference for all users of Acrobat technology. Its detailed explanation of features, extensive presentation of screen displays, and numerous appendices provide the reader with a complete reference for Adobe Acrobat.

I look forward to the many exciting things that you and others will accomplish using Acrobat and the *Adobe Acrobat Handbook.*

Preface

Adobe Acrobat has engulfed my life for the last three years. From my first exposure on June 3, 1990, when I was asked to write a "smoke and mirrors" prototype for demonstrations, until June 11, 1993, when Quality Assurance signed off on the master diskettes and sent them to manufacturing, Acrobat for Windows has been the consuming force in my life. Sure, there have been diversions from time to time—first to write *TypeAlign for Windows* with my good friend and fellow employee, Michael Diamond, and then to develop the frame work for Photoshop for Windows using C++—but I always returned to Acrobat (which was code named *Carousel* at the time). There was even a month-long diversion to write an installer for Windows Illustrator that has become one of the most leveraged code pieces the Applications Program Division has, being used over and over for one product after another. But still, Acrobat was the continuing drive. In the spring of 1992, Michael Diamond was added to the Windows viewer team to concentrate on text handling and printing. Later, in the fall of the same year, Ning Ju Nan was added to complete the Windows Viewer team.

At that point, Adobe Systems began its full-fledged assault on Acrobat. Most of the engineering staff has worked six or seven days a week since that time, with only the year-end break to interrupt the effort. Now Acrobat Exchange, Reader, Distiller, and PDF Writer are ready.

This new technology is a radical change in the way people may access information. With no additional tools other than Acrobat, computer users may now create electronic paper using the programs they are used to using, and exchange those documents—in all their richness and fidelity—with other users, regardless of the receiving user's computer, programs, or fonts. The potential for corporate savings is staggering. The potential for natural resource savings (trees) is also staggering. Corporate documents need not be printed; instead they can be "PDF'ed," written through a new printer "device" called the PDF Writer or distilled through a program that converts PostScript document files into Acrobat files called *PDF files.*

We have seen the word *Xerox* become a verb in general use in our English language because of its incredible ease of use and convenience. I predict that *PDF* will also become just as common a verb. Corporate staffs will receive their employees' manuals as PDF'ed documents. Phone directories will be PDF'ed or distilled and placed on networks for searching. In every conceivable form of information, including chart, photograph, table, and text, PDF documents will appear and be instantly accessible for viewing, searching, and even printing if necessary. And not just in the corporate world. Even students will submit PDF documents to teachers, having PDF'ed their work at home the night before.

Many, many people have been involved in the development and support of this technology. First and foremost is John Warnock, the visionary, missionary, evangelist, technologist, and first user of the feeble and stumbling code produced by the Carousel team (as it was then know). This was his dream and vision. He sold the idea to the board, proselytized to the world the need and solution, fed his unending enthusiasm to the team, steered the direction of the product, and suggested technical solutions to the engineering staff (after all, he wrote PostScript) when difficult problems appeared.

The second is Chuck Geschke. Chuck has been the leader and articulator of the core beliefs and values that underlie the "Adobe culture." To excerpt and paraphrase these beliefs and values as I understand them:

- Thrive on innovation.
- Treat each employee and customer as you would like to be treated.
- Deliver the best and most innovative products.
- License technology on a fair and impartial basis.
- Provide the highest level of service.
- Hire the best, treat them well, and share the success.
- Provide a fair return for the shareholders "...through predictable growth and careful husbanding of our resources."
- For the community, support charitable causes and public-benefit programs.

These beliefs and values pervade themselves throughout Adobe. In over 30 years of programming for different companies, never have I worked at a company that behaves in such a moralistic, caring, and sharing way. It is this family culture, the Adobe culture, that has helped nurture such success for PostScript and promises to do the same for Acrobat. Chuck Geschke is the one individual most responsible for that.

Third is Bob Wulff, the Engineering manager for all nine components of Acrobat. Never before has Adobe produced nine separate products on two separate platforms at the same time. Each component was an incredibly difficult problem. To manage this horrendous task, keeping each product in sync with the other products, analyzing problems, suggesting solutions, and tracking progress, while uncovering the most bugs, deserves admiration.

Two other areas need special recognition. These are the "Core Technology" and Adobe Type Manager (ATM). Without either of these, there would be no Acrobat. Two individuals stand out as having contributed a "critical mass" toward the success of Acrobat. These are Nabeel Al-Shamma and Richard Cohn. Richard should be thought of as the "father of PDF" as no other individual can. Although many worked on the file format, it was Richard's design and code implementation that solved the myriad of problems that Acrobat presented. Never have I met a more unimposing man, humble and pleasant, yet with piercing intensity. The most straightforward and elegant solutions became known as "Richard" solutions. More than once, when Richard was approached with a complex problem, he would respond with, "Why don't you just...," a solution that only someone who can see both the forest and the trees could present.

Nabeel Al-Shamma was the ultimate problem solver, be it on DOS, UNIX, Macintosh, or Windows. Need an ATM that worked before the ATM group could deliver? No problem, just ask Nabeel. Need better error handling? No problem, just let Nabeel add it to the core code and have it work on all four environments. Problem with the deleted resources in the file? No problem, just ask Nabeel and it will be fixed. And on and on it went.

ATM provides the marvelous ability for the creation of substitution fonts to be used in the place of missing fonts on a recipient's system. Without this chameleon font, it would not be possible to render a document for viewing or printing that retained the look and feel of the original document. The group responsible for this critical component deserves special thanks for their efforts.

And last, I want to acknowledge the other myriad components and the people that have developed them that represent components of the Acrobat technology solution. These include the Rasterizers for each platform, the PDF Writers for each platform and the many coming components, announced and not announced, that will provide the most complete solution of any new technology ever introduced. All of these people, too numerous to mention, need special recognition. As for the initial product line, the last page of the Guided Tour PDF file contains a list of these people.

In closing, I look forward to the exciting new world of PDF documents that I know will begin to flood the networks of the world. Good PDF'ing!

—*Ken Grant*
San Jose, CA
August, 1993

We arise daily to negotiate paper blizzards and accretion, oblivious of their social and economic cost. Massive infrastructure rhythms ephemerally unite, producing smudge-graced paper consumed with fleeting glances. Usually, recipients condemn the extruded carriers and their attendant smudge constituencies to causal, ignominious doom. Though many documents genuinely merit more than cursory glances, are they truly worth the tree branches and human bandwidth their copying, delivery, consumption, handling, storage, retrieval, and disposal require? After 500 years of printing and four decades of computing, isn't there yet a better way? These are not whimsical questions.

Consider how paper matter arrives, clattering for attention. Massive manufacturing facilities disgorge uniform cut-sheet rolls following wholesale forest slaughters and their slurry reduction. The earth oozes noxious petroleum, providing fuel and asphalt for fume-belching vehicles to transport paper to printing facilities. There, other transport infrastructures assist properly smudged and folded paper to begin its odysseys. The objective: retinal foveae time-sharing within an increasingly visually-intensive society. The projected impact: usually minimal, if even measurable. For preceding decades, personal time-management consultants advise clients to touch papers at most once. Back to the journey.

Human intellect and hands channel paper rivers, vectoring tributary rivulets towards properly addressed drops. This requires machinery and human bandwidth. Bandwidth means time. Time means money. Human bandwidth (time) means frightful money and concomitant delay. The journey continues.

Malthusian environmentalism aside, consider the fates of arriving papers. Discarding them implies litter, costly recycling, or ancestral reunions in overflowing landfills. Keeping papers (archiving them) implies their mastery and your obedient servitude. Paper occupies considerable space, so perhaps fossilized microfilm or microfiche images suffice (involving more people). But what happens when you can't remember where you saw something? Human bandwidth rummaging costs may well eclipse substantial retrieval costs—just ask lawyers involved in massive legal-discovery actions. And what about pedestrian human delivery delays? They often entail identifiable and sometimes substantial opportunity costs. Federal Express thrives daily by absolutely, positively compressing transit delays.

What we have here is not a failure to communicate—not yet, at least. What we have are wheezing paper-based information distribution systems mightily straining under insatiable requirements dictating additional volume ramp-ups. The storm's fury is yet to arrive as the mythical paperless office personal computer pundits promise increasingly assumes broken covenant status. Historically, personal computing's superlative paper disgorging capabilities simply exacerbate paper problems rather than help abate them. So printed matter deluges continue amplifying, posing increasing social and economic costs. We are truly writing checks we cannot cash. The time fast approaches when the hue and cry must be "Paper? Just say no!"

Conventional solutions simply cannot scale to emerging demands. The recommended way to get the best of problems is to never let them happen. And, so it is with paper.

Acrobat provides a timely departure from traditional paper-based information distribution models. Its first release exhibits singular design elegance and astonishing functional concussion. It blends existing and new mind-set technology to accommodate current printed-material preparation processes while solving numerous distribution, storage, retrieval, and referencing problems. Because Acrobat is electronic, it exhibits substantial distribution time-compression advantages and provides opportunities to discard or archive information without intervening paper reproduction and distribution activities. Text information remains, enabling machine speed archival searches using future extensions Adobe only thinly veils. In contrast to ossified paper documents and their conventional images, Acrobat documents are living documents that transcend their predecessor's paper imprisonment.

Viewing your first personally authored PDF document is a memorably personal experience, granting immediate Acrobat club member status. Today, you can distribute documents to Macintosh and Windows systems. Soon UNIX and DOS will have viewers. While I harbor no particular bias for or against any system, the Windows interface facilities seem oddly superior to Macintosh's interfaces. John, are you listening or working with different fact sets?

Finally, I cannot be completely candid without voicing my single enduring Acrobat disappointment. I deeply regret I have not authored a Reader or Exchange module so I could personally contribute to the initial product's development. Alas, another historic moment silently eludes grasp.

—Dave Schwaderer
El Cajon, California
August, 1993

Acknowledgments

I want to recognize all the wonderful people at Adobe that have made Acrobat such a wonderful product. Although you can find their names listed on the last page of the Acrobat Help file, I want to list them here to further expose their efforts. Their hard work, year after year, shows the dedication to quality products for which Adobe is so recognized.

First is the engineering team lead by Bob Wulff. Bob encouraged me to write this book and has supported my efforts from the beginning. This team, which included myself, was composed of Nabeel Al-Shamma, Doug Brotz, Scott Byer, Richard Cohn, Jim Cole, John Cole, Mike Diamond, Nathan Graham, Steve Hawley, Steve Herskovitz, Peter Hibbard, Paul Holland, Karin Jurcevich, Eoin MacDonell, Ning-Ju Nan, Mike Ossesia, Daryoush Paknad, Mike Pell, Lindsay Sanford, Mike Schuster, and Alan Wootton. Special thanks go to Nabeel Al-Shamma, Richard Cohn, Mike Diamond, and Ning-Ju Nan who reviewed the text of this book and made suggestions for improvement as well as finding various errors.

Next is the international effort including Monique van Gelooven, Anders Hagstrom, Gerard Ho, and Wiegert Tierie.

Then there are all the people in Marketing Communications including Gail Blumberg, Linda Clarke, Lynn Edwards, Lisa Wehrer, Lori Barnett, Lisa Beverly, Kim Brown, Alice Cassidy, Molly Detwiler, Robin Edwards, Elizabeth Fajardo, Karen Gordon, Jill Jones, Janet Miclean, Veronica Ramirez, John Ritter, Susan Verba, Min Wang, and Karla Wong.

In Product Marketing, Rob Babcock led the team, which included John Dawes, Frank Boosman, and Ellen Ablow. Rob should be given special recognition as being the single entity bearing the most pressure for Acrobat's marketing success.

The tremendous effort put forth by Quality Assurance was lead by Jonathan Sjørdal. Many people in his team, as well as others were responsible for various components, such as ATM for the Macintosh and ATM for Windows, including Jim Al-Shamma, Ben Arbogast, Geoff Arnold, John Brooks, Tom Cane, Peter Crandall, Tonya Crutchfield, Christopher Eastwood, Erik Max Francis, Louis Fuh, Jim Gould, Rob Heiser, Curtis Kunz, Steve Mcshurley, Will Naber, Denis Neema, Andrew Otewalt, Deborah Okner-Smith, Harrison Page, Clare Park, Rob Powell, Dina Sakahara, Mark Sonnes, Brent Walker, Greg Walker, Grace Williams, Rick Wulff, Tokuro Yamashiro, and Ada Yue.

Special thanks to Jamie Beverly, Sarah Rosenbaum, and Ed Svoboda.

Included in this Acknowledgment is Dave Schwaderer, who convinced me of the need for this book, took on the effort to secure a publisher, and then co-authored the book.

I want to thank my children Angelique, Larissa, and Scott. Scott's late nights at school enabled me to put in the much needed extra time on Acrobat.

Last, but most importantly, I want to thank my dear, loving wife, Libby, for having endured all the lost time together, not only from the engineering effort for Acrobat, but for this book as well. No one has contributed more to my success, both by her encouragement and her support.

—Kenneth D. Grant

This book was written in two and a half weeks. Contrails and sonic boom have yet to arrive. Such bold undertakings necessarily require teamwork. First, the Adobe Acrobat development and technical support staffs deserve top-drawer accolades. My closing Preface paragraph pretty much sums up my sentiments towards them—I hope they read it. I also wish to thank Jena Yankovich, Adobe Acrobat's Beta Test Coordinator, for admitting me into the program. Johannas Gutenberg would have been envious.

Next, I wish to thank the folks at Sams Publishing for meeting the brutal schedules a 2½-week, marketing drop-in book requires in contracts, schedules, marketing, and white knuckles. Many authors babble about their publishing support, which often seems curiously absent from their books. In this case, hardcore resolve at Sams flattened obstacles. In particular, Tad Ringo went out of his way to scrutinize the manuscript when he could have passed on it. Such dedication does make a difference.

Nabeel Al-Shamma produced a superb technical edit. Technical material accuracy is binary, and Nabeel did his job in product flux amidst development overload. Having done this five times before, I was glad to see his red pen hit portions with which I was unfamiliar.

Finally, I would like to thank John Warnock for taking time to write the Foreword. I hope he is as pleased with the book as I am with the products.

—David Schwaderer

About the Authors

Kenneth D. Grant is a Programming Manager for Adobe Systems Incorporated. He has a B.S. in Physics from Loyola College in Baltimore, Maryland, with graduate work in Physics, Mathematics, and Computer Sciences at American University and George Washington University, and over thirty years of programming experience. He has programmed just about every major computer system developed over the last thirty years, including systems for deep space radar tracking and object identification, scientific data analyses, underwater acoustical detection and signal analysis, business accounting, worldwide law enforcement, medical artificial intelligence, and library management. He has authored or participated in team efforts developing major retail software packages. Included in these are TypeAlign, LaserTalk PC, Window Personal Librarian, Adobe Illustrator, Adobe Photoshop, Adobe Acrobat, and many other software packages.

Ken is an active builder of wooden boats, as well as airplanes, having previously completed two boats and one airplane restoration. He is currently building a 30-foot coastal cruiser and is starting the construction of a composite two-place airplane.

The father of three children and master of one dog (Snow), he resides with his wife and son in San Jose, California.

W. David Schwaderer is an internationally recognized data communications and digital imaging authority. He has authored four data communication and programming books, and took time from his forthcoming *C Programmer's Guide to Digital Image Processing* (Addison Wesley) to write the *Adobe Acrobat Handbook.* He previously worked for EDS, IBM, and two Silicon Valley start-ups, and is currently a consultant on high-performance, visually intensive arenas. He is currently under contract with Sams Publishing to co-author *Industrial Strength Microsoft Windows and NT Programming.*

Introduction

This book provides you with the initial spark to ignite your use of Adobe's Acrobat products, converting the potential of Adobe Acrobat into an actual desktop wallop! This book additionally provides a handy guide to Acrobat product features that are not always obvious to casual users. Whether you are a casual user or a power Acrobat user, there is something here for everyone.

How To Use This Book

Part I of this book contains a quick Acrobat Exchange tutorial and Acrobat product overviews, including product relationships and hardware requirements. Part II contains detailed reference information for Acrobat Reader and Exchange. Part III contains detailed reference information on Acrobat Personal and Network Distiller programs. Part IV contains terse Acrobat product summary reference materials. (Some of these materials appear on the disk accompanying this book as PDF files, enabling you to reference them while using Acrobat Reader and Exchange.) The Appendices contain information that you may only occasionally need to reference, if at all. Finally, the Glossary provides a comprehensive set of Acrobat definitions as well as definitions for associated technologies, where appropriate. (There are a few surprises buried in the Glossary to induce you to read it and familiarize yourself with the terms.)

Understanding Part I enables you to utilize the remainder of the book in a variety of ways, including using it as a reference or as a series of tutorials. Therefore, understanding Part I prior to using the Acrobat products may prove advantageous. To this end, Chapter 2, "Escaping ASCII Prison with Acrobat Exchange," contains a quick tutorial that illustrates several Acrobat Exchange features.

Parts II and III provide user hints in proximity to associated topics where appropriate. Acrobat's features are surprisingly interrelated and often provide numerous ways to accomplish the same result. Reviewing these sections provides an excellent way to select techniques that compliment your personal style.

Finally, readers may wish to copy Part IV and use the copies as reference cards until they become familiar with the products. Alternatively, readers can access some of these materials using the files on the accompanying disk.

PART I

Paradigm Fast Forward

- From Gutenberg to Adobe
- Escaping ASCII Prison with Acrobat Exchange
- Acrobat Reader and Exchange Overview
- Personal and Network Distiller Overview

CHAPTER ONE

From Gutenberg to Adobe

Adobe Acrobat represents a radical change in the way people may distribute and access information, in much the same way that Johannas Gutenberg's printing press changed the way people distributed and accessed information over 500 years ago. To fully appreciate how Acrobat's electronic paper technology will change your life, take a moment now to step back in time to 1450 *Anno Domini.*

Gutenberg's Tears

Yes, there was social order as scribe monks scratched inked quills across parchment. With politically correct Gothic strokes and hand-painted embellishments, perhaps they mused that their cursive efforts embodied quantum leaps over primitive papyrus scrolls. And the annual book a scribe created went to a worthy social cause—namely, it disappeared into a sprawling authoritative hierarchy where knowledge was often power, and thus denied to the uninformed, "unwashed" masses. Meager production rates, and hence high costs, provided natural knowledge barriers, thereby preserving the status quo.

Enter Johannas Gutenberg

Johannas Gutenberg's fledgling moveable-type printing advancement was a confluence of wine press, mechanical engineering, metallurgy, and oil-based ink technology. At its inception, a paltry 10 percent of Europe's population was literate, of which the overwhelming majority belonged to the Catholic church. By 1520, 12 million books existed and 80 percent of Europe's population was literate. Pandora would have revelled; with liberated knowledge guaranteed, the world never looked back at pre-existing publishing methods. Luckily, Luddites did not appear until 355 years after Johannas launched his technology; Gutenberg's ship was long under way.

Publishing quickly evolved in ways that surely astonished the scribes. Social order rapidly transformed. Where information was once transmitted verbally, written information was now revered; the accuracy of the storyteller could now be verified by referring to the printed word. (Tell the fair's storyteller I won't be there this year. I read the book and he doesn't get the ending right.)

Document publishing formats also evolved, eventually coagulating from high-energy, extemporaneously free-form origins. Prefaces, forewords, tables of contents, chapters, footnotes, subscripts, superscripts, fonts in numerous sizes (typefaces), glossaries, indexes, cross references, and bibliographies emerged. (Bibliographies? Who previously needed them with so few books around?) Even woodcutters and engravers joined the ink-rolling extravaganza, developing new illustration techniques for the emerging publishing bonanza. Gutenberg's ship had not only sailed, it was greeted on arrival by wildly cheering throngs. And, other than incremental refinements, it essentially stayed moored moribund for 530 years.

Digital Tarmacks

Fast forward to circa 1981. Two development groups each work feverishly to complete death march development projects. A Cupertino, California effort develops Apple Computer's Macintosh computer. The other project, in Boca Raton, Florida, develops the IBM PC. Both machines exceed commercial adequacy requirements and annex zealous aficionado support. The rest is publishing history, although all does not come up roses without Adobe's periodic intervention.

Adobe to the Rescue

Despite Adobe's PostScript print programming language, users exchanging native electronic document files regularly had to flush the files' incompatibilities, even when using the same systems and document preparation programs. While floppy disk, byte size, and byte ordering problems proved nettlesome, "the font problem" became document interchange's intractable juggernaut. Sending documents to other locations that did not have the required document fonts doomed the documents to incorrect printing or displaying (rendering). Indeed, such rendered documents usually appeared significantly different than intended or, worse, not at all. The problem endured until June 1993, when Adobe Systems Incorporated intervened and introduced electronic paper with its Acrobat product family.

Adobe launched Acrobat's development with a few guiding principles, intending to solve electronic document interchange problems in flexible, permanent, device-independent ways.

- Acrobat must accept output from a variety of document preparation tools such as Power Point, WordPerfect, Word, Frame, and so on. These applications may execute on the same or different computer platforms, generating documents containing rendered text, graphics, bitmap data, and color images, as well as black-and-white images.
- Acrobat must transform document information into files that not only interchange across Acrobat-supported systems, but exhibit efficient compaction for intersystem data transmissions.
- Acrobat must display or print (render) transformed documents identically on supported systems, regardless of the system or program that created the original document.
- Acrobat should capitalize on continuing technology advances, gracefully reflecting improved technology with improved rendering *for all existing documents*, not just recently created ones. Restated, Acrobat's rendering of century-old Acrobat documents must harness the relentless improvements in technology of the intervening years.
- Acrobat must therefore comprise the world's first viable approach to render *living documents*—vibrant, visually luxurious electronic paper documents that endure and flourish independent of origin.

Living Documents

As examples of the profound nature of living documents, consider the following three examples:

If the United States' founding fathers used Acrobat when penning the Declaration of Independence, Constitution, and Bill of Rights, there would not be any crowds milling through the National Archives straining for brief nostalgic glimpses of these fragile, humidity controlled, light-protected, air-conditioned, nitrogen-bathed relics—grand as they are.

If the IRS used Acrobat, widely accessible income tax preparation forms would print on low-cost home printers, averting taxpayers frantic trips to copy forms for last-minute filings.

Acrobat's electronic paper implementation promises relief for the Library of Congress's mounting inventory problems, not to mention electronic library access for every community. Acrobat's initial watershed technology, combined with planned data superhighways, provides a remarkably viable foundation for electronic libraries housing unlimited electronic bookshelves stuffed with perpetually available materials.

Personal Touches

Acrobat users may personalize their compact living documents, without affecting the contents, by adding any of the following optional features:

- Superimposed "sticky" notes
- Bookmarks that can be arranged in hierarchic outline form
- Links—hot spots to click to view optionally magnified document positions
- Thumbnails—miniature page images that turbocharge document page viewing

And, unlike fossilized optical scanning, microfiche, and microfilm approaches, users can electronically search their living documents for text—text that may exist camouflaged within tens of thousands of pages. Acrobat's intermediary electronic paper format enables users to perform their activities on a variety of machines and interchange documents at will.

Preserving Document Fidelity

Acrobat 1.0 meets its daunting challenges admirably. To appreciate Acrobat's audacious scope, consider how Acrobat resolves "the font problem" with device- and resolution-independent mechanisms.

When required document fonts exist on user systems, Acrobat renders documents using actual system fonts. To supplement system fonts, Acrobat includes and uses one symbol font and 13 basic fonts. These two approaches neutralize many font problems.

When fonts are not present on system, Acrobat requests Adobe's Type Manager (ATM) to invoke its internal Adobe *multiple master font* technology, which allows multiple master fonts to masquerade for broad ranges of original font widths, sizes, weights, and type styles. This works because Acrobat's Portable Document Format (PDF) files contain essential font weight, size, style, and character width information, as well as specific font names for the PDF file's associated fonts. Acrobat users can specify that the font substitution use either the multiple master serif or sans serif font, both of which are provided by Acrobat. The chameleon font substitutions are so effective, even a close examination of a rendered document requires intimate knowledge of the original font to detect any discrepancies.

Although these preceding approaches are effective for typical English characters, other characters further complicate font substitutions. Specifically, major computer systems assign different internal codes to represent the same characters. Also, some characters exist in some systems but not others. For example, the Apple Macintosh apple symbol does not exist in the IBM or ANSI character set. This phenomena is particularly nettlesome with foreign characters.

Fonts possessing their own symbol-rendering codes further exasperate the rendering process. For example, different fonts may render the "@" symbol in several different ways. Acrobat solves character encoding problems by using standard encodings, such as Macintosh and Windows, and special exception encodings. As a final resort, Acrobat converts special character symbols into line segments for rendering.

These approaches collectively preserve document fidelity in device- and resolution-independent ways. Therefore, computer display and printer resolution advancements continue to improve document rendering for all existing PDF documents. This is only possible because Acrobat's PDF format is extensible and preserves document rendering data instead of preserving rendered documents. Simply preserving fossilized document images (bitmaps) forever dooms document rendering to specific resolutions, forfeiting the opportunity to exploit inevitable future hardware advancements. Finally, such digital "stone rendering" precludes editing the document in the future.

Storage Benefits

One final Acrobat PDF benefit is PDF file size. Stand-alone CCITT Group 3 FAX letter image files typically consume 50,000 storage bytes and forfeit any chance at resolution enhancement without extensive optical character reading processing. Original native PDF document files only consume between 5,000 and 10,000 storage bytes, a significant reduction by any standard. That means standard 200 megabyte disks hold approximately 30,000 resolution-independent document pages with vastly superior visual content at approximately 0.6 cents per page by 1993 costs.

For CD-ROM storage, the cost differential is even greater. The typical 1993 CD-ROM manufacturing unit cost is $1.00. Such CD-ROMs store approximately 90,000 resolution-independent PDF pages for 0.001 cents per page. At this price, electronic paper significantly eclipses paper and toner costs. Acrobat additionally mounts a full assault on facsimilies as the default electronic mail mechanism. Gutenberg would weep tears of pride for his prodigious invention's progeny.

Summary

A historical watershed moment of this profundity does not occur often. Acrobat arrived 540 years after Johannas Gutenberg set up his shop in Mainz, Germany. There is little doubt Acrobat's electronic paper technology approach will revolutionize the world in ways as inconceivable and profound as did Gutenberg's primitive press. Industries everywhere must necessarily brace for the global shock waves as knowledge distribution models tremble, convulse, and shear. It's a good bet civilization's order will again prove to be thin gruel against such a sharp tool—just ask the flabbergasted monk scribes who watched Gutenberg's ship sail beyond the horizon.

CHAPTER

TWO

Escaping ASCII Prison with Acrobat Exchange

Melissa owns and operates the *Health Club*. She drives customers hard (go, go, go, go, go!!!) with state-of-the-art equipment and fitness programs, expecting only what she expects from herself—the very best *sans* excuses, thank you. This is a regular problem for Dave and Ken, who prepare the Health Club's newsletter. It's not that Ken and Dave are turkeys; they have simply been unable to produce the newsletter reliably because they lacked the proper tools.

Dave prepares the Health Club's newsletter activity schedule using Microsoft's Word for Windows on a PC clone. Ken prepares the articles using another word processor on a Macintosh. Neither system reliably (never) reads the other system's files. Because Ken and Dave reside in different cities, they have mighty problems coordinating their efforts on the tight time frame Melissa (go, go, go, go, go!!!) requires.

Historically, Dave and Ken have dwelled in ASCII prison, a place that requires all entering and exiting text (e.g., newsletter) information to exist as lowest common denominator ASCII text strings. It is a miserably primitive arrangement for folks exchanging documents or, as in this instance, document fragments. Highlighting (boldface, italics, and so on) and formatting? Ha! Not allowed—go directly to jail! Do not pass GO. Do not collect $200.

This month, it is different. Using Acrobat Exchange, Ken and Dave exchange and integrate fully formatted document fragments in a few minutes virtually effortlessly. They each print the documents on different systems and printers, even though neither has all the necessary fonts and applications. Each can visually check the material without having to fax finished documents back and forth, and they can do it in a fraction of the time they previously spent attempting to perform the task. Let's eavesdrop to see how they do it.

NOTE

Don't Be Just a Spectator!

Rock and roll with Dave and Ken! Join the fun! This book's sample disk contains the DOC1.PDF and DOC2.PDF files discussed in the following section. You can actually perform the discussed operations (as Dave is going to ask you to do shortly). Just be sure to make a copy of DOC1.PDF before changing it with Acrobat's sharp tools!

Documents à la Carte, Ken, and Dave

Ken prepares a three-page newsletter using his Macintosh word processor like he always does. Pages one and three contain Health Club news; page two is a holding page that Dave replaces with the monthly activity schedule. Previously, Ken printed the document on a printer and faxed it to Dave. Now, Ken prints the document to a file using Acrobat Exchange's PDF Writer.

PDF Writer is an Acrobat Exchange module that pretends to be a printer, but instead produces an electronic paper PDF file. Ken does not leave his word processor application to use PDF Writer. Rather, he uses his system's Printer Setup feature to select PDF Writer as the current printer. Now, instead of faxing a paper document to Dave, Ken just transfers a PDF file, named DOC1.PDF, to Dave.

Unlike a fax image, DOC1.PDF contains all the necessary document information. Its transmission occurs many times faster than a fax transmission because of its superior compression. (For more information on using PDF Writer, see Chapter 13, "Exchange's PDF Writer.") However, Dave is busy with another project, so he asks you to insert his monthly activity file into the DOC1.PDF file he has received from Ken. Dave also used PDF Writer to create an electronic paper version of his activity schedule, naming the file DOC2.PDF.

Getting Started

Start Acrobat by clicking the Acrobat icon. Acrobat presents a standard Open dialog box, illustrated in Figure 2.1. Select DOC1.PDF as the file for Acrobat to initially open.

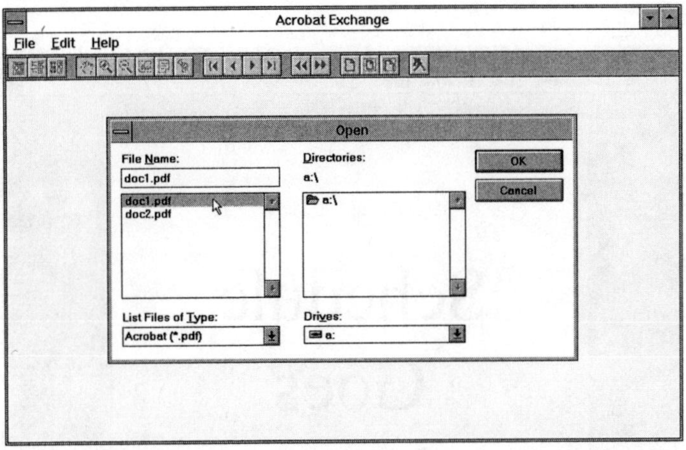

Figure 2.1. The initial Open dialog box.

Because you know Ken has included a "sticky note" text annotation to the file, first search for the note. Such notes are not part of the newsletter and are easily deleted from the file without altering the actual newsletter. (Chapter 9, "Document Notes," discusses text annotation notes in more detail.) Select the Find **N**ext Note command (see Figure 2.2); Figure 2.3 shows the result. Double-click the revealed Note icon to open the note (see Figure 2.4). Drag the Note window up off the page's text by dragging the note's title bar.

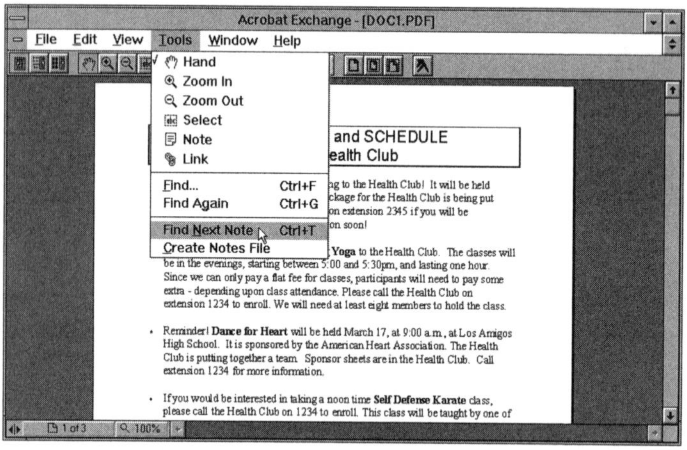

Figure 2.2. Selecting the Tools menu's Find Next Note command.

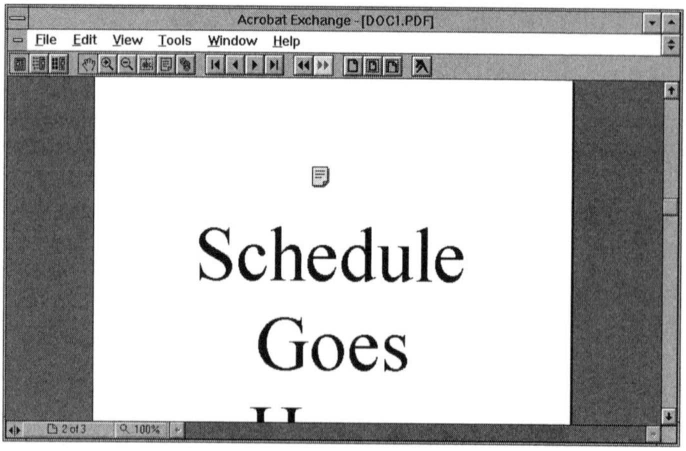

Figure 2.3. An iconized note.

Adjust the page view by using the Hand tool and dragging it up the screen (see Figure 2.5). (Chapter 6, "Document Browsing," discusses Acrobat's many ways to browse pages and adjust page views.) Next, reveal DOC1.PDF's page thumbnails by clicking the tool bar's Page and Thumbnails button (see Figure 2.6). Figure 2.7 shows the resulting thumbnails on the left side of the screen. Actually, Ken created these thumbnails using Acrobat Exchange after creating DOC1.PDF using PDF Writer. (Thumbnails provide miniature graphical page representations users can use to alter page views as discussed in Chapter 11, "Document Thumbnails.")

Figure 2.4. An open note.

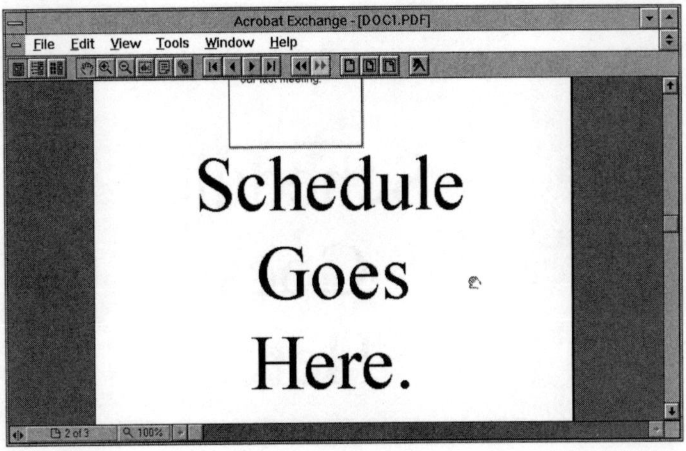

Figure 2.5. Page browsing using the Hand tool.

Figure 2.6. Selecting the Page and Thumbnails button from the tool bar.

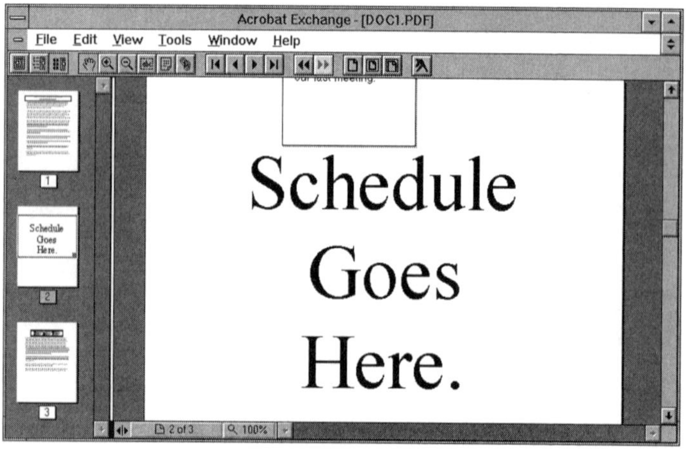

Figure 2.7. The resulting thumbnails and page view.

Deleting a Page

You need to replace DOC1.PDF's second page with Dave's DOC2.PDF activity schedule. Therefore, you must delete page 2. Then, you must insert DOC2.PDF after the first page. Select the **D**elete Pages... command (see Figure 2.8); then select the OK button in the Delete Pages dialog box (see Figure 2.9). Figure 2.10 shows the result. Notice that now there are only two thumbnails and that the document's page 2 is now the last document page.

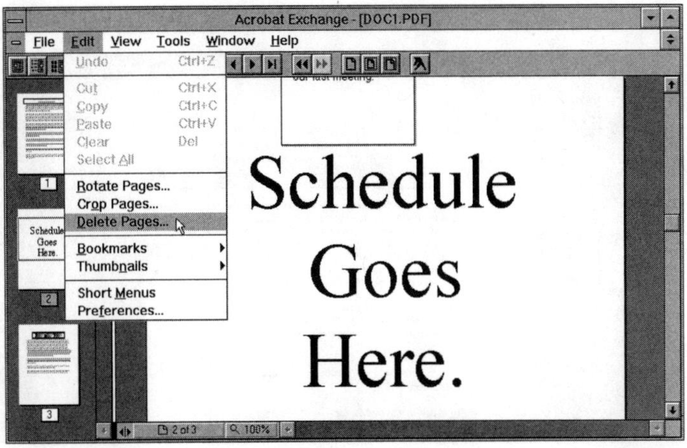

Figure 2.8. Selecting the Edit menu's Delete Pages... command.

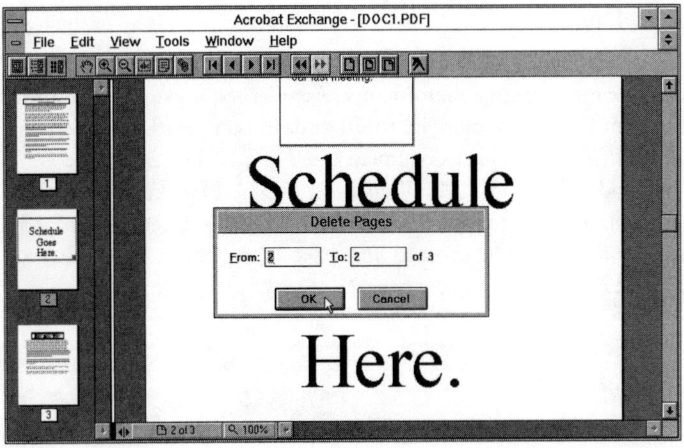

Figure 2.9. The Delete Pages dialog box.

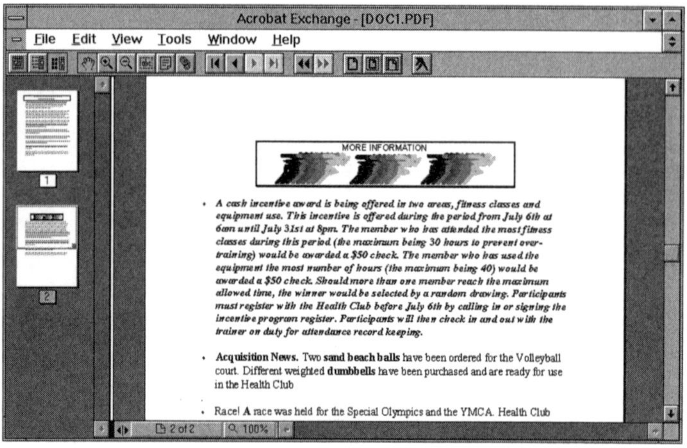

Figure 2.10. The resulting active page view.

Inserting a Page

Now you need to insert DOC2.PDF after page 1 of the current document. However, to maximize internal performance, Acrobat requires you to save the current document before any more insertion or deletion operations. Therefore, you must **S**ave the now two-page document (see Figure 2.11). Select the Inser**t**... command (see Figure 2.12); then select DOC2.PDF from the Insert dialog box that appears after selecting the Inser**t**... command (see Figure 2.13). Indicate that the file should be inserted *after* page 1 (see Figure 2.14). Alternatively, you could insert the file *before* page 2.

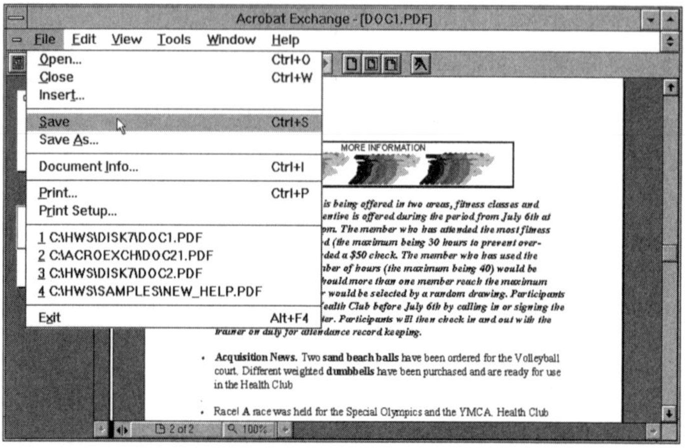

Figure 2.11. Selecting the File menu's Save command.

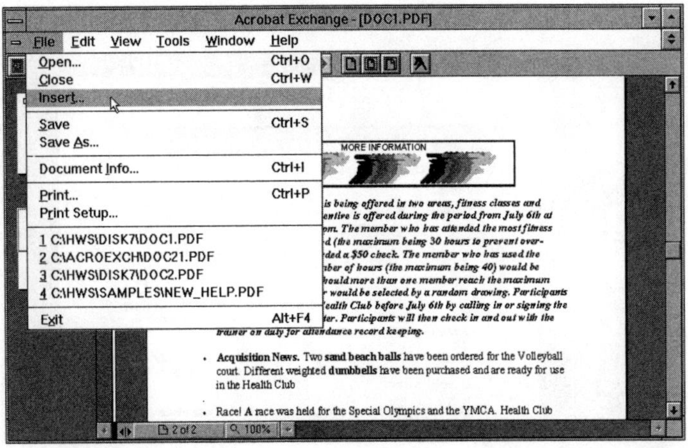

Figure 2.12. Selecting the File menu's Insert command.

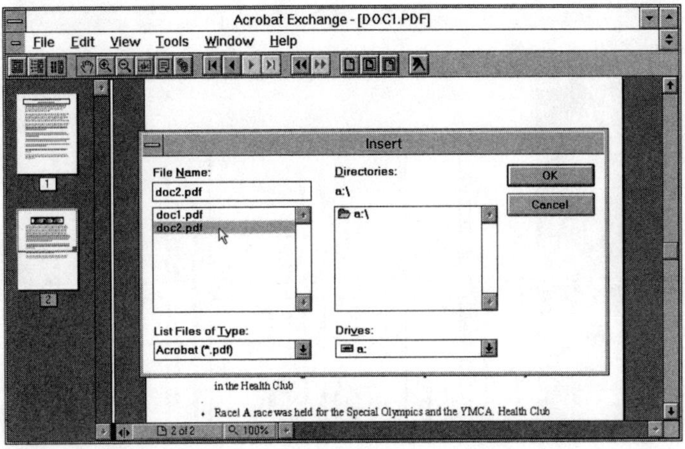

Figure 2.13. The Insert dialog box.

Rotating a Page

Figure 2.15 shows the result of the Insert operation. Note that there are now three thumbnails, but the second is completely gray. This is because you need to create a thumbnail for the inserted page. Note also that this page is in *landscape* mode, which is why it appears unaesthetically rotated. To fix this, select the **R**otate Pages... command (see Figure 2.16). To rotate the page clockwise, you need the top of the page to rotate to the right, and you only want to rotate page 2. Figure 2.17 shows the Rotate Pages dialog box, from which you can select these options. Figure 2.18 shows the result of rotating the page. Note that the thumbnail is also rotated, but it is still gray.

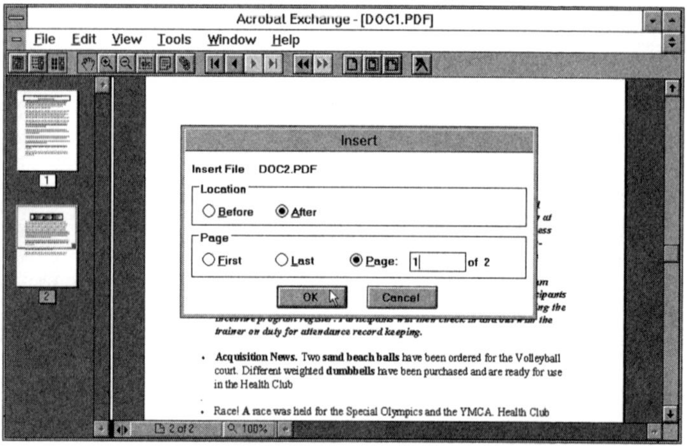

Figure 2.14. Inserting the page after page 1.

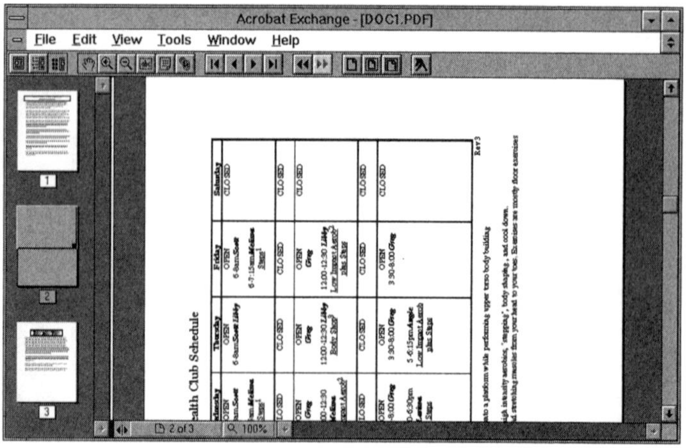

Figure 2.15. The active page view following the Insert operation.

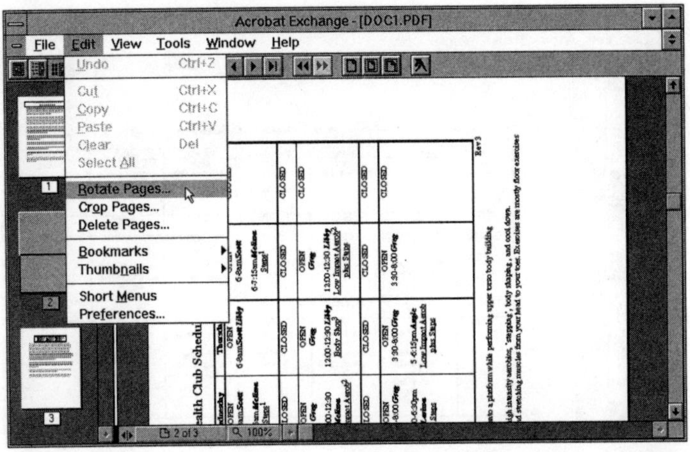

Figure 2.16. Selecting the Edit menu's Rotate Pages command.

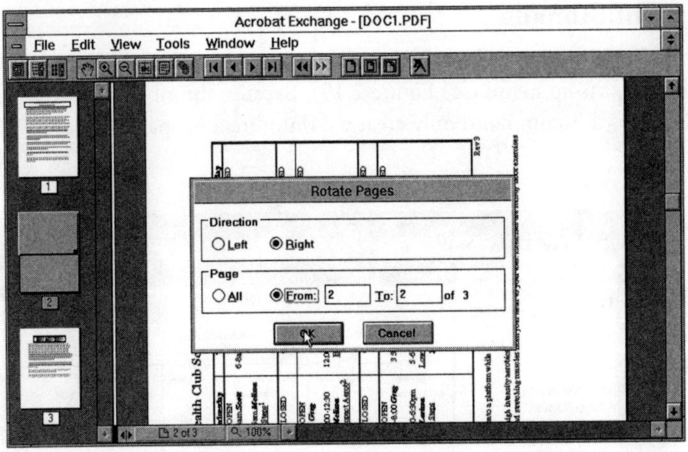

Figure 2.17. The Rotate Pages dialog box.

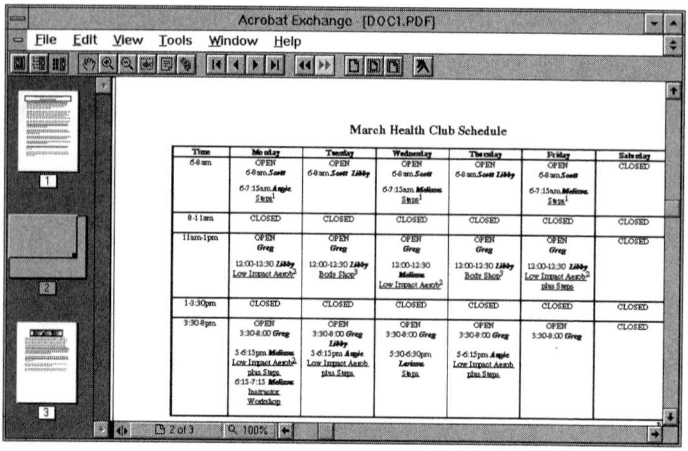

Figure 2.18. The resulting active page view after the Rotate Pages operation.

Creating Thumbnails

Create a thumbnail for page 2 by selecting the **C**reate All... command from the Thumb**n**ails pop-up menu (see Figure 2.19). Because thumbnails exist for pages 1 and 3, this command only creates a thumbnail for page 2 (see Figure 2.20).

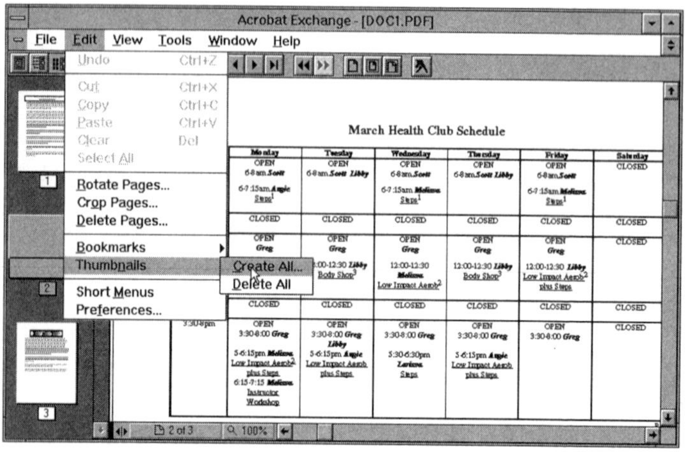

Figure 2.19. Selecting the Edit menu's Create All Thumbnails command.

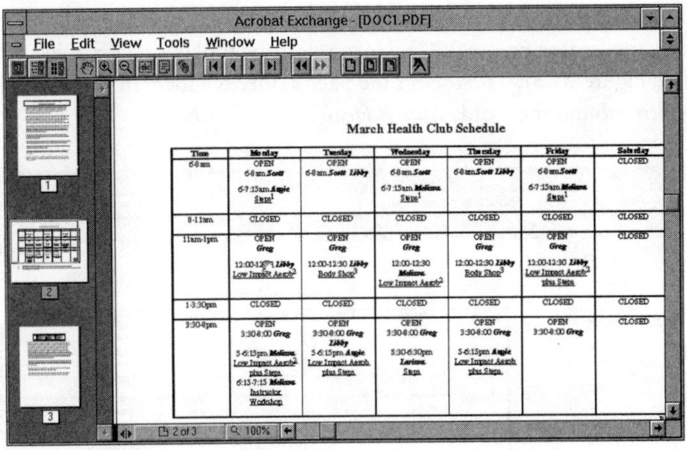

Figure 2.20. The resulting active page view.

Adding a Bookmark

Prepare to add a bookmark for the new page by clicking the tool bar's Bookmarks and Page button (see Figure 2.21). The bookmarks Ken created appear in place of the thumbnails. You can click bookmarks to display associated document portions or pages. (Chapter 10, "Document Bookmarks," discusses bookmarks in more detail.)

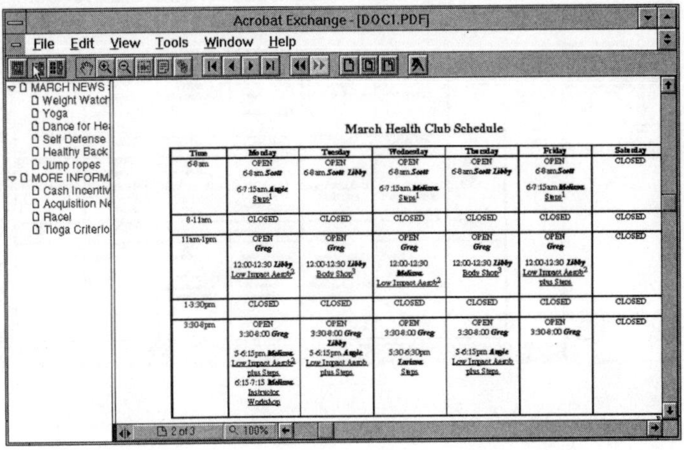

Figure 2.21. The active page view after selecting the Bookmarks and Page button.

To add a bookmark, select the bookmark under which you want the new bookmark to appear (see Figure 2.22). Next, select the tool bar's Text Selection tool (see Figure 2.23). Then select the page's title, as shown in Figure 2.24 (notice the box around the words *March Health Club Schedule*).

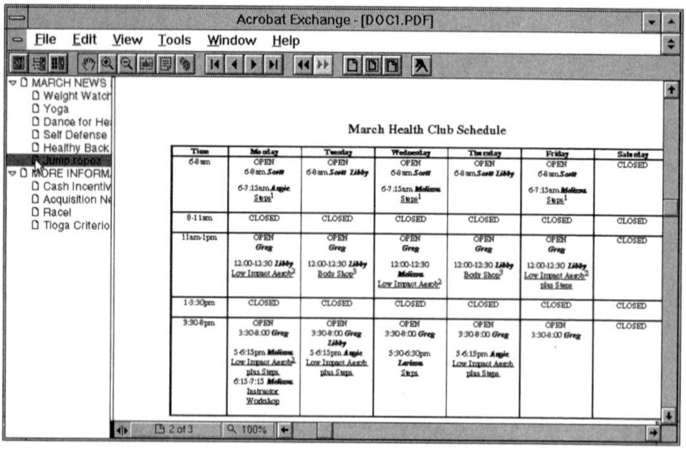

Figure 2.22. Selecting a bookmark prior to inserting a new entry.

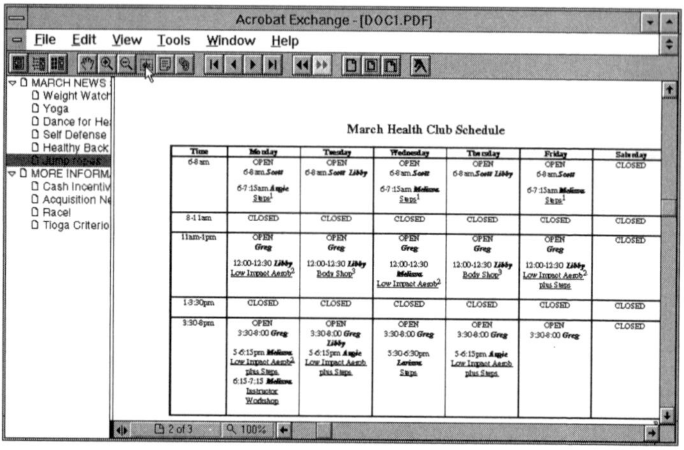

Figure 2.23. Selecting the Text Selection tool.

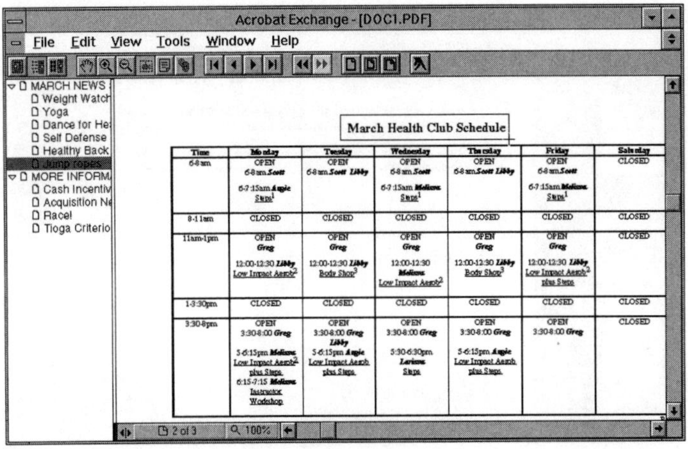

Figure 2.24. Selecting document text prior to copying it to the Clipboard.

After releasing the button, press the following key combinations:

- *Ctrl+C* to copy selected text to the Clipboard
- *Ctrl+B* to create a new bookmark after the selected bookmark (Jump ropes)
- *Ctrl+V* to copy the Clipboard text to the bookmark text area
- *Ctrl+LeftArrow* to move the new bookmark's indentation level to the left

Creating a Note

To redisplay the thumbnails, click the tool bar's Thumbnails and Page button and press the PageDown key to move to the next page (page 3). There, you notice an error in the *Tioga Criterion* topic. Rather than an endurance race from Yosemite National Park's Tioga Pass to Mount Whitney and back, as Melissa would have organized, it was really a raucous Roman toga, wine, and cheese party organized by her brother Greg. Compelled to subtly call attention to this error, you decide to send a note to Ken.

Select the tool bar's Note tool (see Figure 2.25), and then drag the cross-hair cursor to delineate the note's shape (see Figure 2.26). Figure 2.27 shows the note that awaits your text; Figure 2.28 shows the completed note (get a spell checker, Dave!).

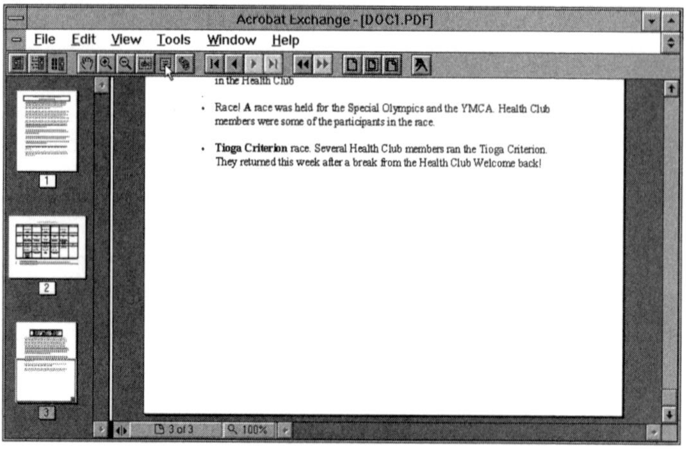

Figure 2.25. Selecting the Note tool.

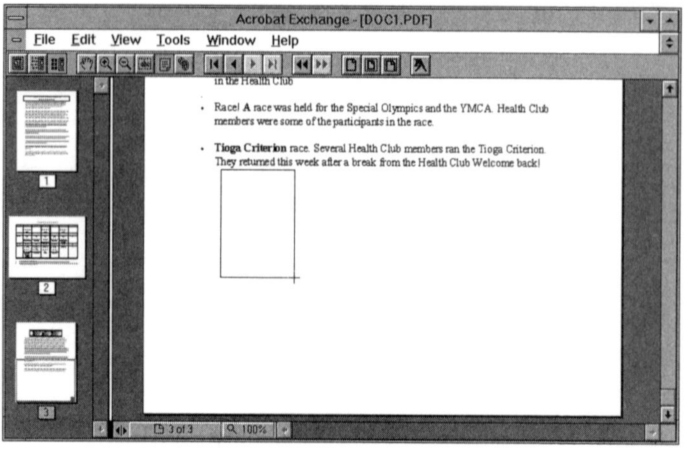

Figure 2.26. Drawing the note's shape.

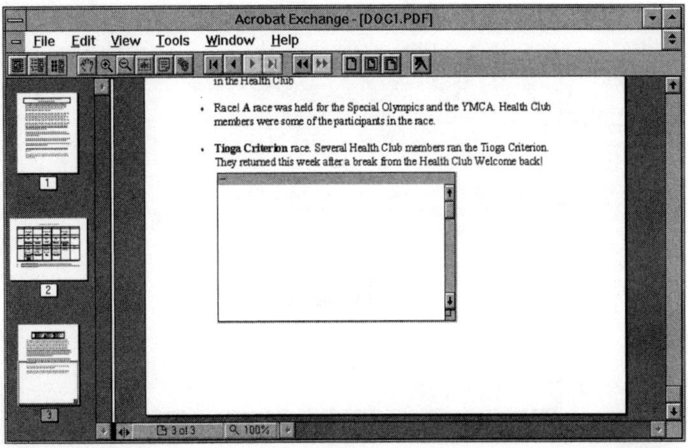

Figure 2.27. The Note window.

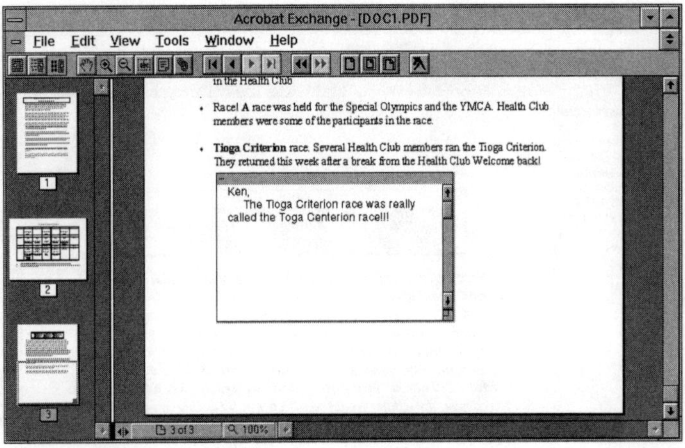

Figure 2.28. The completed note.

Executing a Link

Finally, click outside the note and move to the bottom of page 1 by successively pressing the PageUp key. Ken has created a hypertext link over the words *Click here for more info!!!*. Place the cursor on this area and click it (see Figure 2.29). Figure 2.30 shows the result—the page jumps from page 1 to page 3. (Chapter 12, "Document Hypertext Links," shows how to create and modify hypertext links.)

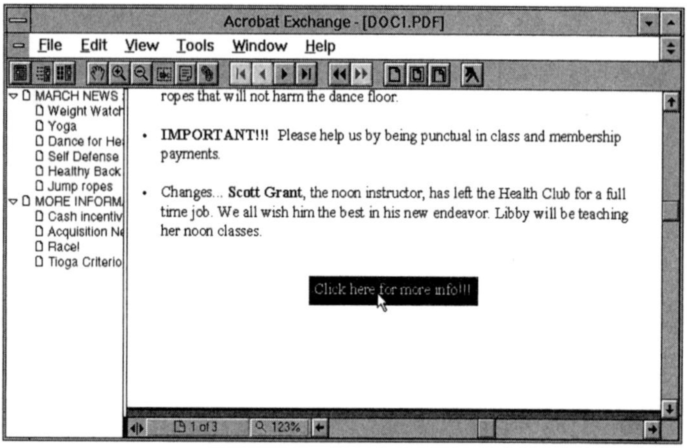

Figure 2.29. Clicking a hypertext link.

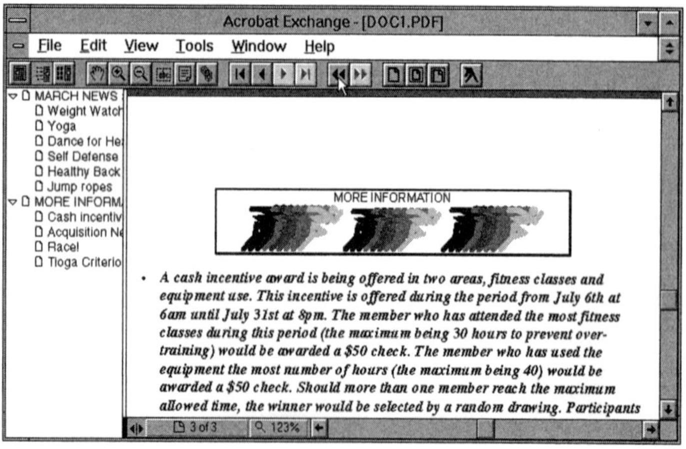

Figure 2.30. The active page view after jumping to the link.

Finally, you save the document, as before, and then select the File menu's Exit command to end the application. You now have an updated DOC1.PDF file that Dave can transfer back to Ken. Ken will view the note and then fix his Bacchic error. Ken does not have to delete the note he sent Dave because Ken attached it to page 2. You deleted page 2 and, in doing so, deleted all sticky notes attached to that page.

NOTE

The remainder of this book is a working handbook that will enable you to escape ASCII jail with Acrobat. (Proceed directly to GO. Collect $200.) Be sure to wave good-bye to those flabbergasted monk scribes loitering on the shoreline!

CHAPTER

THREE

Acrobat Reader and Exchange Overview

Acrobat Reader and Exchange enable you to view Adobe Acrobat Portable Document Format (PDF) files. Exchange users can optionally enhance the documents for other Reader and Exchange users that view Acrobat's electronic paper documents on Windows and Macintosh systems. Adobe has already announced Reader and Exchange versions for DOS and UNIX systems, as well as Acrobat Publishers Tools that will provide a variety of extensions to existing Acrobat products, including popular searching software to locate text sequences and patterns.

PDF is a PostScript-language–based file format that describes documents that contain any combination of text, graphics, grayscale images, and color images in a resolution- and device-independent meta-file format. Documents can range in size from one-inch-by-one-inch single-page documents to documents containing thousands of 45-inch-by-45-inch pages. Any application that prints can create PDF files containing a luxurious blend of fonts, graphics, and images.

Other Acrobat components—PDF Writer, Personal Distiller, and Network Distiller—transform application print information into PDF files. PDF Writer converts the output calls from Windows Graphical Device Interface (GDI) or Apple Quick Draw into PDF files. Personal Distiller and Network Distiller transform PostScript output into PDF files. Any Reader or Exchange user can view any PDF file regardless of the type of system that created it.

Viewing PDF Files

Reader and Exchange programs operate within application windows. Figure 3.1 illustrates Windows Exchange with one document displayed within a single application window. Both Reader and Exchange can have up to 10 simultaneous document windows. Figures 3.2 and 3.3 show four document windows that are cascaded and tiled, respectively.

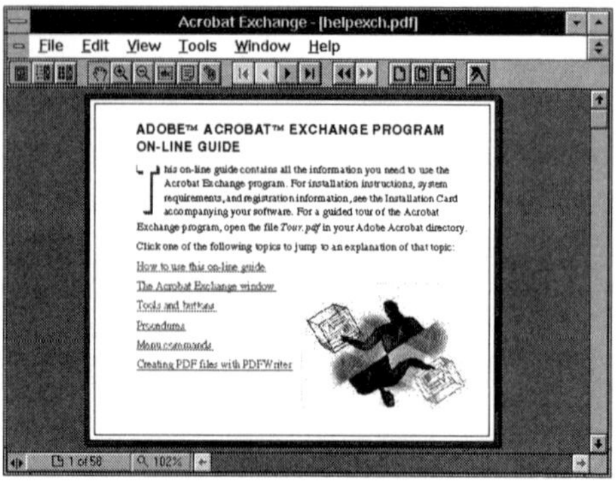

Figure 3.1. A single document window.

Each document window is independent of other document windows and contains three windows:

- *Page window*—displays a portion (screen) or all of a document page
- *Thumbnail window*—displays miniature graphical representations (thumbnails) of document pages
- *Bookmark window*—displays named views (destinations) of document pages, optionally arranged in a hierarchic outline form

Acrobat Reader and Exchange enable you to define independent document window *panes*, which enable you to view the page window through a *Page View pane* and bookmarks or thumbnails through an *Overview pane.*

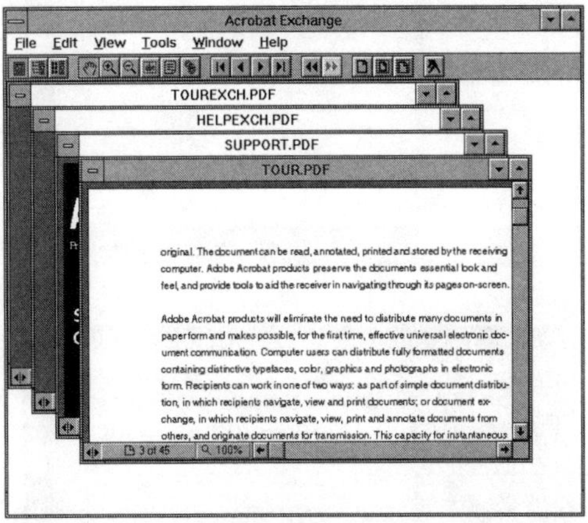

Figure 3.2. Four cascaded document windows.

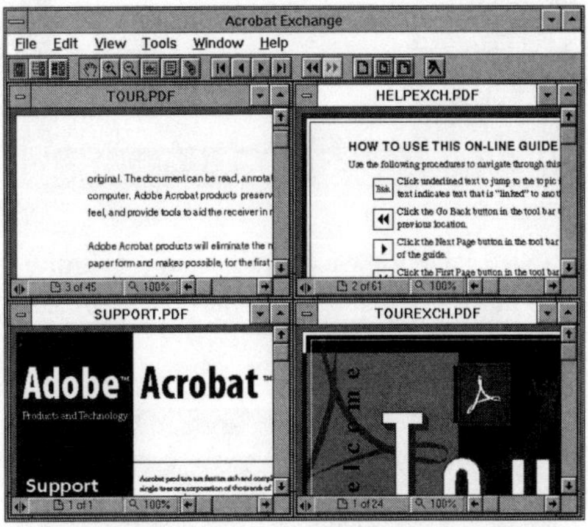

Figure 3.3. Four tiled document windows.

Figure 3.1 illustrated a document window that only displays a page window through a Page View pane. Figures 3.4 and 3.5 illustrate a document window that displays both a Page View pane and an Overview pane that reveal the Bookmark and Thumbnail windows, respectively.

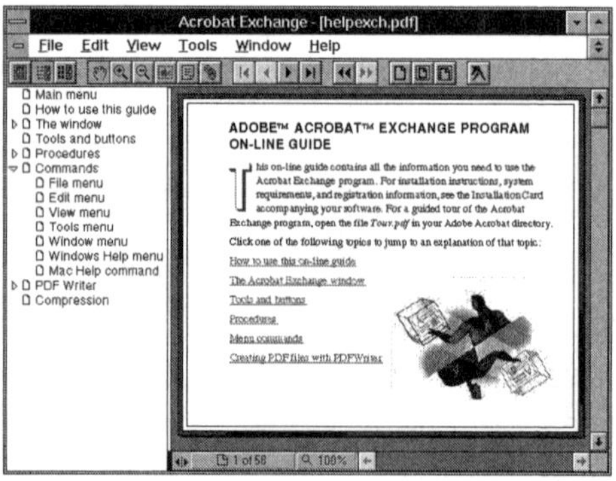

Figure 3.4.
A document window displaying both the Bookmark window and the page view.

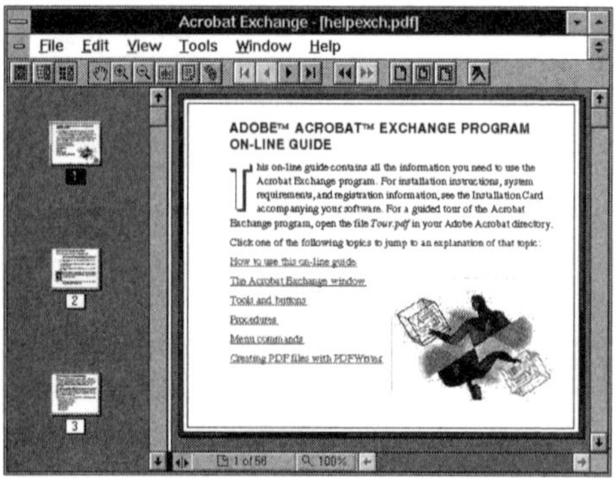

Figure 3.5.
A document window displaying both the Thumbnail window and the page view.

Just as Figure 3.1 illustrated that a Page View pane can occupy an entire document window, Figure 3.6 illustrates that an Overview pane can also occupy the entire document window.

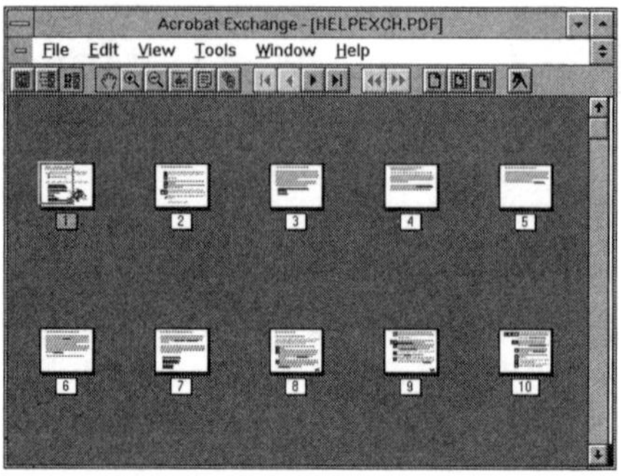

Figure 3.6.
A document window filled by the Overview pane.

Page Numbers and Numbers on Pages

Many different page-numbering schemes exist, and a typical book may use more than one numbering scheme. A book may have an unnumbered preface, a table of contents numbered with lowercase Roman numerals (i, ii, iii), chapter pages numbered with Arabic numerals (1, 2, 3), and appendix pages numbered to indicate the page within that appendix (for example, Appendix B would start with pages B-1, B-2, and so on). Because of the virtually unlimited possibilities, Acrobat makes no attempt to provide synchronization between numbers printed on pages and PDF file pages. Acrobat uses simple order-based page numbering, which usually corresponds to the page numbers printed on the pages.

This may initially be confusing, because PDF page rotation, crop page, insert page, and delete page operations require PDF page numbers, not document page numbers. The notion of printed page numbers is obsolete with Acrobat's electronic paper technology. All Acrobat page-based operations apply to the logical PDF file page order you encounter as you sequentially browse through documents from beginning to end. PDF files that have three index pages before the document page printed with the page number 1 have all Acrobat page numbering offset by three.

Thus, when you want to insert pages before the page printed as page one, select Insert Before and type 4 in the Page Number field of the Insert dialog box. In practice, you will rapidly adapt to Acrobat page numbering, ignoring printed page identifiers in preference for Acrobat page numbers displayed at the bottom of Page View panes or under associated page thumbnails.

Document Window Anatomy

Using Acrobat Exchange for Windows as an example, individual document windows contain the following elements (refer back to Figures 3.2, 3.4, and 3.5 to inspect how these elements appear on-screen):

- *Document window sizing handles*—four of them, one at each corner of the document window
- *Document Close button*—double-clicking this button closes a document window
- *Document Title bar*—displays the document name
- *Maximize button*—fills the available application window area with the document window

- *Minimize button*—reduces the document window to an icon within the application window
- *Vertical scroll bar*—permits vertical screen and page scrolling within documents
- *Horizontal scroll bar*—permits horizontal scrolling within documents
- *Status bar*—contains the Magnification Level and Page Number windoids
- *Magnification Level windoid*—displays the current magnification level for the document window; clicking it changes the magnification level
- *Page Number windoid*—displays the current PDF document page number for the document in the document window's Page View pane
- *Pane Width control*—dragging this button horizontally controls pane sizes

Application Window Anatomy

The Application window contains the following Acrobat items (refer back to Figure 3.5 to inspect how these elements appear on-screen):

- *Window sizing handles*—four of them, one at each corner of the document window
- *Application Close button*—double-clicking this button ends the application
- *Title bar*—names the application and, optionally, the document in the document window if the document window is maximized
- *Maximize button*—maximizes the application window
- *Minimize button*—reduces the application window to an icon
- *Menu bar*—displays application commands
- *Optional tool bar*—displays various tool and button icons

Both application and document windows can display Restore buttons that have different effects depending on the state of the window. Application Restore buttons restore the application window to a previous state. Document window Restore buttons restore document windows to their previous states. Note that the Restore buttons in Figures 3.2 and 3.3 are in different positions than the Restore buttons in Figures 3.1, 3.4, and 3.5. Figure 3.7 shows a maximized document window; Figure 3.8 shows a document window that is not maximized.

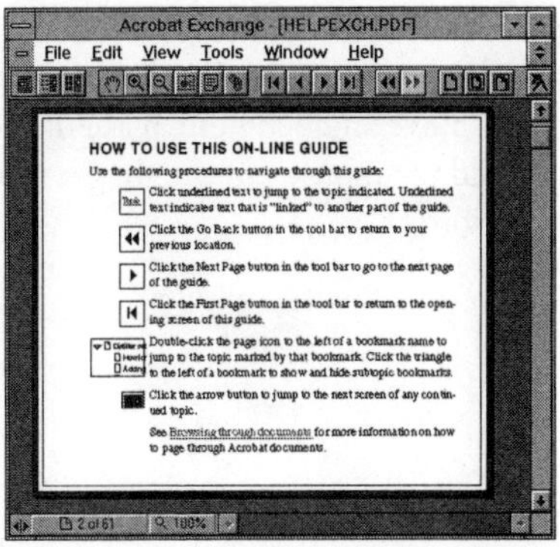

Figure 3.7.
A maximized document window.

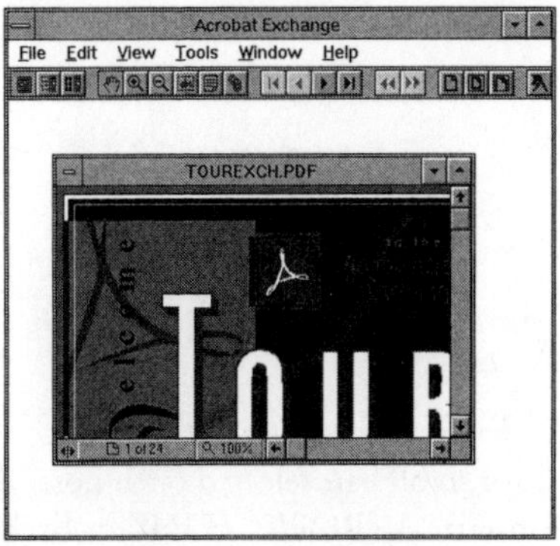

Figure 3.8.
A document window that is not maximized.

Reader and Exchange Features

Both Acrobat Reader and Exchange enable you to view PDF documents. Acrobat Reader is a cost-reduced, functional subset of Acrobat Exchange, and as such, retains many Exchange features. However, it does not enable you to alter PDF documents.

Notes

Exchange users can attach electronic notes to displayed document pages for other Exchange or Reader users to view. These notes appear on document pages as either closed iconized notes or open "sticky" notes. You can drag the currently selected note on the Page View pane to reveal document content previously obscured by them. Because the note placement is on the same page view, you cannot move the notes to other document pages.

Figures 3.9, 3.10, and 3.11 illustrate the three states of attached notes: iconized and closed, open but not selected, and open and selected. To move a closed iconized note, place the cursor on the note icon, press and hold the mouse button, and drag the note icon to another position. To place the note icon there, release the mouse button. To move an open note, place the cursor over the window's title bar, press and hold the mouse button, drag it to the new position, and release the mouse button.

Figure 3.9.
An iconized note (enlarged here for clarity).

Figure 3.10.
A deselected open note.

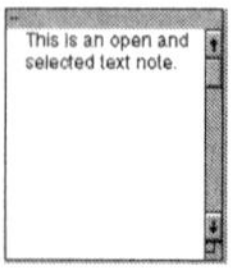

Figure 3.11.
A selected open note.

Selected iconized notes are gray; deselected notes are yellow. Deselected open notes do not have a window title or scroll bar; selected open notes do. If you are using Windows, you can customize ACROEXCH.INI for Exchange or ACROREAD.INI for the Reader file to make open notes varying colors (see Appendix F, "Reader and Exchange INI File Settings"). You also can use the More Preferences dialog box. You can size and scroll through an open selected note window when it contains more text than is visible in the text window. Double-clicking a note icon opens a note window. Double-clicking a window's upper-left corner close box control closes an open note.

Thumbnails

Thumbnails are miniature graphical representations of document pages. The thumbnail for the active document visible in the Page View pane also has a view box, which you can resize and drag to other positions on the same page using the Hand tool. To move the view box to another thumbnail, click the desired page's thumbnail and the view box moves to the thumbnail, appearing centered over the click point if possible. To resize a view box, drag the view box's resizing handle to a different location, or you can also press Shift and click within the view box. Although the Hand tool does not convert to an arrow cursor, the cursor still draws a new view box outline. When a thumbnail is completely gray, the thumbnail does not exist.

Distillers, but not PDF Writer, may automatically create PDF files with thumbnails; Exchange users can create them for existing PDF files. Clicking the tool bar's Thumbnails and Page button or choosing the View menu's Thumbnails and Page command displays document page thumbnail images in the Overview pane (see Figures 3.12 and 3.13). Page cropping and rotation erases affected page thumbnails, thus introducing holes in the thumbnail collection. Acrobat Exchange users can restore missing thumbnails by using the Create All command in the Edit menu's Thumbnails submenu.

Figure 3.12. Selecting the Thumbnails and Page button from the tool bar.

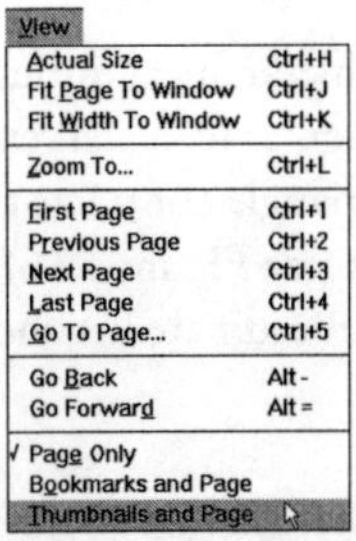

Figure 3.13. Selecting the Thumbnails and Page command from the View menu.

Bookmarks

Bookmarks are named PDF document destinations appearing in Acrobat Reader and Exchange bookmark windows. Destinations are specific document page views, each at specific magnification levels. Bookmarks enable you to display page view destinations by double-clicking a page icon to the left of the bookmark name. Bookmarks may appear in any bookmark list position, independent of their associated document destinations. Using optional indentation, a document's bookmark list can be a hierarchical outline of the document; a bookmark may appear subordinate to other bookmarks and have subordinate entries itself.

Clicking the Bookmarks and Page button or choosing the View menu's Bookmarks and Page command (see Figures 3.14 and 3.15) displays document bookmarks as a list within the document window's Overview pane. If none appear in the Overview pane, none exist and you must create them. Double-clicking the bookmark's page icon to the left of the bookmark name moves the active page view to the bookmark's destination.

Figure 3.14.
Selecting the Bookmarks and Page button from the tool bar.

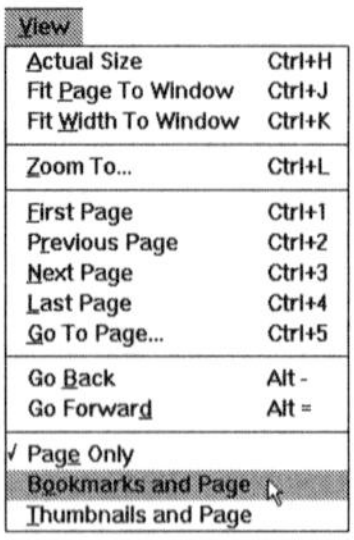

Figure 3.15.
Selecting the Bookmarks and Page command from the View menu.

When a bookmark list arrangement is a hierarchical outline, subordinate bookmarks are indented and have a triangular icon that either points down or to the right. Clicking a down-pointing triangle contracts the subordinate list and makes the triangle point to the right (see Figure 3.16). Clicking a right-pointing triangle expands a contracted subordinate list and makes the triangle point down (see Figure 3.17).

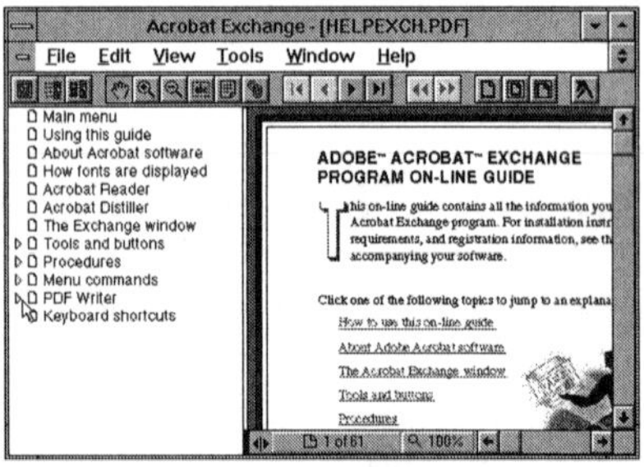

Figure 3.16.
A bookmark with a right-pointing triangle and its subordinate list contracted.

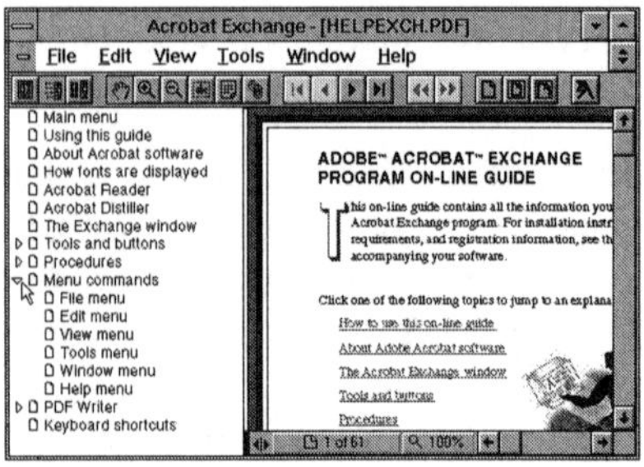

Figure 3.17.
A bookmark with a down-pointing triangle and its subordinate list displayed.

Hypertext Links

By using Exchange, you can connect related information by adding Link buttons to document pages. When Reader and Exchange users click Link buttons, the Page View pane displays the link's destination. Just as with bookmarks, link destinations are specific document page views, each at specific magnification levels. Link buttons may or may not have a box outline. Visible Link buttons have a rectangular outline around them. Invisible Link buttons do not have a box drawn around them, so visual clues usually signal their position. The tool bar's Go Back button provides you with a convenient way of returning from a link destination. After viewing the Link button's destination, clicking the Go Back button returns the Page View pane to the Link button's location.

To create a link between two document parts, draw a Link button around any page part, display the document area to which the Link button should link, and set the position using the displayed dialog box. Exchange users can edit existing Link buttons and destinations.

Navigation Stack

You can view documents by browsing sequentially or by skipping around using page jumps, thumbnails, bookmarks, link buttons, and so on. When the Page View pane displays a new view, Reader and Exchange records the document location and magnification level in the next available slot in the document's *navigation stack*.

Navigation stacks can hold 64 entries before discarding the earliest views. You can retrace earlier stack recorded views towards the stack's beginning by using the tool bar's Go Back button or the View menu's Go **B**ack command. When you retrace towards earlier views, you can return to subsequent views by using the tool bar's Go Forward button or the View menu's Go Forwar**d** command. This is a very powerful technique when used with links, bookmarks, and thumbnails.

PDF Writer

PDF Writer is a printer driver that installs with Exchange. PDF Writer accepts printer output and converts it to PDF format. PDF Writer is easy to use, but does exhibit some limitations. To escape these limitations, create PostScript file output and then process the PostScript output with Acrobat Distiller.

Page Insertion and Rotation

Many enterprises use incompatible document preparation products, and then piece together their output into composite documents. Exchange enables PDF document insertions within other PDF documents, thereby preserving these enterprises' existing document preparation procedures and product investments. When one product produces landscape mode (sideways) pages, Exchange enables you to rotate the page to portrait mode for easier viewing later.

Exchanging PDF Files Across Systems

Perhaps the most exciting Acrobat feature is its disparate computer system file sharing. Both Macintosh and DOS Acrobat programs can access files created and modified by either system by using a 7-bit, character-coded, line-oriented file format that is insensitive to the different text line termination schemes.

The Macintosh uses only a carriage return, but DOS-based systems use a combination of a carriage return followed by line feed. This normally complicates file interchange, because these schemes are typically incompatible for application programs. Acrobat is insensitive to such schemes, so files created on one system can be updated on the other, intermixing lines terminated in one system's scheme with lines terminated in the other's.

Another file interchange issue involves byte-ordering within data elements. Macintosh systems and DOS systems use apparently incompatible data storage approaches. Again, Acrobat solves the problem by using a character-based stream similar in concept to Adobe's PostScript approach.

A third issue involves physical data transfer between different systems. There are many ways to accomplish this. The first is direct disk reading. Several Macintosh applications allow Macintoshes to read DOS disks. *Apple File Exchange* is a good example of an application that provides this capability. Installing such packages on Macintoshes provides the exchange capability.

CAUTION

Avoid using options to convert DOS line terminators into Macintosh line terminators and vice versa. This option is sometimes available in check boxes specifying carriage return replacements with carriage return and line feeds and visa versa. Such replacements damage Acrobat PDF files.

However, PDF file structure facilitates recovery of damaged files. When Acrobat opens damaged files, it attempts to repair the file and informs you with a message box while the repair process proceeds.

A second way Acrobat exchanges files is through network access, such as with Novell's NetWare.

TIP

Acrobat PDF file network use is completely transparent; you need not concern yourself except to keep filenames short enough so DOS sees the name accurately. To prevent DOS access problems, Macintosh, Windows, DOS, and UNIX users should name files using the eight-dot-three format (XXXXXXXX.ZZZ). This is true even if transfers are between two Macintoshes, because many E-mail programs cause name truncation problems.

For all the environments to recognize PDF files, the file must end with the *.pdf* extension. It is also useful for E-mail programs that can recognize attached Acrobat files ending in .pdf and launch Acrobat at attachment double-clicks.

A third file-exchange method attaches PDF files to electronic mail messages. This introduces the possibility of networking components, such as bridges, corrupting files. In some instances, the network bridges or mail systems themselves assume that files are text and may inappropriately fragment files, appending line terminators within the PDF file. Such anomalies usually are not serious impediments and network administrators can rectify the problems when notified.

Exchange Full Menus vs. Short Menus vs. Reader Menus

Acrobat Exchange provides two menu command formats. Full menus display all Acrobat commands; short menus provide the most commonly used commands. When full menus are in effect, two tools—the *Link* and *Note* tools—appear in the tool bar that are absent when short menus are in effect.

The reader menus are a subset of Exchange's short menus. In addition to not having a PDF Writer, you cannot perform any of the following operations using Reader:

- Create notes
- Create/delete thumbnails
- Create/delete bookmarks, reorganize lists, and change destinations
- Create/delete links; move, resize, and change the visibility of Link buttons; and change link destinations
- Change or save documents
- Combine documents or use the Insert command
- Delete, crop, or rotate pages
- Cut, paste, or clear the Clipboard

Apple Differences

The Macintosh enables you to perform the following operations with Reader and Exchange:

- Use the Return key for PageDown and use the Shift+Return key combination for PageUp.
- Hold down the Option key while creating Exchange Notes to keep the Note tool selected after note creation.
- Hold down the Option key while creating Exchange Links to keep the Link tool selected after link creation.
- Click the document Close box while holding down the Option key to close all open documents.
- Select all note or bookmark text by pressing Command+A.
- Activate PDF Writer's Page Setup box by holding down the Ctrl key and selecting Page Setup. If this fails, you can select the PDF Writer from the Chooser or select the Control Panel's PDF Writer shortcut activation key.

TIP

With many Macintosh applications, holding down the Ctrl key and choosing the File menu's Print command creates PDF files without changing PDF Writer Chooser settings. This is known as the *PDF shortcut.*

When Macintosh Exchange or Reader substitutes fonts, the cursor appears as a spinning letter *a.*

Windows Differences

Windows enables you to perform the following operations with Reader and Exchange:

- Ctrl+click the Note tool while creating Exchange notes to keep the Note tool selected after note creation.
- Ctrl+click the Link tool while creating Exchange links to keep the Link tool selected after link creation.
- Shift+click and drag existing thumbnail View boxes to draw new View boxes. Notice that the Hand tool does *not* change to an arrow during this operation.
- Tile and cascade documents.
- Select bookmarks by using either Shift+click or Ctrl+click.

There is no Select All command in Windows Exchange or Reader. There is, however, an Overview Pane-Only view. Just drag the Pane Width control all the way to the right.

Windows System Requirements for Reader and Exchange

Windows systems must have the following *minimum* requirements to use Reader and Exchange:

- A 386 or higher processor
- 4MB of RAM
- One 1.44MB 3.5" floppy-disk drive or network access for installing Acrobat software
- PostScript Printer or other Windows-compatible output device
- A hard disk with 5.5MB for the software and 5.0MB free afterwards
- MS-DOS 5.0 or later version with Windows 3.1 or later version running in the 386 Enhanced mode
- VGA, Super VGA, or higher-resolution display adapter supported by Windows 3.1

To *fully* exploit the Windows version of Reader and Exchange, Adobe recommends the following system requirements:

- A 486 or better Intel processor
- 8MB or more of RAM

Windows Network Distiller systems require at least one LAN adapter card.

Macintosh System Requirements for Reader and Exchange

Macintosh systems must have the following *minimum* requirements to use Reader and Exchange:

- A 68020 processor
- One 800K or Apple SuperDriver floppy-disk drive or network access for installing Acrobat software
- 2MB of RAM for System 7; 2.5MB of RAM for System 6
- A hard disk with 7.0MB free for installation and 3.5MB after installation
- Macintosh System 6.0.5 or later, including System 7
- A PostScript Printer or other Macintosh-compatible output device

To *fully* exploit the Macintosh version of Reader and Exchange, Adobe recommends the following system requirements:

- 4MB of application RAM
- Macintosh System 7.1 or later
- A Macintosh II, PowerBook, Centris, or Quadra

Macintosh Network Distiller systems require a network connection.

CHAPTER FOUR

Personal and Network Distiller Overview

Acrobat Distiller transforms PostScript files from PC, Macintosh, and UNIX systems into Portable Document Format (PDF) documents for viewing and printing in Acrobat Reader and Exchange. Distiller-created PDF documents retain all formatting, graphics, and photographic images that the original documents contain. Although PDF Writer can also create PDF files, in some instances the files it creates lack visual fidelity.

There are two versions of Acrobat Distiller:

Personal Distiller
Network Distiller

Each Acrobat version has a Windows and a Macintosh version. For grammatical simplicity, product names cite Windows versions unless otherwise stated.

To use either Distiller version, create document PostScript language files by opening documents, choosing a PostScript printer, and printing the PostScript document files using standard application and system services.

Personal Distiller enables you to create PDF files on your personal machine. You can process files using standard *drag-and-drop*, *Open*, and *Save As...* procedures. Network Distiller lets network users access a network server that performs PDF conversions. While network servers create PDF documents, user computers are available to perform other activities. After PDF file creation, network users copy their PDF files where needed.

Network Distiller has a few features Personal Distiller does not that facilitate its network use. These features allow Network Distiller to watch user-specified network subdirectories for work. Here's how you use Network Distiller:

1. Make the necessary connections to network the subdirectories that Network Distiller monitors. These work source and output destination directories are Network Distiller's *In* and *Out directories*, respectively.
2. Copy the PostScript document file to an In directory monitored by Network Distiller. Creating the PostScript file directly in the In directory eliminates this step.
3. Distiller discovers and reads the PostScript file in the In directory, creates a PDF document, and places the PDF document file in the associated Out directory.
4. When Distiller finishes, you can retrieve your PDF document from the associated Out directory.

A single Network Distiller server can monitor multiple network subdirectories; multiple Network Distiller servers can monitor a given In directory. In network environments where PCs and Macintoshes can share files, Macintosh Network Distiller servers can process PC In subdirectories and PC Network Distiller servers can process Macintosh In folders. It's all very flexible.

PDF Writer vs. Distiller

Acrobat Exchange provides *PDF Writer*, a special printer driver. PDF Writer creates PDF files by behaving like a printer, but it creates electronic PDF files instead of printed paper pages. However, PDF Writer cannot create high-quality PDF files for some kinds of documents. Distiller must create the PDF files in such instances.

For example, many high-end graphics and page-layout programs create documents containing Encapsulated PostScript (EPS) graphics. PDF Writer cannot create high-quality PDF files for documents containing EPS graphics because it uses bitmap preview images accompanying the EPS file instead of EPS graphics. Also, many applications offer PostScript printer features unavailable with other printers. To create PDF files with features normally available only with PostScript printers, use Distiller.

Finally, Distiller allows color image compression to differ from grayscale image compression. However, PDF Writer forces color and grayscale images to use the same compression method.

Distilling PostScript Files

Distiller needs two things to create error-free PDF files:

Valid PostScript files
Access to the PostScript Type 1 fonts that the documents use

To ensure that your PostScript files are valid, print your documents on a PostScript printer before creating their PostScript files. Usually, PostScript files include the Type 1 fonts that the documents use. Otherwise, they must be available to Distiller. System administrators can set up Network Distiller to find document fonts.

Distiller Windows System Requirements

Windows systems must have the following *minimum* requirements to use Distiller:

- A 386 processor
- 8MB of RAM
- A hard disk with 5MB free
- One 1.44MB 3.5" floppy-disk drive
- MS-DOS 5.0 or later version with Windows 3.1 or later version running in 386 Enhanced mode

To *fully* exploit the Windows version of Distiller, Adobe recommends the following:

- 12MB of RAM
- A hard disk with at least 12MB free

- A 486 or better Intel processor, or a 386 processor with an 80387 math coprocessor

Windows Network Distiller systems require at least one LAN adapter card.

Distiller Macintosh System Requirements

Macintosh systems must have the following *minimum* requirements to use Distiller:

- A Macintosh II, PowerBook, Centris, or Quadra with a 68020 processor or better
- One 800KB or Apple SuperDriver floppy-disk drive
- 6MB of RAM
- A hard disk with 10MB free
- Macintosh System 6.0.5 or later, including System 7

To *fully* exploit the Macintosh version of Distiller, Adobe recommends the following:

- A Macintosh Centris or Quadra
- 12MB of RAM
- Macintosh System 7.1 or later

Macintosh Network Distiller systems require at least one LAN adapter card.

PART

II

Reader and Exchange Viewing Engines

- Opening PDF File Documents
- Document Browsing
- Page View Magnification
- Miscellaneous Functions
- Document Notes
- Document Bookmarks
- Document Thumbnails
- Document Hypertext Links
- Exchange's PDF Writer
- Acrobat Reader and Exchange Menu Reference
- Troubleshooting

CHAPTER

FIVE

Opening PDF File Documents

When Acrobat Reader or Exchange begins initial execution, a logo box appears, followed by a standard Open dialog box that enables initial file selection (see Figure 5.1). After opening a file, the standard File menu Open command enables other files to open. The following discussion summarizes the various ways users can open files using Windows Reader and Exchange as an example.

Opening PDF Documents

There are six ways to open PDF documents with Windows Exchange or Reader. You can do any of the following:

- Use the File menu's **O**pen command
- Use Program Manager File menu's Run command with a filename on the command line
- Double-click a file listed in File Manager that ends in *.pdf*
- Drag one or more selected files from a File Manager list onto either an open or iconized Acrobat window
- Drag a PDF document to the program name listed in File Manager
- Use a program that uses DDE to instruct Acrobat to open a PDF document. Under several Windows desktop managers, you may also drag a PDF file to a desktop Quick Access icon to launch Acrobat.

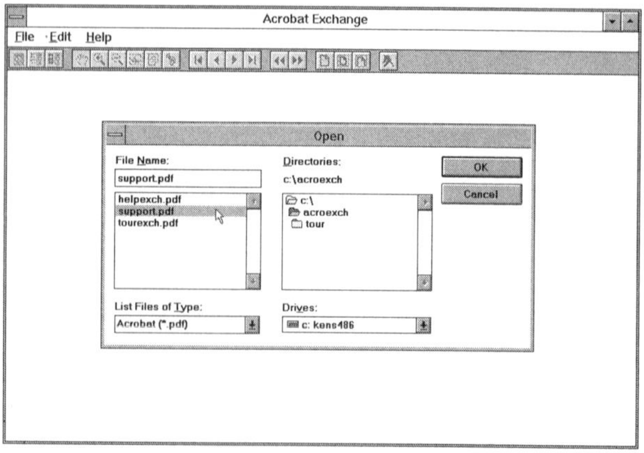

Figure 5.1. Standard system Open dialog box.

Although you can make multiple File Manager selections by either Shift+clicking or Ctrl+clicking files listed in File Manager, dragging these multiply-selected files to Acrobat Exchange or Reader only works if Acrobat is already running. Due to apparent Program Manager inconsistencies, dragging multiply-selected files to the File Manager's program name results in only the first file opening.

Acrobat Document Icons

Windows also iconizes document files in Program Manager groups. This provides a Macintosh-like user interface for document files appearing as desktop folder icons. As an example, create an Acrobat group in the Program Manager by using the Program Manager File menu's **N**ew... command (see Figure 5.2), select Program **G**roup from the New Program Object dialog box, and then click OK (see Figure 5.3). Using File Manager, click and drag a PDF document file to the newly created Acrobat program group. The document icon is the Acrobat Exchange or Reader icon, but its title is the file's name without the .pdf extension (see Figure 5.4).

Figure 5.2. Selecting the Program Manager's File menu's New... command.

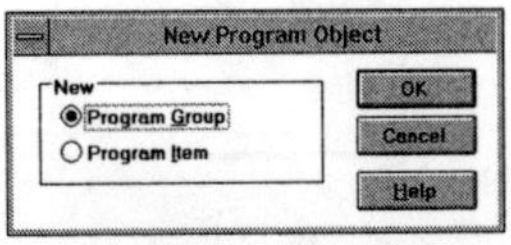

Figure 5.3. The New Program Object dialog box.

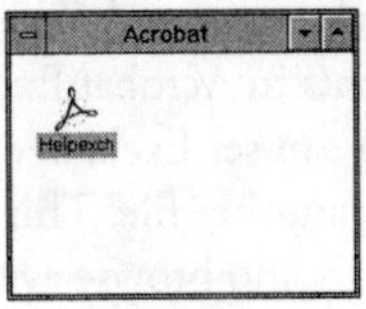

Figure 5.4. The Program Group shows an Acrobat document using the program icon.

Click the icon to select it, and then select the **P**roperties... command in the File Manager's File menu (see Figure 5.5). Figure 5.6 is the resulting dialog box, with the title selected. Type the title (in this example, `Exchange Help`) and then click the Change Icon... button. Figure 5.7 shows the icons available in Acrobat Exchange, the program associated with the PDF document. Using the mouse, click the PDF document icon and click OK. Then click OK in the Program Item Properties dialog box. The resulting group will now show a PDF document with its associated document icon (see Figure 5.8) and will cause the document to open in Acrobat Exchange or Reader when it is double-clicked. You may create separate groups of PDF documents or place these into other groups as desired.

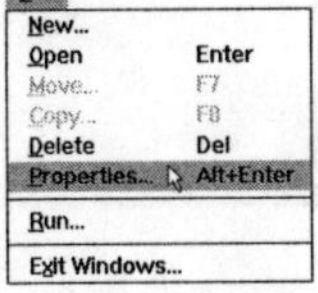

Figure 5.5. Selecting the File Manager's File menu's Properties... command.

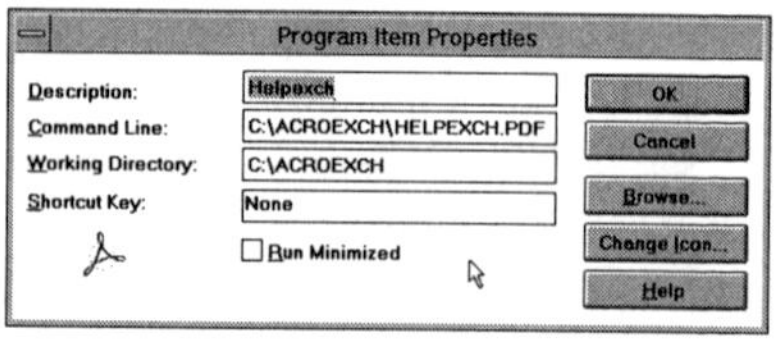

Figure 5.6.
The Program Item Properties dialog box.

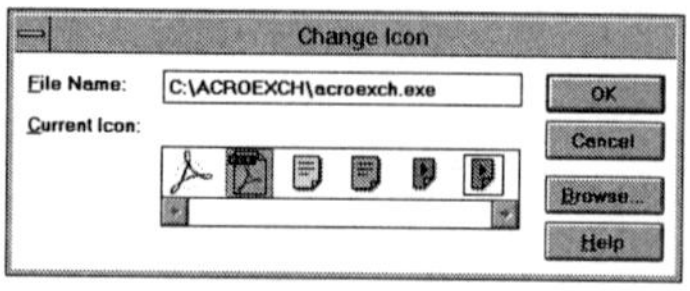

Figure 5.7.
The Change Icon dialog box.

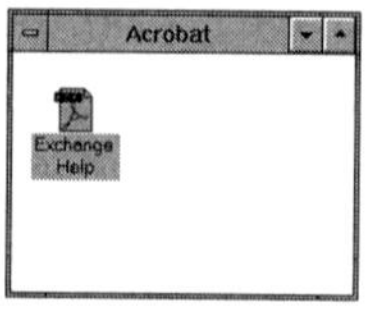

Figure 5.8.
The Program Group shows an Acrobat document using the program icon.

Figure 5.9 shows dragging a selected file listed in File Manager that resulted from the File Manager File menu's Search command. The resulting file "hit list" ending in *.pdf* can manage documents in Acrobat Exchange or Reader. Using the More Preferences feature, you can set Exchange or Reader to close PDF files that are open before you open another file. This enables you to use File Manager to assemble PDF file hit lists and browse available documents. This is especially useful on networks, where users may locate thousands of documents. By placing the File Manager list next to Acrobat Exchange or Reader, you can browse all day, simply double-clicking files ending in .pdf or dragging them to Acrobat.

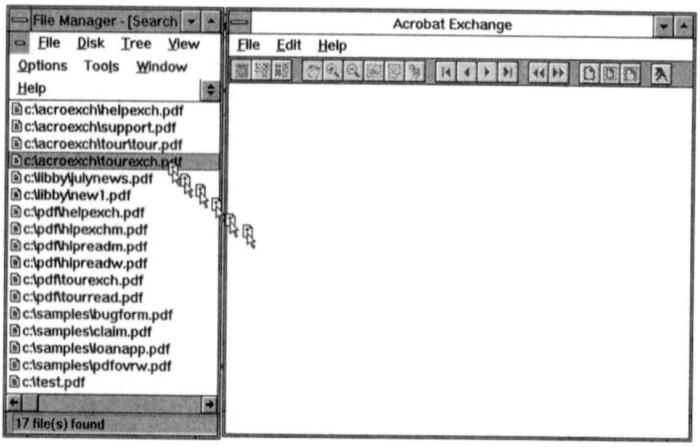

Figure 5.9.
Dragging a selected document from the File Manager to Acrobat Exchange.

TIP

Developer's Tip: A Dynamic Data Exchange (DDE) command is available for simple document viewer control from other applications. This allows current Windows document management programs to add simple DDE protocols and use the Acrobat Exchange or Reader as an internal viewer.

The DDE command is registered in the registration data base under

```
AcrobatClass->Shell->Open->DDEexecute
```

Server applications can send the DDE command `[FileOpen(1%)]` to Acrobat Exchange or Reader to open documents. (Note: the 1% is the full pathname of the target file to open.) If the viewer has set More Preferences to Close All on Open, Exchange or Reader does not run out of document windows when many documents open in this manner.

CHAPTER SIX

Document Browsing

Acrobat Reader and Exchange offer numerous ways to browse documents. One or more of them will surely meet your needs.

Browsing the Current Page

Clicking the tool bar's Hand tool (see Figure 6.1) and dragging the Hand tool on the active page view (see Figure 6.2) adjusts active page views without magnification level changes. The horizontal scroll bar enables you to make horizontal adjustments to the active page view. The vertical scroll bar enables you to make vertical adjustments to the active page view within the current page or provides jumps to other pages.

Figure 6.1.
Selecting the Hand tool from the tool bar.

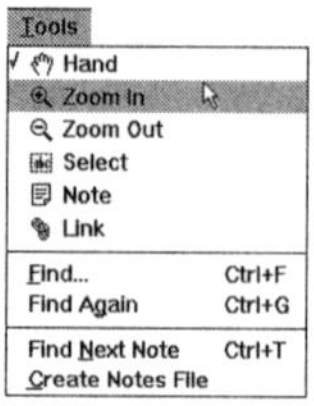

Figure 6.2.
The Tools menu.

Clicking a thumbnail moves the view box to the clicked thumbnail. Dragging the thumbnail's view box (see Figure 6.3) on the active thumbnail changes the active page view without changing the magnification level. Clicking inside the view box and dragging it creates a new view box, although the Hand tool does not transform to an arrow icon.

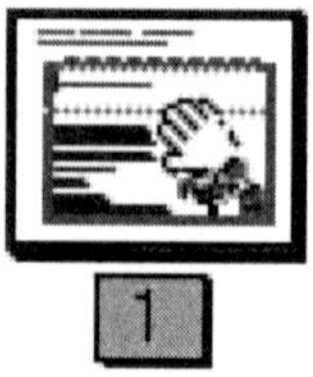

Figure 6.3.
The thumbnail view box (enlarged here for clarity).

Moving to Relative Pages

To move to the top of the preceding page, select the View menu's Previous Page command (see Figure 6.4) or click the tool bar's Previous Page button (see Figure 6.5). Otherwise, press the Up Arrow or Left Arrow key.

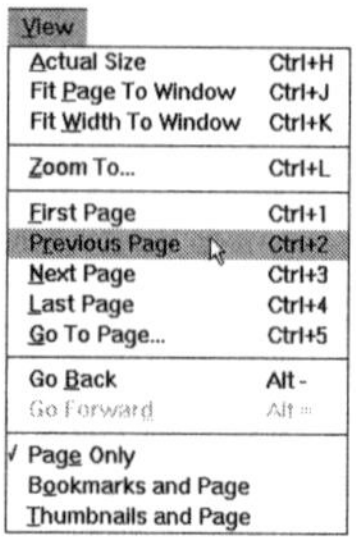

Figure 6.4.
Selecting the View menu's Previous Page command.

Figure 6.5. Clicking the tool bar's Previous Page button.

To move to the top of the following page, select the View menu's **N**ext Page command (see Figure 6.6) or click the tool bar's Next Page button (see Figure 6.7). Otherwise, press the Down Arrow or Right Arrow key.

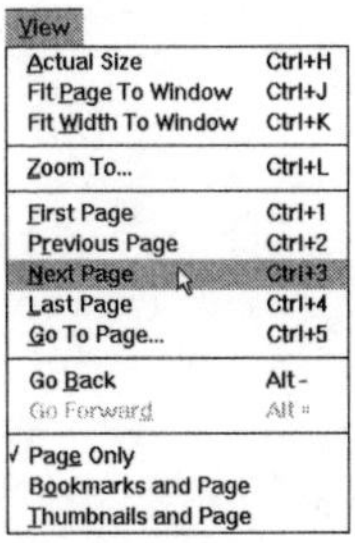

Figure 6.6. Selecting the View menu's Next Page command.

Figure 6.7. Clicking the tool bar's Next Page button.

Adjusting Page View Screens

Pressing the PageUp key moves one screen toward the top of the document. Pressing the PageDown key moves one screen toward the end of the document.

Moving to Specific Pages

Acrobat Reader and Exchange enable you to move gracefully between pages using numerous techniques. These techniques enable you to select a variety of target destinations with minimal effort.

Moving to the First Page

To move to the first page of a document, click the tool bar's First Page button (see Figure 6.8) or select the View menu's **F**irst Page command (see Figure 6.9). Otherwise, press the Home key.

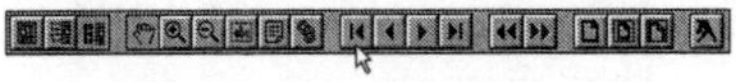

Figure 6.8. Clicking the tool bar's First Page button.

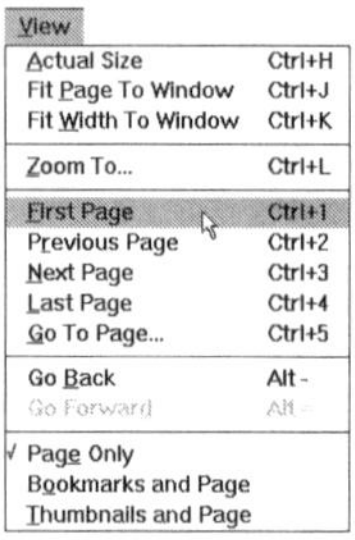

Figure 6.9. Selecting the View menu's First Page command.

Moving to the Last Page

To move to the last page of a document, click the tool bar's Last Page button (see Figure 6.10) or select the View menu's Last Page command (see Figure 6.11). Otherwise, press the End key.

Figure 6.10. Clicking the tool bar's Last Page button.

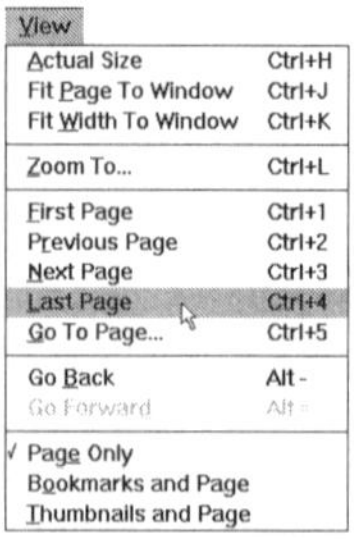

Figure 6.11. Selecting the View menu's Last Page command.

Moving to a Specific Page

There are a couple of ways to move to a specific page within a document. One is to drag the slider in the vertical scroll bar until the selected page number appears (see Figure 6.12).

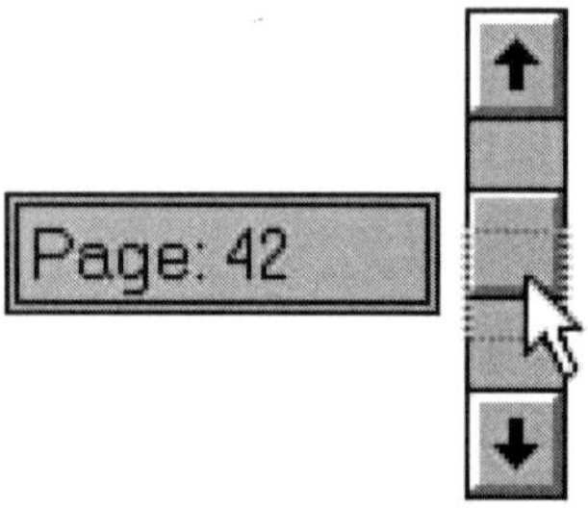

Figure 6.12. Sliding the vertical scroll bar to move to a specific page (enlarged here for clarity).

Another way to move to a specific page is to select the View menu's **G**o To Page... command (see Figure 6.13) or click the Status Bar Page Number box (see Figure 6.14); then enter the desired page number in the Go To dialog box (see Figure 6.15).

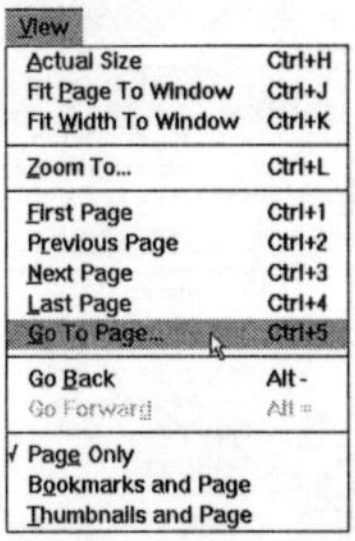

Figure 6.13. Selecting the View menu's Go To Page... command.

Figure 6.14. The Page Number box (enlarged here for clarity).

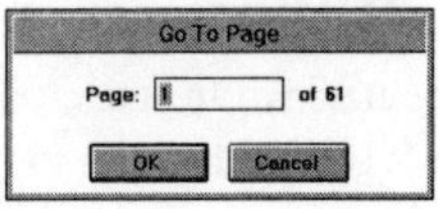

Figure 6.15. The Go To Page dialog box.

Bookmarks

To view a bookmark's destination, double-click the bookmark's page icon (see Figure 6.16).

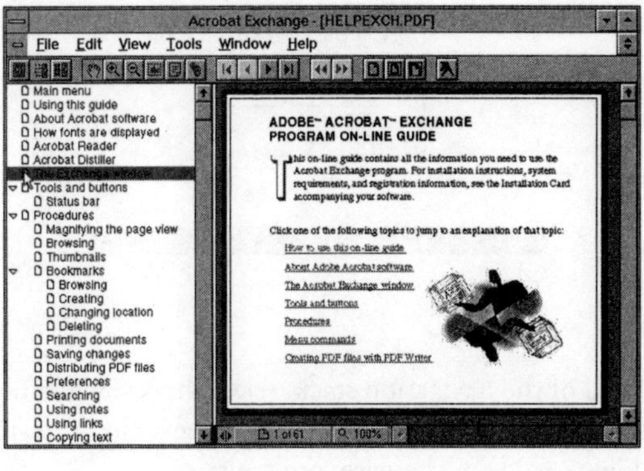

Figure 6.16. Clicking a bookmark's page icon.

Thumbnails

To jump to a page, expose and click the page's thumbnail (see Figure 6.17). The click point is the center of the active view, if possible.

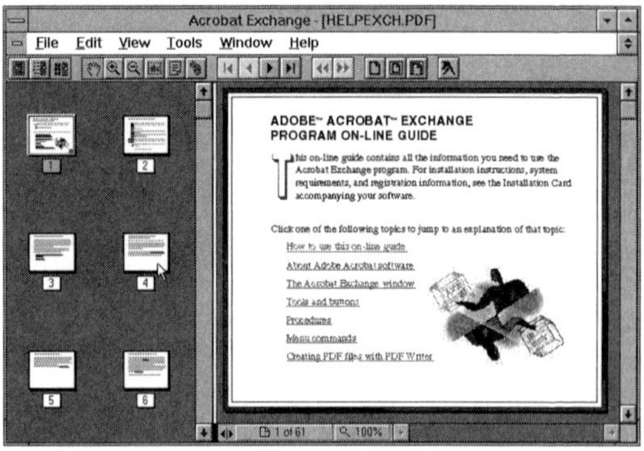

Figure 6.17. Clicking a thumbnail.

Page View Retracing Using the Navigation Stack

To navigate toward the beginning of the navigation stack, select the View menu's Go **B**ack command (see Figure 6.18) or click the tool bar's Go Back navigation button (see Figure 6.19). Otherwise, press Alt+hyphen (Alt+–).

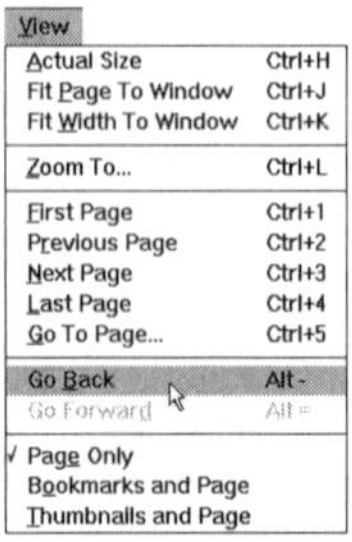

Figure 6.18. Selecting the View menu's Go Back command.

Figure 6.19. Clicking the Go Back navigation button.

To navigate toward the end of the navigation stack, select the View menu's Go Forwar**d** command (see Figure 6.20) or click the tool bar's Go Forward navigation button (see Figure 6.21). Otherwise, press Alt+=.

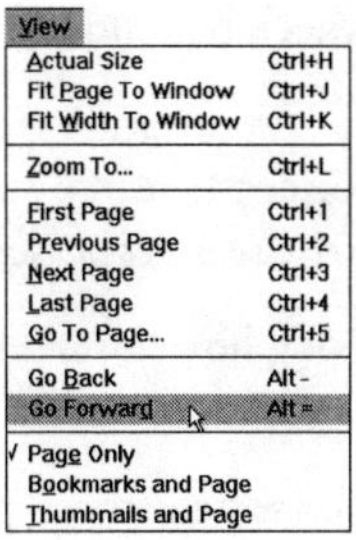

Figure 6.20. Selecting the View menu's Go Forward command.

Figure 6.21. Clicking the Go Forward navigation button.

String Searching

To search for a character string, select the Tools menu's **F**ind... command (see Figure 6.22) or click the tool bar's Find tool (see Figure 6.23). Otherwise, press Ctrl+F.

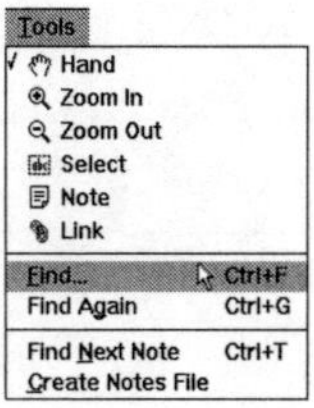

Figure 6.22. Selecting the Tools menu's Find command.

Figure 6.23. Selecting the Find tool from the tool bar.

When the Find dialog box appears, enter the search string in the Find What text box (see Figure 6.24).

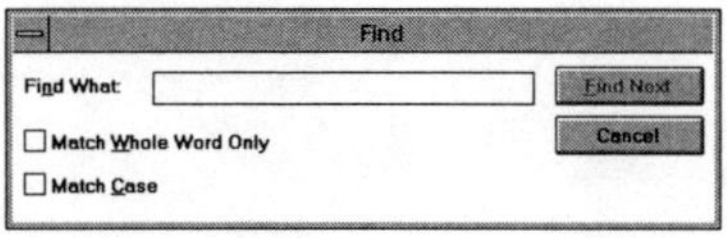

Figure 6.24. The Find dialog box.

Selecting the Match Whole Word Only check box indicates the search string letters must match the source string in length.

Selecting the Match Case check box indicates the search string letters must match the source string in capitalization (the search is case sensitive).

Click the Find Next button. The Find dialog box closes and page view highlights the word if it finds a match.

To find the next occurrence of the previous search string, press Ctrl+G or reselect the Tools menu's **F**ind... command. Click Find Next. The Find dialog box closes and page view highlights the word if it finds a match.

CHAPTER SEVEN

Page View Magnification

Acrobat Reader and Exchange offer a variety of ways to alter page view magnifications. Collectively, these techniques comprise a surprisingly powerful toolkit that reveals Acrobat's numerous design considerations.

Using the Zoom Tools

Zoom tools provide a quick way to double or halve the current magnification level. Changing magnification levels really enables Acrobat Reader and Exchange rendering capabilities to shine.

Making Global Page View Changes

Select the Tools menu's Zoom In or Zoom Out command (see Figures 7.1 and 7.2) or click the desired tool bar Zoom tool (see Figures 7.3 and 7.4). Clicking the selected tool on the active page view changes the magnification level, and the click point becomes the center of the page view. After clicking the page, drag the tool horizontally. The shape of the selected area is similar to the shape of the Document pane.

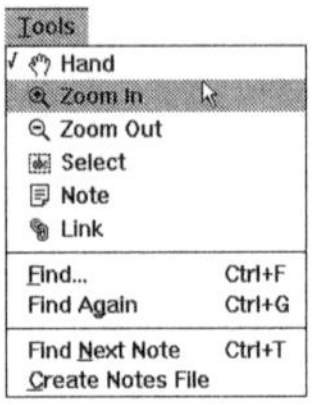

Figure 7.1. Selecting the Tools menu's Zoom In command.

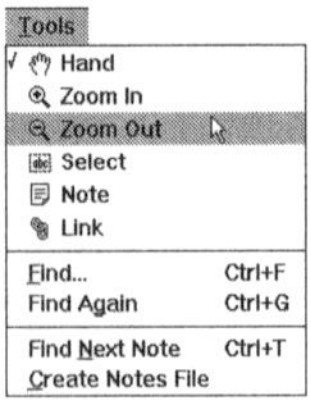

Figure 7.2. Selecting the Tools menu's Zoom Out command.

The Zoom In tool doubles the magnification level up to a maximum of 800 percent.

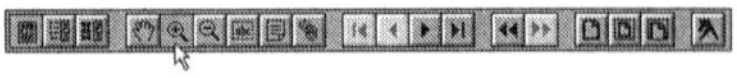

Figure 7.3. Selecting the Zoom In tool from the tool bar.

The Zoom Out tool halves the magnification level down to a minimum size of 12 percent.

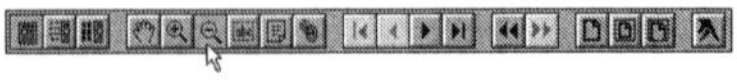

Figure 7.4. Selecting the Zoom Out tool from the tool bar.

Selecting Page View Areas

Click the desired tool bar Zoom tool or select the Tools menu's Zoom In or Zoom Out command. Select a rectangle by dragging the tool on the active page view.

The Zoom In tool (see Figure 7.5) expands the rectangular area so that it fills the Page View pane, if possible.

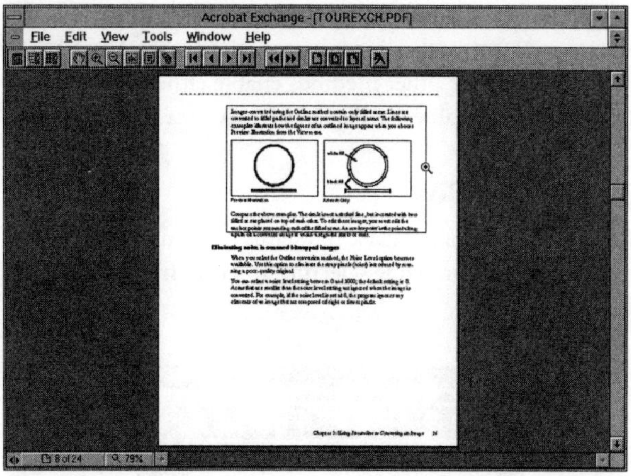

Figure 7.5. Using the Zoom In tool.

The Zoom Out tool (see Figure 7.6) shrinks the active page view to fit within the rectangular area.

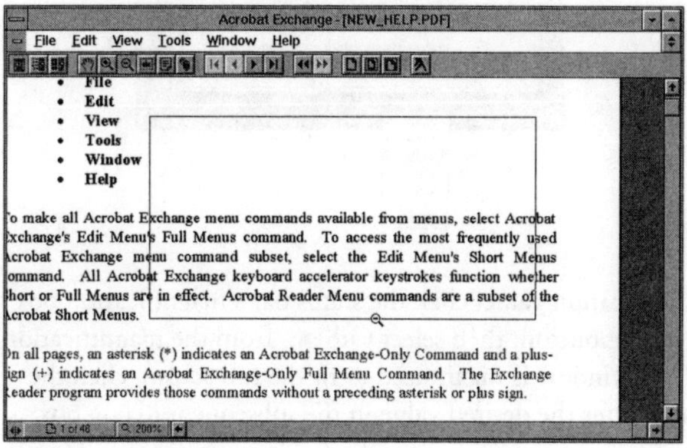

Figure 7.6. Using the Zoom Out tool.

To toggle the selected Zoom tool, hold down the Ctrl key while the selected Zoom tool is over the active page view.

Changing the Magnification Level Without Using the Zoom Tools

Zoom tools provide quick and easy ways to alter page view magnification levels. However, there are numerous other ingenious methods that Acrobat Reader and Exchange provide. These other methods enable either greater precision in selected magnification values or displayed page area.

Status Bar Magnification Box

To use a preselected magnification value, click the status bar's magnification box and hold down the mouse button while selecting an entry from the magnification list (see Figure 7.7).

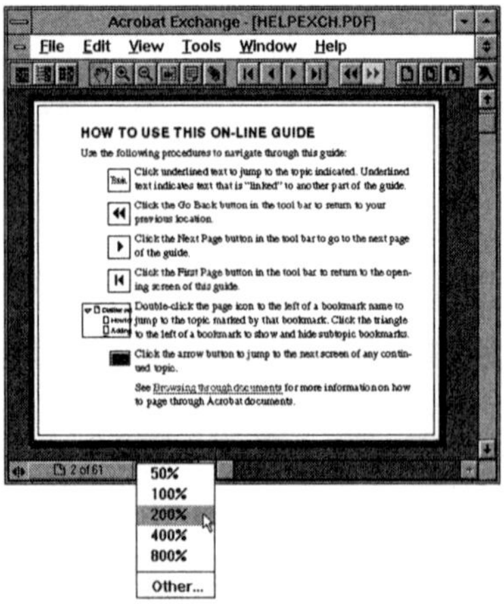

Figure 7.7. The magnification box entry list.

To use a custom magnification value, click the status bar's magnification box and hold down the mouse button; then select Other... from the magnification list. Alternatively, if the window is maximized to fit the full screen, click the magnification box and enter the desired value in the subsequent dialog box (see Figure 7.8).

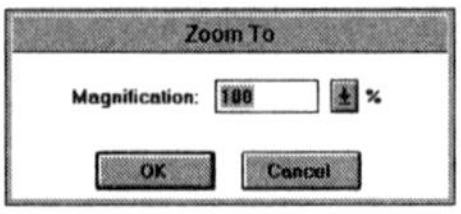

Figure 7.8. The Zoom To dialog box.

Thumbnail View Box

You can expose the thumbnails and resize the active page view's view box by dragging the view box handle (see Figure 7.9).

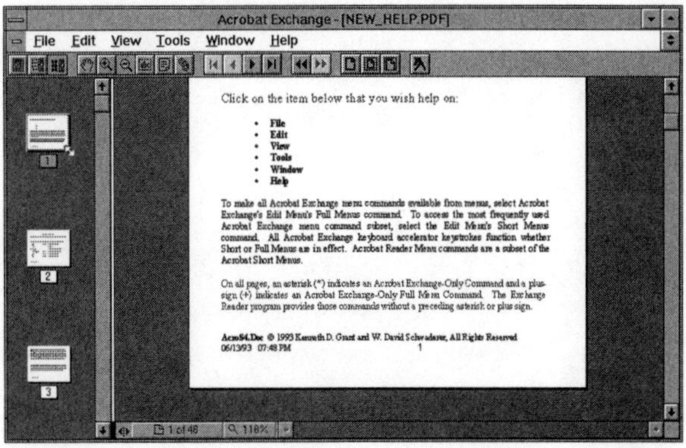

Figure 7.9. Dragging the view box's handle.

Tool Bar Magnification Buttons

Clicking the tool bar's Actual Size, Fit Page to Window, and Fit Width to Window buttons (see Figure 7.10) causes the following changes to the magnification of the active page view:

- *Actual Size button*—the magnification level changes to 100 percent.
- *Fit Page to Window button*—the magnification level changes to a value that enables the entire page to be displayed.
- *Fit Width to Window button*—the magnification level changes to a level that enables the current page width to completely appear within the Page View pane.

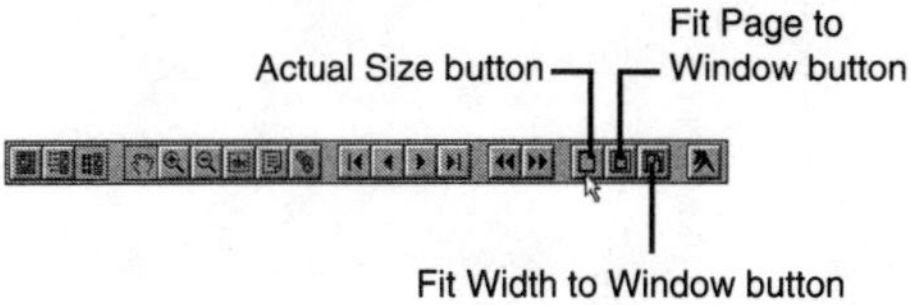

Figure 7.10. The Actual Size, Fit Page to Window, and Fit Width to Window buttons on the tool bar.

Making Changes from the Keyboard

Pressing the Ctrl key in conjunction with the plus key (+) *from the numeric keypad* doubles the magnification level up to a maximum of 800 percent. Pressing the Ctrl key in conjunction with the minus key (–) *from the numeric keypad* halves the magnification level down to a minimum of 12 percent.

Chapter Eight

Miscellaneous Functions

Acrobat Reader and Exchange provide numerous features that do not fall into the previously discussed categories. This chapter enumerates these features and their capabilities.

Copying Text to Clipboards

Select the Tools menu's Select Text command (see Figure 8.1) or click the tool bar's Text Selection tool (see Figure 8.2). The mouse pointer becomes a cross hair over the Page View pane. Click and drag the cursor to highlight the selected text. To start over, click anywhere.

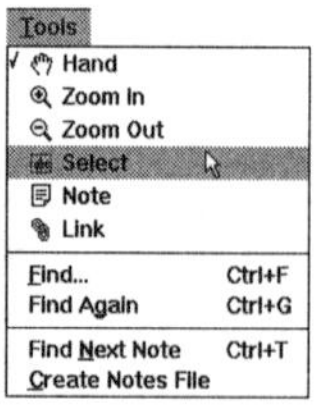

Figure 8.1.
Selecting the Tools menu's Select Text command.

Figure 8.2.
Selecting the Text Selection tool from the tool bar.

TIP

Marking text can seem confusing. Dragging the Text Selection tool over document text line fragments may or may not select the entire line, depending on how the application generates text output. As little as one character may be selected. Therefore, completely enclose all desired text to avoid unanticipated results.

Choosing the Edit menu's **C**opy command copies selected text to the Clipboard (see Figure 8.3).

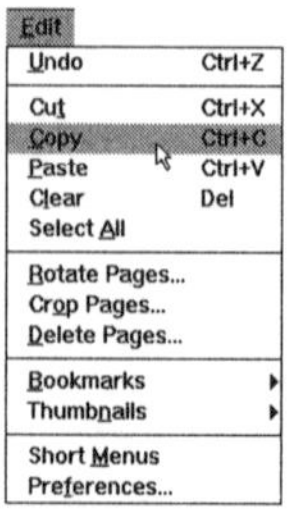

Figure 8.3.
Selecting the Edit menu's Copy command.

Select the Window menu's Show Clipboar**d** command (see Figure 8.4) to view selected text in a window titled *Clipboard Viewer*. Switch to other applications and paste the text elsewhere or paste it into bookmark names.

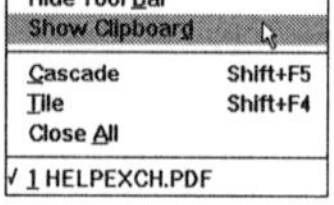

Figure 8.4.
Selecting the Window menu's Show Clipboard command.

TIP

In Windows Reader and Exchange, if the Clipboard Viewer window is not completely visible, selecting the Windows menu displays the Hide Clipboard command.

Deleting Document Pages (Exchange Only)

To delete document pages, select the Edit menu's Full **M**enus command. Select the Edit menu's **D**elete Pages... command (see Figure 8.5) and the Delete Pages dialog box will appear (see Figure 8.6). Enter the page range to delete and click OK, and then save the document.

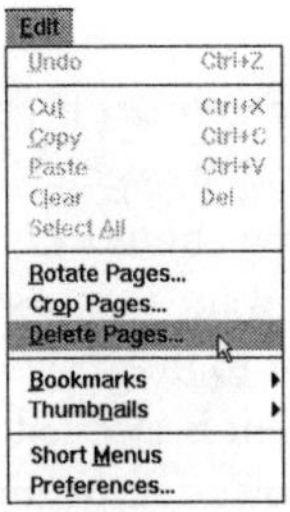

Figure 8.5. Selecting the Edit menu's Delete Pages command.

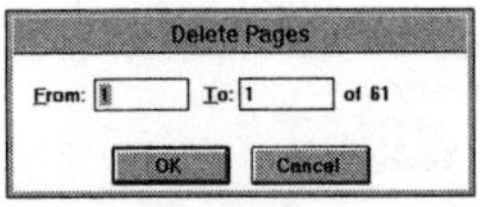

Figure 8.6. The Delete Pages dialog box.

Inserting Document Pages (Exchange Only)

To insert document pages, select Full Menus. Select the File menu's Inser**t**... command (see Figure 8.7) and the Insert dialog box will appear (see Figure 8.8).

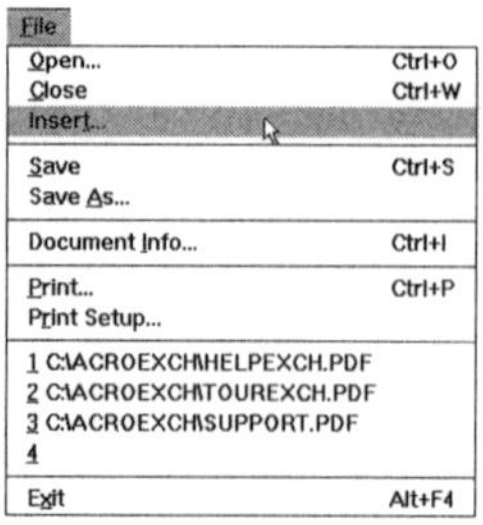

Figure 8.7.
The File Menu's Insert... selection.

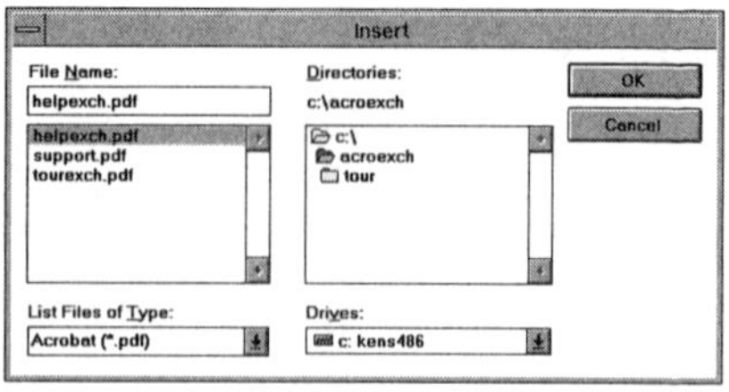

Figure 8.8.
The Insert dialog box.

Enter the document into which you want to insert pages, click OK, and another dialog box appears (see Figure 8.9). By default, the file inserts after the last page. Enter in the Page box the page number before or after which to insert the document. Select Before if you want to insert the document before the specified page; select After if you want to insert the document after the specified page. Click OK and the document is inserted at the specified location. Save the document file before you attempt any other actions.

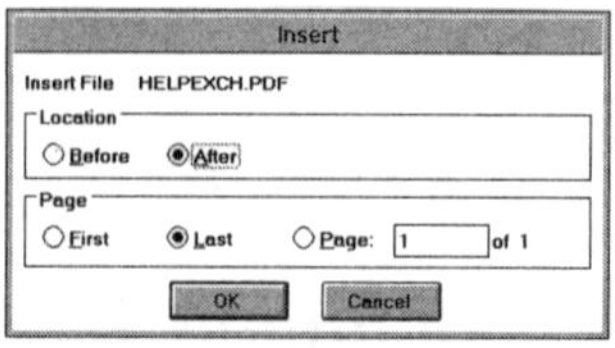

Figure 8.9.
Selecting where to insert the file.

Cropping Page Margins (Exchange Only)

To crop page margins, select Full Menus. Select the Edit menu's Crop Pages... command (see Figure 8.10) and the Crop Pages dialog box will appear (see Figure 8.11).

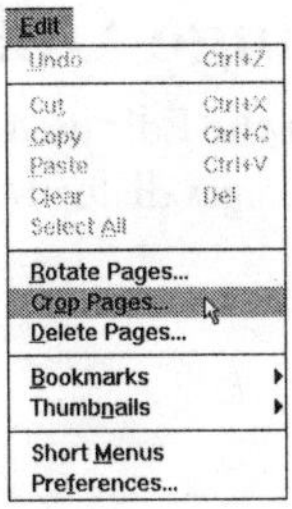

Figure 8.10. Selecting the Edit menu's Crop Pages... command.

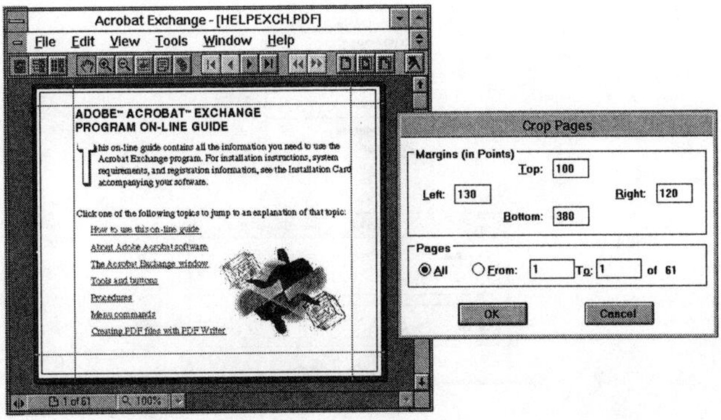

Figure 8.11. The Crop Pages dialog box.

The previously defined page margin point values for the current document appear in the margin boxes (72 points equal one inch). Enter new Top, Bottom, Left, and/or Right margin point values. When entering new margin values, lines appear in the Page View pane indicating the new margins. Enter the page range to which the new margins apply or accept the default, All pages. Clicking OK closes the Crop Pages dialog box. The selected document pages display with new margins and deleted thumbnails (see Figure 8.12).

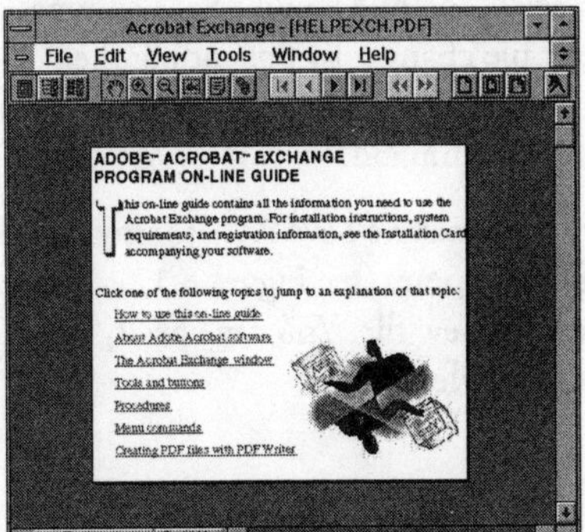

Figure 8.12. The resulting cropped page.

Rotating Pages (Exchange Only)

To rotate pages, select Full Menus. Select the Edit menu's **R**otate Pages... command (see Figure 8.13). The Rotate Pages dialog box will appear (see Figure 8.14).

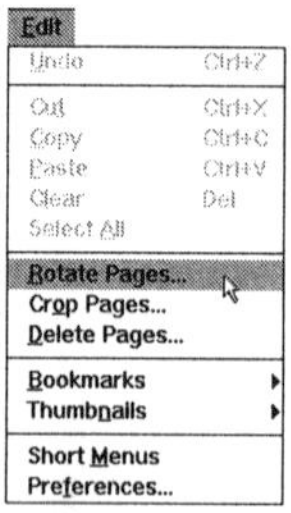

Figure 8.13. Selecting the Edit menu's Rotate Pages... command.

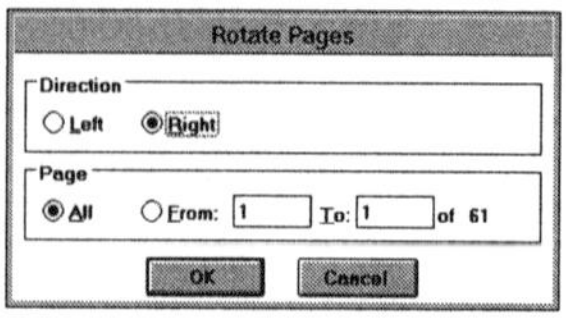

Figure 8.14. The Rotate Pages dialog box.

Select the direction to rotate the pages: either Left (counterclockwise) or Right (clockwise). Specify the range of pages to rotate or accept All pages as the default. When you click OK, the Rotate Pages dialog box closes and the specified pages are rotated, deleting their thumbnails.

Saving Document Changes (Exchange Only)

To perform an incremental save, select the File menu's **S**ave command (see Figure 8.15). This saves all current file changes by appending them to the end of the file. Using the **S**ave command always increases the size of existing files. To shrink file size, use the Save **A**s... command.

To save a new PDF file, select the File menu's Save **A**s... command (see Figure 8.16) and the Save As dialog box appears (see Figure 8.17). This command cleans up the current file by creating a new file. You can specify the same name for the new file and thus create a fresh file copy.

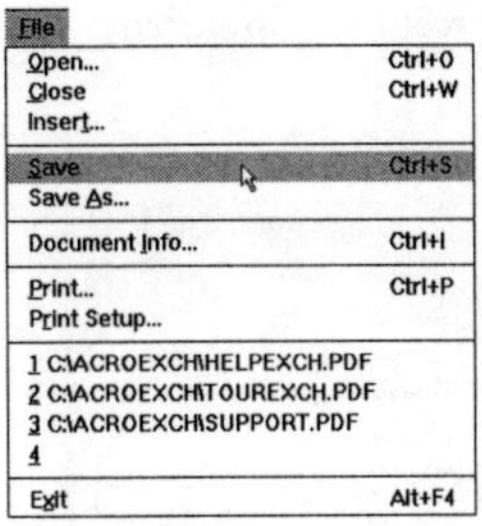

Figure 8.15. Selecting the File menu's Save command.

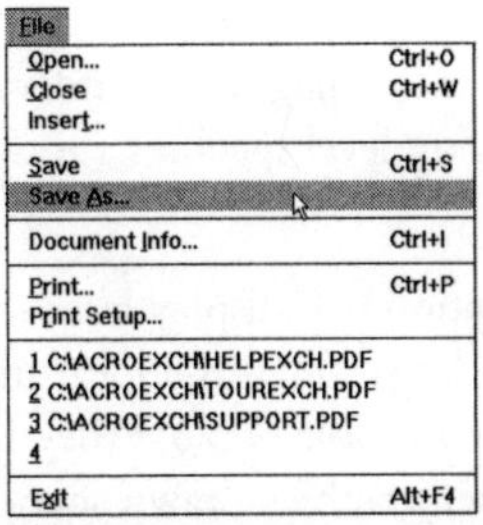

Figure 8.16. Selecting the File menu's Save As... command.

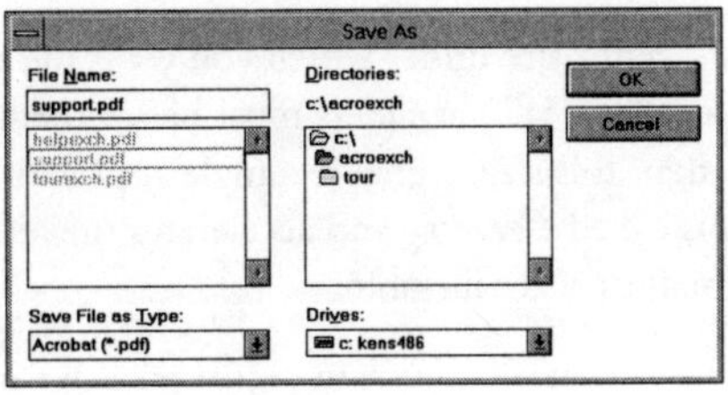

Figure 8.17. The Save As dialog box.

Setting Preferences (Program Initialization Values)

To set program initialization values, select the Edit menu's Preferences... command (see Figure 8.18).

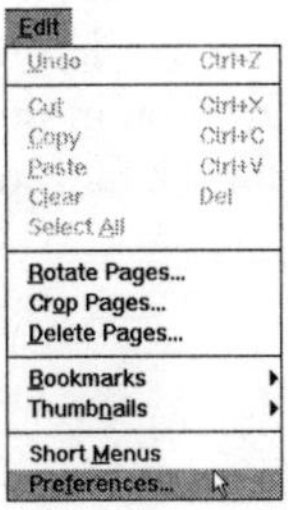

Figure 8.18. Selecting the Edit menu's Preferences... command.

There are five preferences to set in the resulting Preferences dialog box (see Figure 8.19).

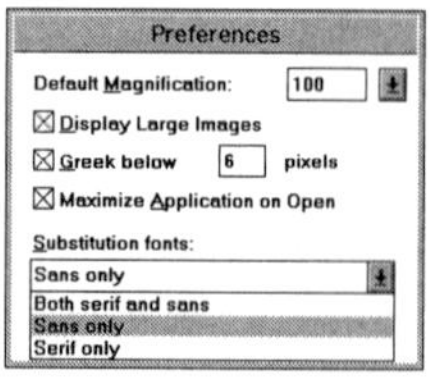

Figure 8.19. The Preferences dialog box.

In the Default Magnification box, enter the magnification level you want for the Page View. The default magnification level specifies a zoom level that is in effect when new documents open.

Checking the Display Large Images option will display large images in the document. If your documents contain large, slow-to-appear images, you can disable their rendering. Images are recognizable because they are rendered as bands. This option does not affect other graphics-drawn shapes, lines, and filled areas.

In the Greek Below box, enter a point size under which you want the text to be Greeked. The Greek size specifies how tall characters must be for them to be rendered. If characters are less than this size, a gray rectangle appears in place of the characters. This process is called *Greeking* and accelerates the representation of characters that are so small they are illegible.

Checking the Maximize Application on Open box does just what it says. If Maximize Application on Open is selected, Acrobat fills the screen with the application's window when it starts.

From the Substitution Fonts list, select whether you want to use both the Serif and Sans Serif fonts, only the Sans Serif, or only the Serif multimaster font for font substitution. Substitution fonts should normally be set to Both Serif and Sans for best substitution. If you have trouble printing to a PostScript printer and generate blank pages or VM error messages, your printer may be running out of memory. Using Serif Only or Sans Only uses less memory. When you are finished setting your preferences, click OK. You must exit Windows and restart (or just restart if using a Macintosh) for the font substitution option to take full effect.

Additional Windows Features

Additional Windows features enable you to make some customizations for Windows Exchange or Reader. While simultaneously holding down the Ctrl+Shift+M key combination, select the Edit menu's Preferences... command. Figure 8.20 shows the resulting More Preferences dialog box.

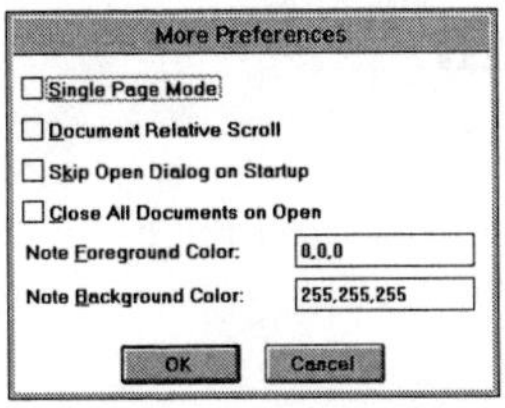

Figure 8.20.
The More Preferences dialog box.

Checking the Single Page Mode option switches the scroll bar to *page relative* mode. In this mode, the top of the vertical scroll bar represents the top of the current page, and the bottom of the vertical scroll bar represents the bottom of the page. When using this mode, you do not move between pages when you use the vertical scroll bar.

Checking the Document Relative Scroll option sets the scroll bar to move relative to the document, not just from page to page. If, for example, the document had two pages and the vertical scroll bar slider, or thumb, was positioned three-quarters of the way down its length, the resulting display would be positioned halfway down page 2 instead of at the top of page 2.

Checking the Skip Open Dialog on Startup option causes Acrobat Exchange or Reader to not request a filename to open on launch. This is useful if you launch Acrobat as an icon with the `LOAD=` line in the WIN.INI Windows file. Checking the Close All Documents on Open option is useful for browsing. Subsequent requests to open a file cause any and all open PDF documents to close before the requested file is opened.

The last two fields enable you to customize annotation colors. You can change these fields and their resulting colors only if there aren't any notes currently open on any open document. The three numeric values represent the foreground (text) and the background (the note) component color values of red, green, and blue, respectively. For example, if you want white text on a blue background, enter the values `255,255,255` for the Note Foreground Color and `0,0,255` for the Note Background Color. The component values range between zero and 255. No blanks or characters are allowed. The results are dependent on the display adapter.

These features are provided for users who want slightly different configurations, but these features are not guaranteed to work with all systems. Some existing keyboards do not allow the dialog activation. For those systems, Appendix F, "Reader and Exchange INI File Settings," shows the equivalent settings for the acroexch.ini or acroread.ini file.

Displaying Document Creation Information

To display the Document Info dialog box, select the File menu's Document Info... command (see Figures 8.21 and 8.22).

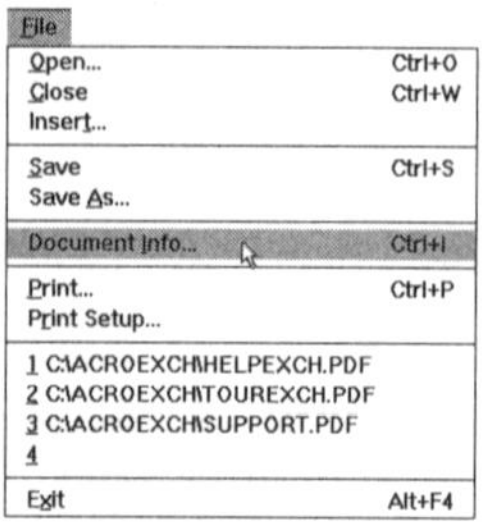

Figure 8.21. Selecting the File menu's Document Info... command.

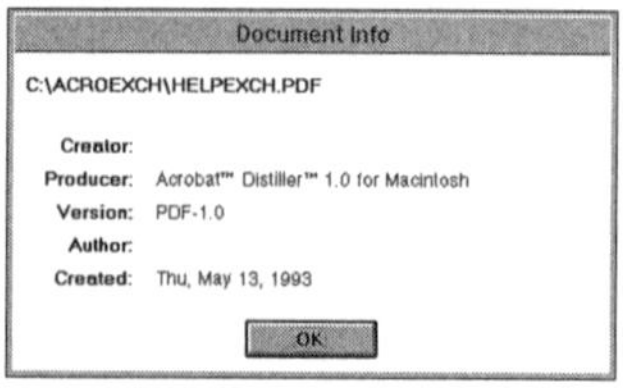

Figure 8.22. The Document Info dialog box.

TIP

Pressing the Ctrl+Shift key combination (Option+Shift on the Macintosh) while selecting the File menu's Document Info... command produces a Document Info dialog box with font substitution data (see Figure 8.23).

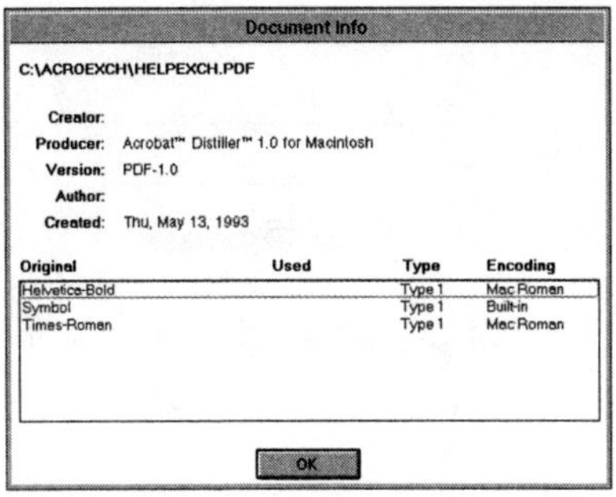

Figure 8.23. The Document Info dialog box with font data.

Printing

To set up a printer, select the File menu's Print Setup... command (see Figure 8.24). The Print Setup dialog box will appear (see Figure 8.25).

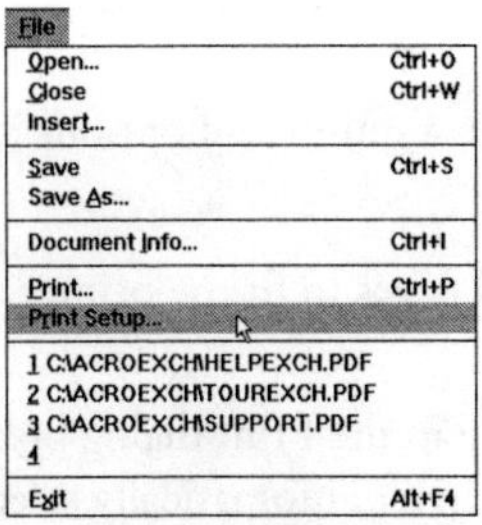

Figure 8.24. Selecting the File menu's Print Setup... command.

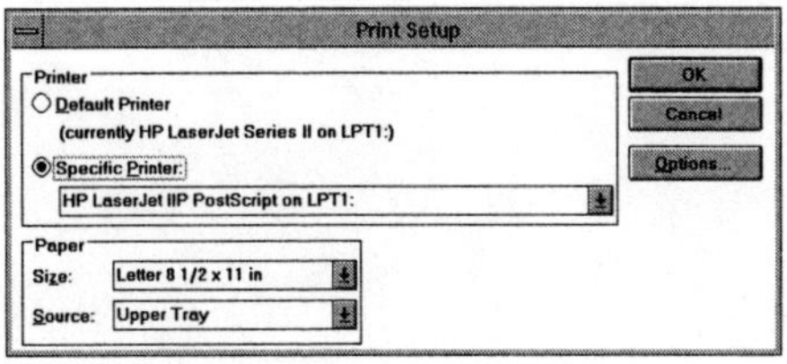

Figure 8.25. The Print Setup dialog box.

To print, select the File menu's **Print...** command (see Figure 8.26). The Print dialog box will appear (see Figure 8.27).

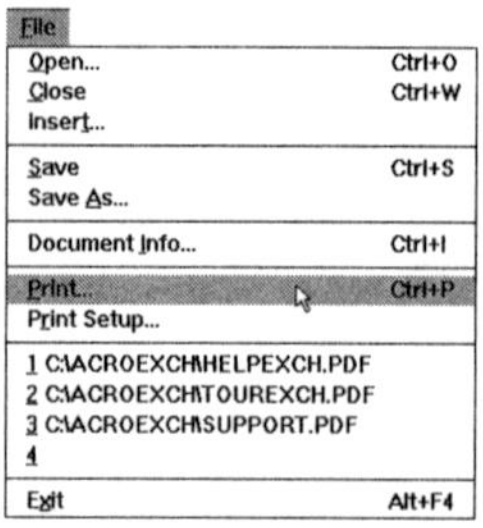

Figure 8.26. Selecting the File menu's Print... command.

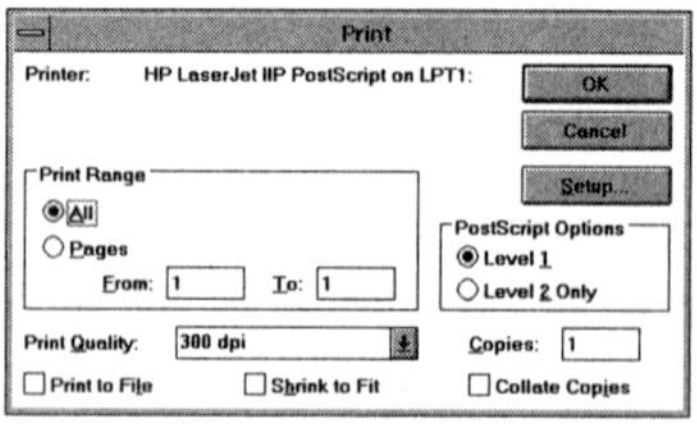

Figure 8.27. The Print dialog box.

The Print dialog box presents you with a number of options. Select the following:

- *Shrink to Fit*—shrinks oversized pages to fit the printer's current paper size.
- *PostScript Options*—appears only in the Print dialog box for PostScript printers. The Adobe PSPrinter driver automatically selects appropriate printer PostScript options. The Level 2 option accelerates printers capable of PostScript Level 2.

C H A P T E R

NINE

Document Notes

We've all used those colorful sticky paper notes on real paper documents, so it should come as no surprise that Acrobat Exchange enables you to attach electronic sticky notes to electronic paper documents. If you are using Windows, you can even select the color of the notes.

Note Essentials

There are many operations essential to using the document notes in Acrobat Exchange. The following sections enumerate these operations.

Opening Notes

To open a note, double-click the Note icon (see Figure 9.1). The note may be gray or yellow, depending on whether it is selected or deselected, respectively.

Closing Note Windows

To close a note window, double-click the close box in the note window's upper-left corner (see

Figure 9.2). This reduces the note to an icon. Note icons reside anywhere on the active page view. The note can remain open while it is an icon.

Figure 9.1.
A Note icon (enlarged here for clarity).

Figure 9.2.
Closing a note window.

Resizing Notes

To resize a note, select the open note and drag the window handle to adjust the note to the desired size (see Figure 9.3). Notice that the text reflows in the note as you resize it.

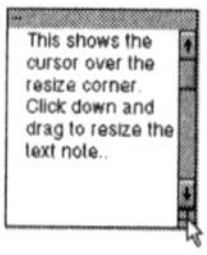

Figure 9.3.
Resizing a note window.

Deleting Notes (Exchange Only)

To delete a note, first close the note window if it is already open. If the note is an icon, click the note to turn it gray. Press Delete, Clear, or the Backspace key to delete the note.

Creating Individual Notes (Exchange Only)

To create individual notes, select the Edit menu's Full Menus command. Then select the Tools menu's Note command (see Figure 9.4) or click the tool bar's Note tool (see Figure 9.5). When the mouse pointer is over the Page View pane, the mouse pointer becomes a cross hair.

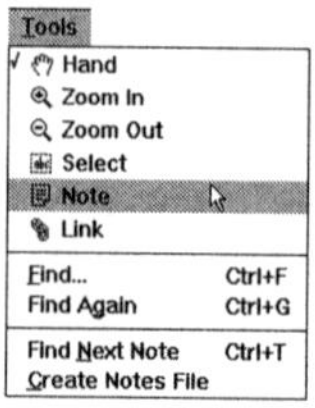

Figure 9.4.
Selecting the Note tool from the Tools menu.

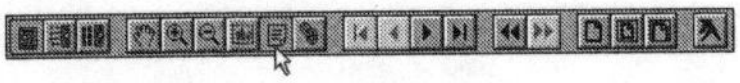

Figure 9.5.
Selecting the Note tool from the tool bar.

Sizing the Note Window

To use the default setting, click where you want to place the upper-left corner of the note. The note will be approximately 2 inches deep by 3 inches wide.

To set a custom size for your note, drag the cross-hair cursor down and to the right. The maximum size for your note is approximately 4 inches deep by 6 inches wide.

You can enter the text into the note and manipulate it by optionally using Cut, Copy, Paste, Clear, and Undo. The text will scroll if it does not fit inside the note window.

TIP

To create multiple notes (Exchange only), hold down the Ctrl key when selecting the tool bar's Note tool or the Tools menu's Note command. Otherwise, the Note tool is deselected after a note is created. Clicking another tool deselects the Note tool.

Creating Note PDF Files

To create note PDF files, select the Tools menu's **C**reate Notes File command (see Figure 9.6). This creates a new PDF file that contains all the note text and appears in a new document window (Figure 9.7). Reader users can only print the new file or copy its information to the Clipboard.

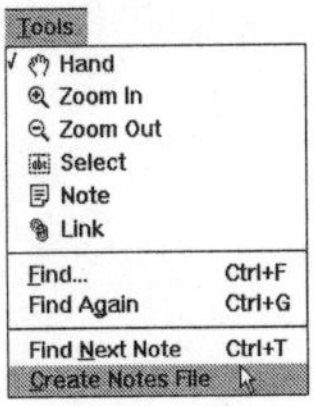

Figure 9.6.
Selecting the Tools menu's Create Notes File command.

Figure 9.7.
A sample output window.

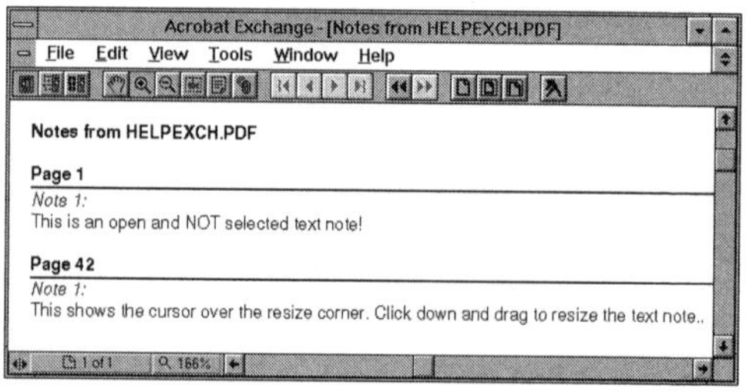

CHAPTER TEN

Document Bookmarks

Bookmarks are named destinations within a document. When you click a bookmark's page icon, you jump to the associated document location. It displays at the magnification level selected when the bookmark was created.

Bookmark Essentials

There are many operations essential to using Acrobat's document bookmarks. The following sections enumerate these operations.

Exposing Bookmarks

To expose a bookmark, select the View menu's Bookmarks and Page command (see Figure 10.1) or click the tool bar's Bookmarks and Page button (see Figure 10.2).

Destination Viewing

To view the destination of a bookmark, double-click the bookmark's page icon. The associated destination appears in the Page View pane.

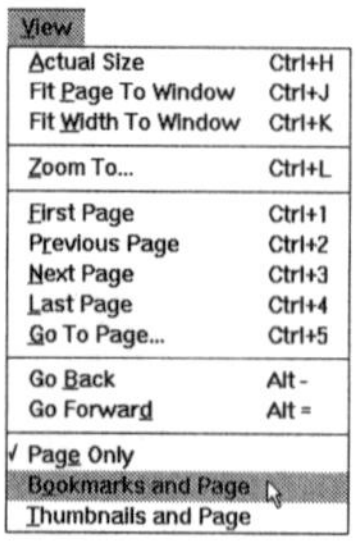

Figure 10.1. Selecting the View menu's Bookmarks and Page command.

Figure 10.2. Selecting the Bookmarks and Page button from the tool bar.

Expanding a Subordinate List

To expand a subordinate list, click the right-pointing bookmark triangle. The triangle will turn into a down-pointing triangle and the subordinate list will be revealed (see Figure 10.3).

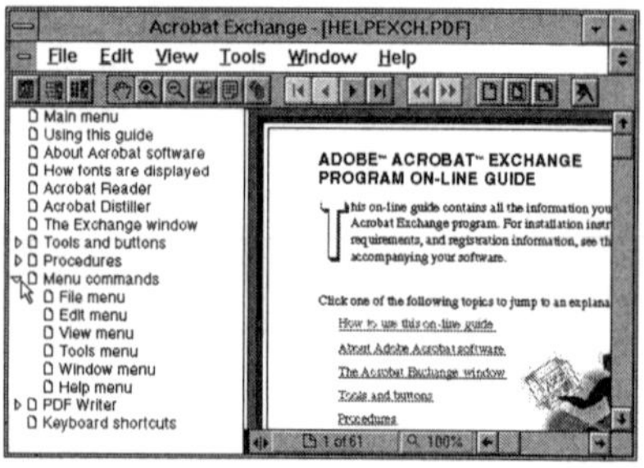

Figure 10.3. Expanding a subordinate list.

Contracting a Subordinate List

To contract a subordinate list, click the down-pointing bookmark triangle. The triangle will turn into a right-pointing triangle and the subordinate list will contract (see Figure 10.4).

Creating a Bookmark (Exchange Only)

To create a bookmark, select the Edit menu's Full Menus command. Move to the desired active page view. Expose bookmarks as described earlier in this chapter. If the bookmark list exists, expand the list as necessary and click the bookmark under which you want to place the new bookmark. (The default position is the bottom of the list if you do not select a bookmark.)

Select **B**ookmarks from the Edit menu, and then select the submenu's **N**ew command (see Figure 10.5). Alternatively, you could press Ctrl+B in the Short Menus. A new untitled bookmark entry appears. Enter the name of the bookmark or paste it from the Clipboard.

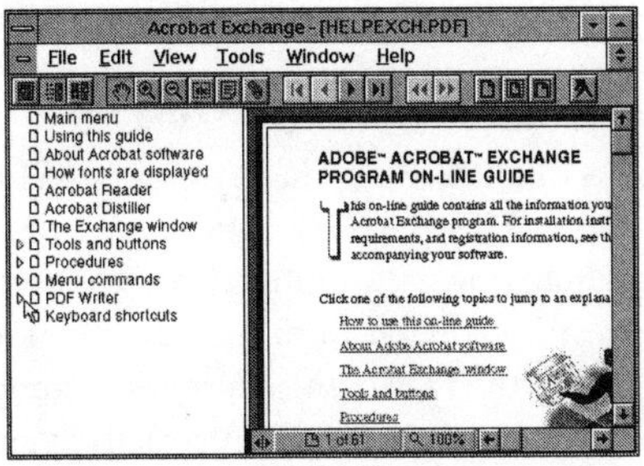

Figure 10.4. Contracting a subordinate list.

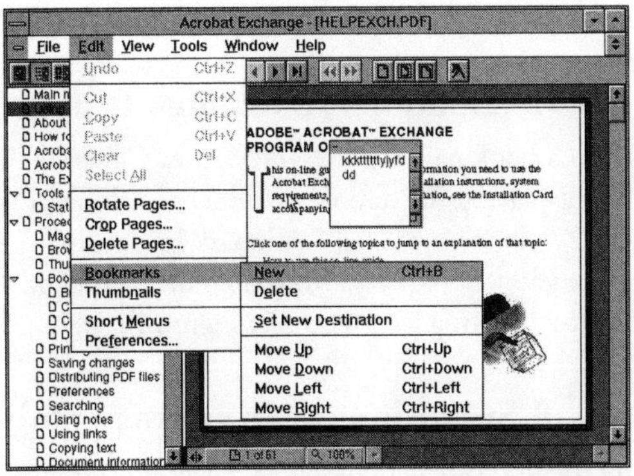

Figure 10.5. The Edit menu's Bookmarks submenu.

TIP

Pressing Ctrl+C, Ctrl+B, Ctrl+V (Command+C, Command+B, Command+V on a Macintosh) selects marked text from annotations and PDF documents to paste into Acrobat bookmark names. This enables you to select, for example, Table of Contents headings with the Text Selection tool, and quickly paste them as bookmark names.

Renaming a Bookmark (Exchange Only)

To rename a bookmark, click the bookmark name. You can then retype the name, or you can paste the new name from the Clipboard.

Simple Indenting to the Right (Exchange Only)

Select the bookmark you want to indent by clicking the bookmark's page icon. Next, select **B**ookmarks from the Edit menu. A submenu will pop up (see Figure 10.5), from which you should select the Move **R**ight command, or you can press Ctrl+RightArrow.

Bookmark List Reordering (Exchange Only)

To reorder a bookmark list, select Full Menus. Then you can select the Bookmark you want to move by clicking the bookmark's page icon. To select two or more bookmarks, hold down the Shift key while you click the bookmarks' Page icons. Select **B**ookmarks from the Edit menu to reach the submenu (see Figure 10.5), and then select the appropriate command: Move **L**eft, Move **R**ight, Move **U**p, or Move **D**own. Alternatively, use the Ctrl+LeftArrow, Ctrl+RightArrow, Ctrl+UpArrow, or Ctrl+DownArrow key combinations, respectively.

Changing Bookmark Destinations (Exchange Only)

To change the destination of a bookmark, select Full Menus. Generate the desired active page view by displaying the desired document position at the desired magnification level. Select the intended Bookmark by clicking the bookmark's page icon. Then select **B**ookmarks from the Edit menu and then **S**et New Destination from the resulting submenu (see Figure 10.5).

Delete Bookmarks and Subordinates (Exchange Only)

To delete a bookmark and its subordinate bookmarks, select Full Menus. Then select the bookmark you want to delete by clicking the bookmark's page icon. Hold down the Shift key while you click the icon if you want to select two or more bookmarks. Finally, select **B**ookmarks from the Edit menu and then D**e**lete from the resulting submenu (see Figure 10.5).

CHAPTER ELEVEN

Document Thumbnails

Thumbnails are miniature graphical page representations. They enable you to identify pages and adjust document page views, using the thumbnail view box and sizing the thumbnails.

Thumbnail Essentials

There are many operations essential to using Acrobat's document thumbnails. The following sections enumerate these operations.

Exposing Thumbnails

To expose thumbnails, select the View menu's Thumbnails and Page command (see Figure 11.1) or click the tool bar's Thumbnails and Page button (see Figure 11.2). The exposed thumbnail has a number under it, which represents the physical page relative to the first page in the document. If there is an asterisk next to it, the thumbnail (which is normally scaled to one-eighth of the actual size) is scaled down even more so the thumbnail is no bigger than a thumbnail of an 11-by-11-inch page.

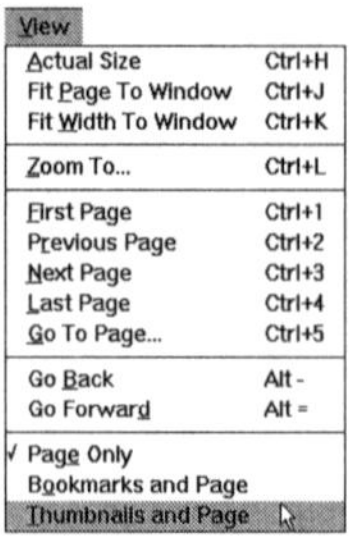

Figure 11.1. Selecting the View menu's Thumbnails and Page command.

Figure 11.2. Selecting the Thumbnails and Page button from the tool bar.

Page Jumps

To jump to a new page, click the desired page's thumbnail. The click point is the center of the page view, if possible.

Active Page View Adjustments

To make adjustments in an active page view, drag the current page's thumbnail view box on the thumbnail (see Figure 11.3), or click the thumbnail to relocate the center of the view box. Dragging the view box handle resizes the view box, adjusting the active page view magnification (see Figure 11.4). You may also drag the view box around on the thumbnail by clicking and dragging the view box. If you click and drag outside of the view box, you create a new view box, which replaces the current view box when you release the mouse button. The active page view then adjusts to the new view. On the Macintosh, the view attempts to dynamically change while you drag or size the view box. Under Windows, you may also Shift+click the inside of a view box and drag it to create a new view box.

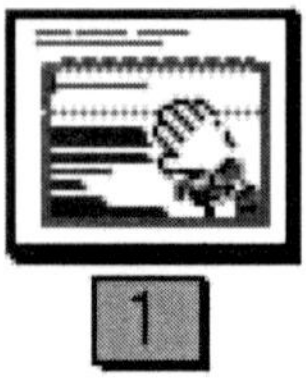

Figure 11.3. Dragging the thumbnail view box (enlarged here for clarity).

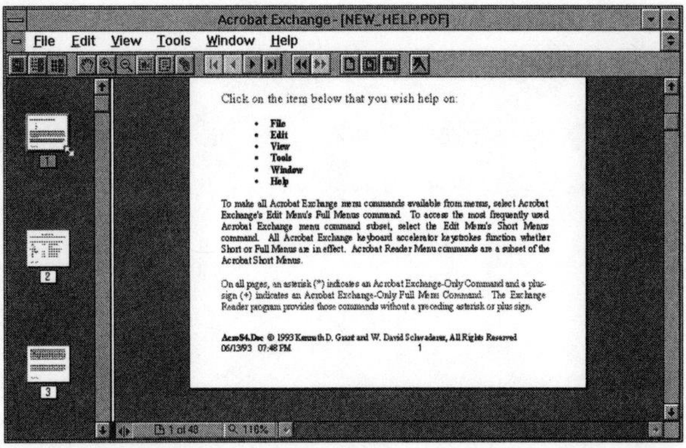

Figure 11.4. Dragging the view box handle.

Creating Thumbnails (Exchange Only)

To create missing thumbnails, select Full Menus. Then select Thumb**n**ails from the Edit menu. From the resulting submenu, select the **C**reate All... command (see Figure 11.5) and the Create All Thumbnails dialog box appears (see Figure 11.6). Only missing thumbnails are created.

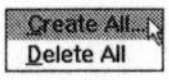

Figure 11.5. Selecting Create All... from the Thumbnails submenu.

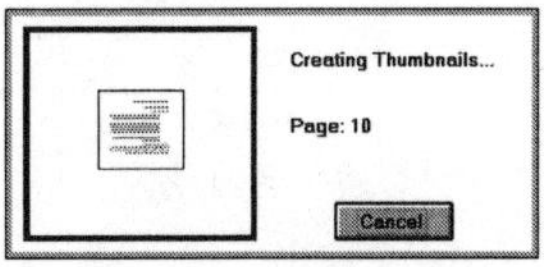

Figure 11.6. The Create All Thumbnails dialog box.

Deleting Thumbnails (Exchange Only)

To delete thumbnails, first select Full Menus. Next, select Thumb**n**ails from the Edit menu, and then select **D**elete All from the resulting submenu (see Figure 11.7). Cropping and rotating pages deletes their associated thumbnails. Deleted thumbnails appear gray.

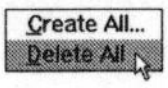

Figure 11.7. Selecting Delete All from the Thumbnails submenu.

CHAPTER

TWELVE

Document Hypertext Links

Hypertext links enable you to jump to document destinations by clicking on the Link buttons found within documents. When using Acrobat Exchange, you can create hypertext links other Reader and Exchange users can use. After jumping to a hypertext location, you can return to the Link button by using the navigation stack.

Using a Link

To use a link, click anywhere inside the Link button. The cursor becomes an arrow when it is positioned over either visible or invisible Link buttons.

Creating Individual Links (Exchange Only)

To create an individual link, first select the Edit menu's Full Menus command. Generate the desired active page view for the Link button's placement. Next, select the Tools menu's Link command (see Figure 12.1) or click the tool bar's Link tool (see Figure 12.2).

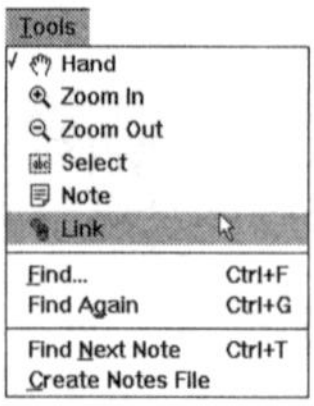

Figure 12.1.
Selecting the Link tool from the Tools menu.

Figure 12.2.
Selecting the Link tool from the tool bar.

The mouse pointer becomes a cross hair over the Page View pane. Holding down the mouse button and dragging it over an active page view draws a Link button, as shown in Figure 12.3. Simply clicking the active page view produces a warning message (see Figure 12.4).

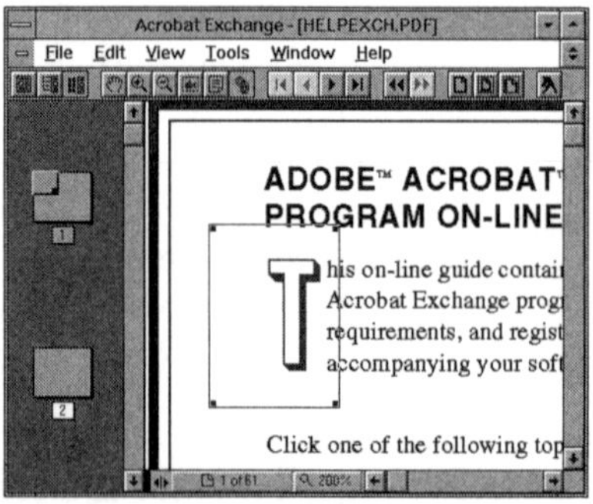

Figure 12.3.
Creating a Link button.

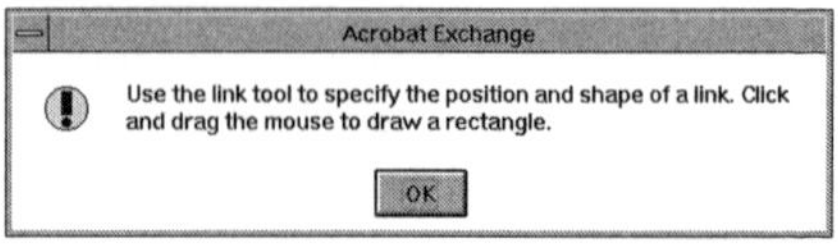

Figure 12.4.
A link creation warning box.

After the link creation dialog box appears, generating a document page view and clicking OK associates a destination with the Link button. Clicking OK before you produce a new page view produces the warning shown in Figure 12.5.

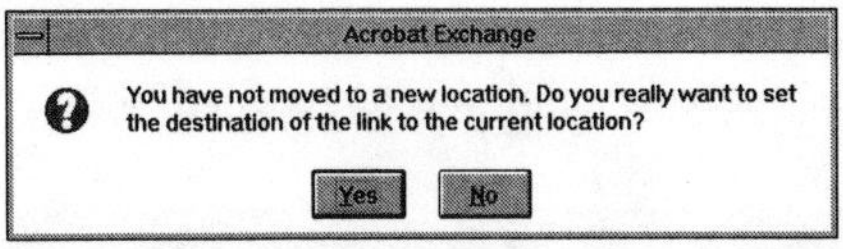

Figure 12.5. Another link creation warning box.

TIP

To create multiple links (Exchange only), hold down the Ctrl key when you select the tool bar's Link tool or Tools menu's Link command. Otherwise, the Link tool will deselect after link creation. Clicking another tool deselects the Link tool.

Releasing the mouse button displays the Link button and displays the Create Link dialog box (see Figure 12.6). For invisible links, select the Invisible Link option.

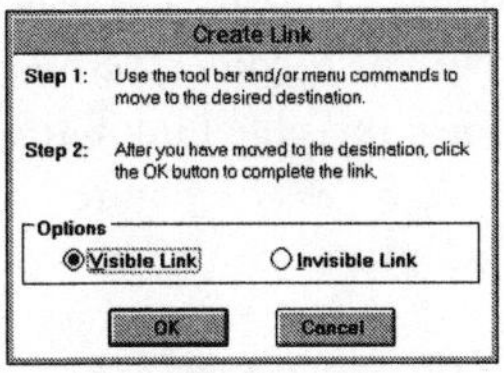

Figure 12.6. The Create Link dialog box.

Finally, generate the desired active page view destination. Click OK to close the dialog box and redisplay the Link button's page view.

Manipulating Link Buttons

Sometimes when using Exchange, you need to modify Link buttons or their associated destinations. For example, when a destination page is deleted and replaced with an updated page, you must redefine the Link button's destination. As always, Acrobat products provide the necessary means for you to accomplish your objectives.

Moving Link Buttons (Exchange Only)

To move a Link button, click the tool bar's Link tool or select the Tools menu's Link command. The mouse pointer becomes a cross hair, displaying all active page view invisible Link buttons. Then position the cursor inside the button and drag the button to a new location (see Figure 12.7). The Link tool does not automatically deselect because a link was not created.

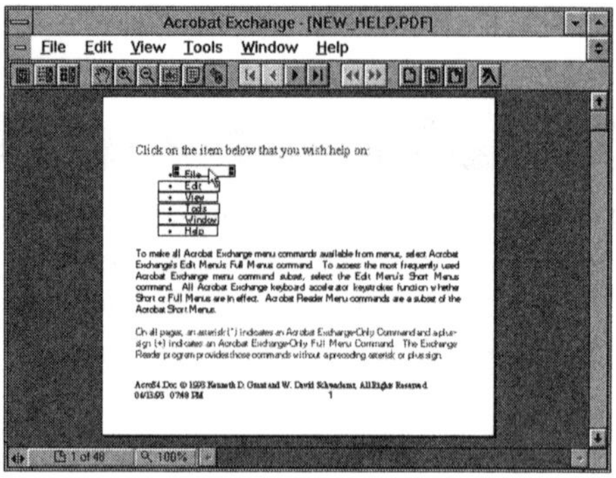

Figure 12.7. Dragging a Link button.

Resizing Link Buttons (Exchange Only)

To resize a Link button, click the tool bar's Link tool or select the Tools menu's Link command. The mouse pointer becomes a cross hair over the page view pane, displaying all active page view invisible Link buttons. Then select the Link button and drag the button's handles (see Figure 12.8). The Link tool does not automatically deselect because a link was not created.

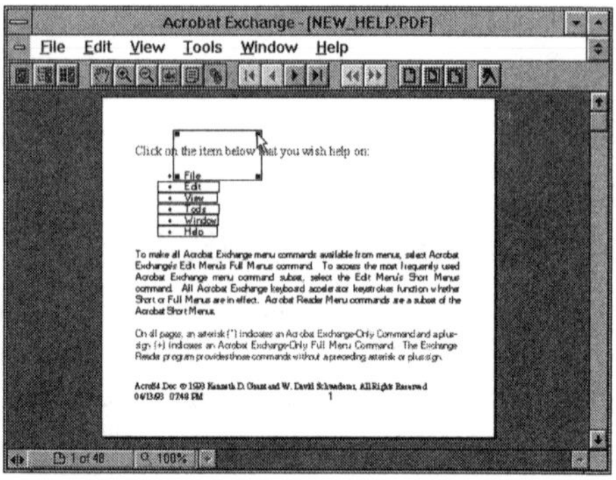

Figure 12.8. Dragging a Link button's sizing handle.

Changing Link Button Destinations (Exchange Only)

To change the destination of a Link button, click the tool bar's Link tool or select the Tools menu's Link command. The mouse pointer becomes a cross hair over the Page View pane, displaying all active page view invisible Link buttons. Double-click the desired Link button to reveal the Edit Link dialog box (see Figure 12.9). Generate the desired active page view destination and click OK.

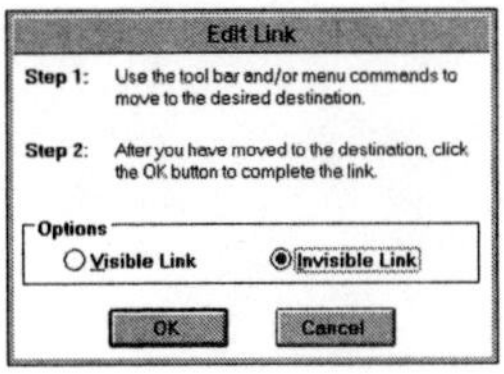

Figure 12.9. The Edit Link dialog box.

Changing Link Button Visibility (Exchange Only)

To change the visibility of a Link button, click the tool bar's Link tool or select the Tools menu's Link command. The mouse pointer becomes a cross hair over the Page View pane, displaying all active page view invisible Link buttons. Double-click the desired Link button to reveal the Edit Link dialog box. Select either Visible Link or Invisible Link, and then click OK.

Deleting Link Buttons (Exchange Only)

To delete a Link button, click the tool bar's Link tool or select the Tools menu's Link command. The mouse pointer becomes a cross hair over the Page View pane, displaying all active page view invisible Link buttons. Click the victim Link button and press the Backspace, Clear, or Delete key.

CHAPTER

THIRTEEN

Exchange's PDF Writer

The PDF Writer driver installs with Acrobat's Exchange program. It creates PDF files by receiving non-PostScript print information from an application and converting that information into PDF files. Although potentially more convenient than Acrobat's Network or Personal Distiller, PDF Writer document processing for Encapsulated PostScript (EPS) images or documents using unique non-PostScript printer features is not always successful. For example, PDF Writer converts EPS images to bitmap images, which display poorly if they display at all. When PDF Writer produces unsatisfactory results, use Acrobat's Network or Personal Distiller. Your system administrator or Adobe dealer can provide you with more Distiller program information.

Using PDF Writer

To create a PDF file using PDF Writer:

1. Start the application and open a document.
2. Select the File menu's Print Setup... command.
3. When the system's Print Setup dialog box appears, select PDFWriter on FILE: in the Installed Printers drop-down list (see Figure 13.1).

Figure 13.1.
The Print Setup dialog box.

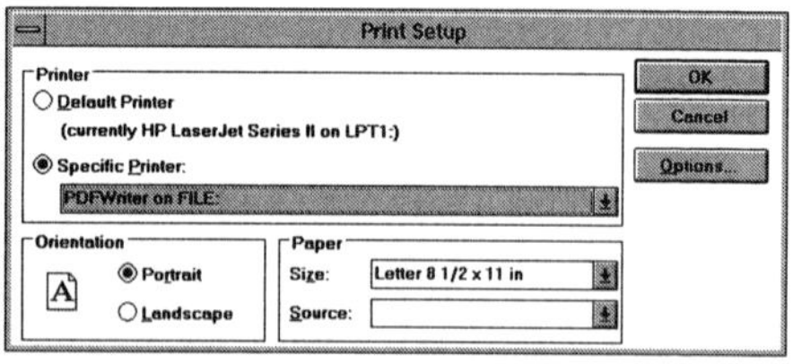

4. Select Options.... The PDFWriter on FILE: dialog box appears (see Figure 13.2).

Figure 13.2.
The PDFWriter on FILE: dialog box.

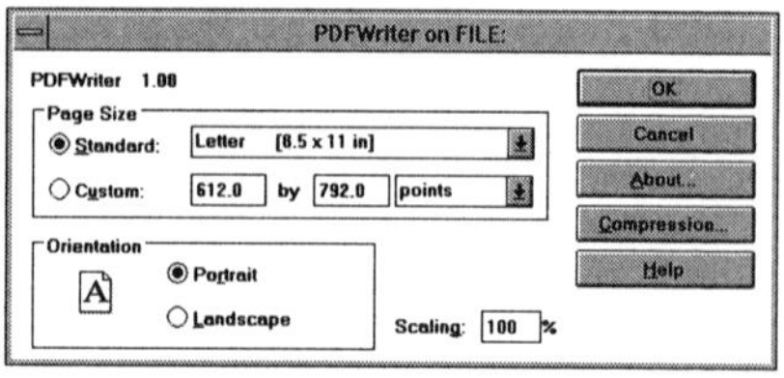

5. From the PDFWriter on FILE: dialog box, select the printer paper size from the Page Size Standard drop-down list or enter the page dimensions for Custom size document pages (see Figures 13.3 and 13.4).

6. Select Compression... to display the Compression Options dialog box (see Figure 13.5) if you need to change the default compression settings.

Figure 13.3.
Selecting a page size from the Standard drop-down list.

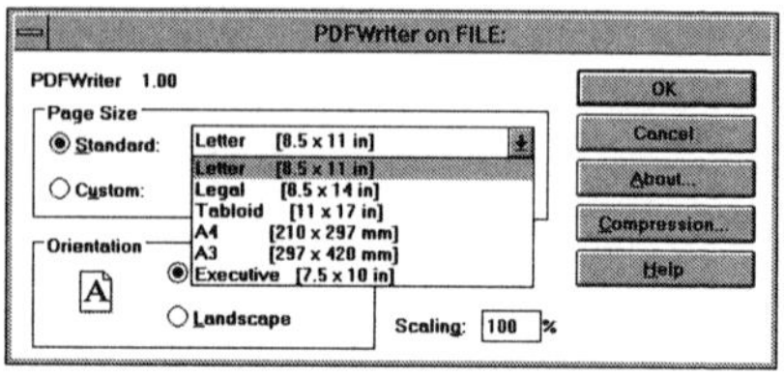

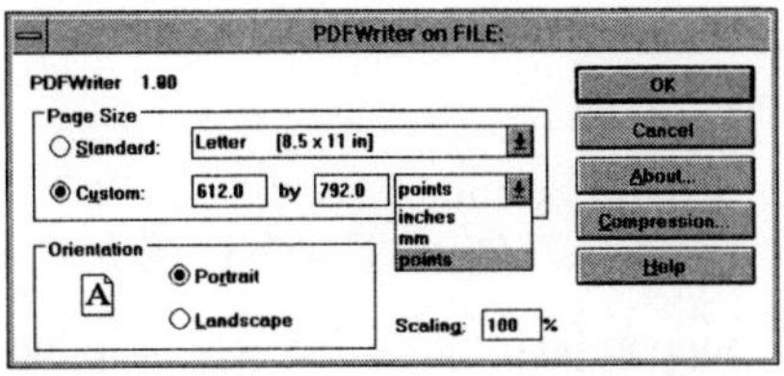

Figure 13.4. Selecting a Custom page size.

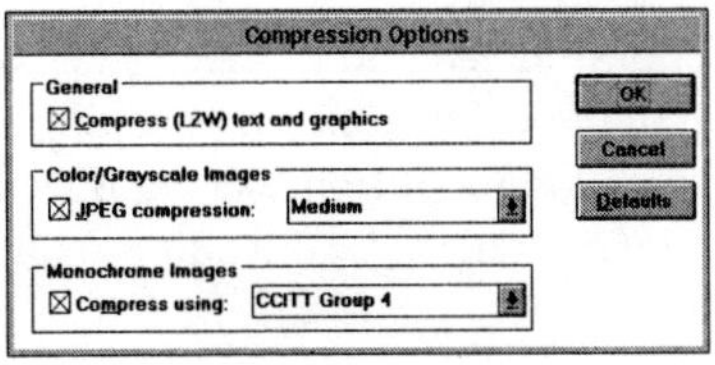

Figure 13.5. The Compression Options dialog box.

7. Click OK when the printer settings are satisfactory. Click OK in the Print Setup dialog box to close the dialog box.
8. Select the application File menu's Print command, select the desired print settings, and select OK.
9. When the Print PDF File dialog box appears, name the PDF file, select its destination directory, and click OK.

PDF Writer returns to the application after creating the PDF file. To create additional PDF files, open the appropriate documents and repeat the steps. When you are finished creating PDF files, follow these steps to use your normal printer:

1. Select Print Setup from the File menu.
2. Select Default Printer.
3. Click OK.

PDF Writer Hints

PDF Writer is a powerful Acrobat Exchange component. However, to maximize its utility, you should be aware of its limitations and use Acrobat Distiller when these limitations are exceeded.

Printing

Although EPS is the preferred way of dealing with placed images, text, and graphics for PostScript, the PDF Writer does not support EPS files, so do not put EPS file enclosures in your document.

If they are *images*, save them as TIFF files and place them in your document as TIFF items.

If they are *text or graphics*, try to save and place them as PICT (if Macintosh) or BMP (if Windows). This enables you to bypass Distiller.

Because PDF Writer does not support fill patterns, don't use them in application output. Use different grayscale shades or colors to differentiate drawing areas.

If printing documents on PostScript printers or to Distiller generates PostScript errors as a result of invalid PostScript files, try printing the file to PDF Writer directly and printing to PostScript from Acrobat Exchange or Reader. This bypasses invalid PostScript output by offending applications.

Launch Failure Numbered Error Messages

If you receive a numeric error message when you try to use PDF Writer, refer to Appendix G, "Reader and Exchange Launch Failure Numbered Error Messages."

Compression Settings

Scanned-color and grayscale-image files can be very large. A single scanned-color photograph's file can exceed several megabytes. To minimize the size of PDF file color and grayscale images, PDF Writer provides several compression options. You can also compress bilevel (black-and-white) images, and text and graphics as well. Specify compression options in the Compression Options dialog box. The Compression Options dialog box contains the settings detailed in the following sections. Usually, the defaults should be acceptable and you should not need to alter the compression settings.

Text and Graphics Compression

Selecting the Compress (LZW) Text and Graphics check box tells PDF Writer to LZW compress text and graphics. Document text and graphics include everything other than bitmap data. The LZW compression is a *lossless* compression method (it preserves detail). If Acrobat used a *lossey* compression method with text, *outpz cxq gsrffd.* You likely understand what that would mean now.

Color/Grayscale Image Compression

Selecting the JPEG Compression check box tells PDF Writer to JPEG compress color and grayscale bitmaps. The JPEG compression method loses detail, but represents an attempt to reduce image information amounts with minimum detail loss. You specify the compression amount when you select JPEG compression, ranging from Low, for the minimum compression, to High for maximum compression (see Figure 13.6). The Low and Medium-Low options have an almost imperceptible loss of detail. However, the Medium-High and High options may lose significant detail. At these settings, images may acquire blocky, quilted appearances.

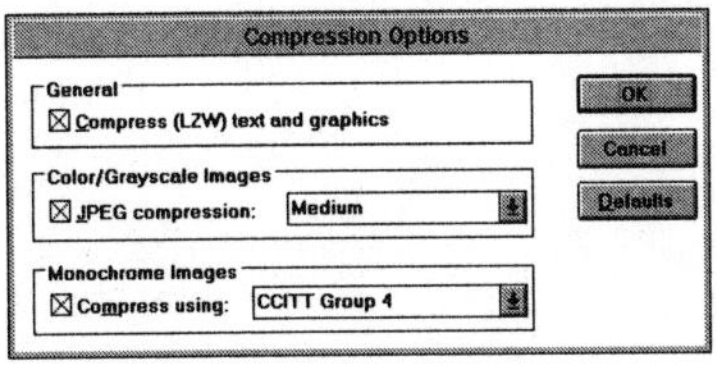

Figure 13.6.
Selecting the level of JPEG compression.

Bi-level (Monochrome) Image Compression

Bi-level images are images that only contain two colors, such as black and white. Adobe Acrobat refers to such images as *monochrome* images. However, because monochrome VGA monitors display grayscale images, we use the term *bi-level* in this book to avoid confusion.

Bi-level image compression methods are lossless. Selecting the Compress Using check box tells PDF Writer to compress bi-level bitmaps using the method specified to the right of the check box (see Figure 13.7).

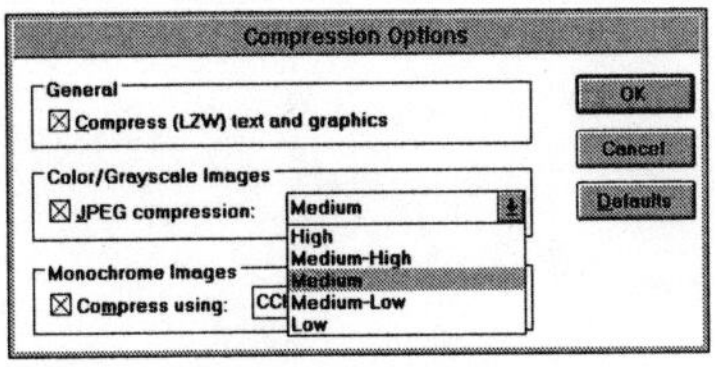

Figure 13.7.
The Compress Using check box options.

- ◆ *CCITT Group 3* is the compression method most facsimile machines use to compress individual bi-level bitmap rows.
- ◆ *CCITT Group 4* is a general-purpose compression method that usually provides better compression than CCITT Group 3 compression.
- ◆ *LZW* compression provides the best compression for images containing repetitious patterns.
- ◆ Adobe's *Run Length* compression implementation provides the best compression for images that primarily contain large areas of solid white or black.

Defaults

The Defaults button tells PDF Writer to restore all default compression option settings, which are as follows:

- Compress text and graphics
- Compress color and grayscale images with the JPEG compression method, using the Medium compression option
- Compress monochrome images with the CCITT Group 4 compression method

CHAPTER FOURTEEN

Acrobat Reader and Exchange Menu Reference

When viewing documents, the Acrobat Reader and Exchange program windows provide six menus. The menu bar displays their names:

- File
- Edit
- View
- Tools
- Window
- Help

To make all of the Acrobat Exchange menu commands available from the menus, select the Full Menus command from Acrobat Exchange's Edit menu. To access the most frequently used subset of Acrobat Exchange menu commands, select the Edit menu's Short Menus command. All Acrobat Exchange keyboard accelerator keystrokes function whether Short or Full Menus are in effect. Acrobat Reader menu commands are a subset of the Acrobat Short Menus.

File Menu Commands

Figure 14.1 shows the File menu. Table 14.1 describes the File menu commands when a document window exists. In the Table, an asterisk (*) indicates an Acrobat Exchange-only command, and a plus sign (+) indicates an Acrobat Exchange-only Full Menu command. The Exchange Reader program provides those commands without a preceding asterisk or plus sign.

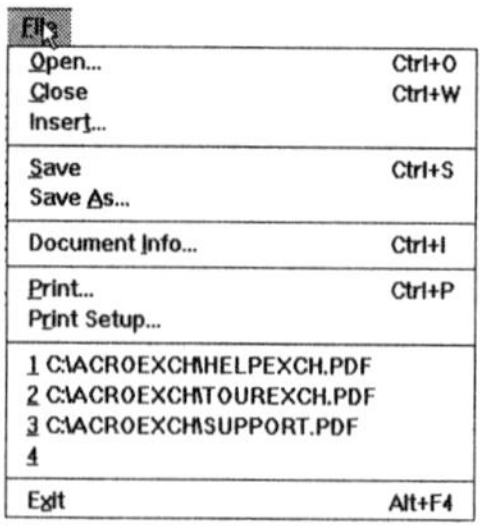

Figure 14.1.
The File menu.

Table 14.1. The File menu commands.

File Menu Entry	*Shortcut*	*Description*
Open...	Ctrl+O	Open another document
Close	Ctrl+W	Close current document
+Inser**t**...		Insert a PDF document in current document
***S**ave	Ctrl+S	Save current document
*Save **A**s...		Save current document using a different name
Document **I**nfo...	Ctrl+I	Display document's authoring information
Print...	Ctrl+P	Print current document
P**r**int Setup...		Set up the printer
1 C:\Kid$\Melissa.Pdf		Great document #1
2 C:\Kid$\Gregory.Pdf		Great document #2
3 D:\BowWow\Charlie.Pdf		Great document #3

File Menu Entry	*Shortcut*	*Description*
4 D:\BowWow\Katie.Pdf		Great document #4
E**x**it	Alt+F4	We're outta here!

Open (Ctrl+O) displays the standard system Open dialog box. The standard system Open dialog box also appears when the program begins. The List Files of Type box contains a default *Acrobat (*.pdf)* entry that sets the filename value in the File Name box. This value limits the displayed drop-down file list to files having the *.pdf* extension. Choosing the *All files (*.*)* entry displays all current directory files including, say, Macintosh PDF files without the *.pdf* extension. Entering different values in the File Name box produces different file selection lists. Double-clicking entries inside the Directories box changes the current directory to the selected directory. Finally, clicking the Drives box and making the appropriate selection changes drives.

Close (Ctrl+W) closes the active document window. You can also close an active document window by double-clicking the window's upper-left corner Control Menu box. When the active document contains changes that have not been saved, the Exchange program prompts you to save the changes before closing the document window. Closing a document window without saving changes discards the changes.

Inser**t** displays the Insert dialog box. After you select an insertion PDF file, the Insert dialog box displays (see Figure 14.2). Use the Insert dialog box to specify the location in the current document where the inserted document is to be placed.

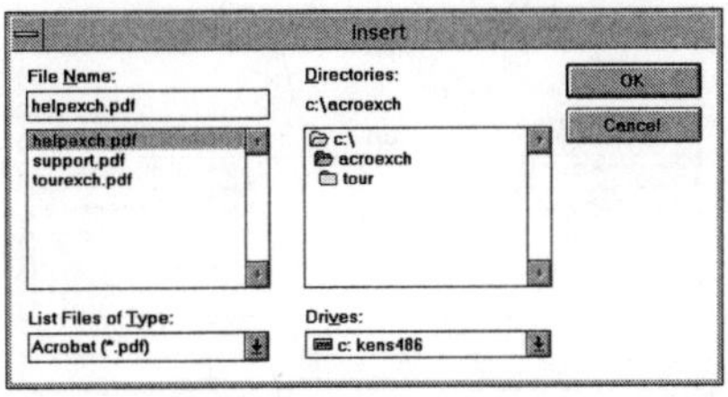

Figure 14.2.
The Insert dialog box.

Save (Ctrl+S) preserves document changes made since the document was opened or last saved. You cannot save changes to read-only or locked documents. For read-only or locked documents, use the Save **A**s... command to create a new document with the changes. Using Save is faster, but it performs incremental updates that usually result in larger files than using Save As.

Save **A**s... displays the standard Save As dialog box (see Figure 14.3). Use Save **A**s... to make document copies and to reduce PDF file sizes after successive file modifications. Using the Save **A**s... command rewrites a file from scratch, removing the effect of obsolete incremental changes.

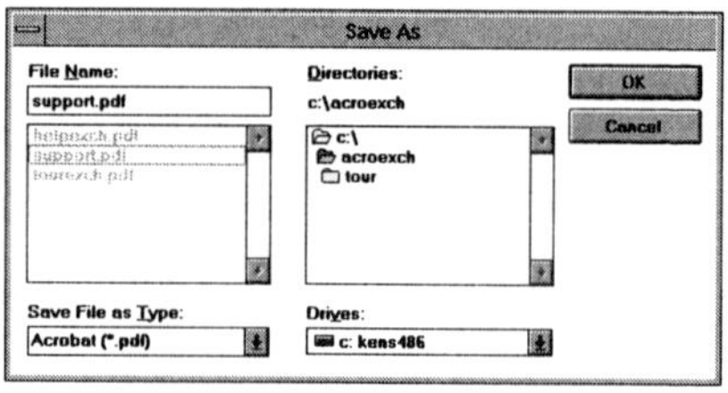

Figure 14.3.
The Save As dialog box.

Document **I**nfo (Ctrl+I) displays active document information in the Document Info dialog box (see Figure 14.4). Holding down the Ctrl and Shift keys while selecting the File menu's Document Info command produces a Document Info dialog box with font substitution data (see Figure 14.5).

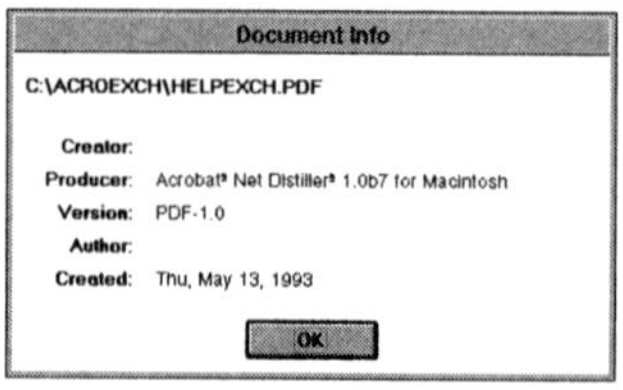

Figure 14.4.
The Document Info dialog box.

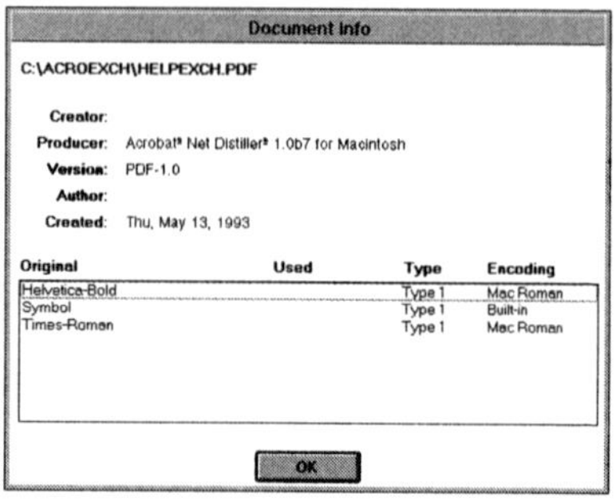

Figure 14.5.
The Document Info dialog box with font data.

Print (Ctrl+P) displays a standard system Print dialog box (see Figure 14.6) that enables you to optionally display the Print Setup dialog box (see Figure 14.7). The Print dialog box also provides additional PostScript Level 2 printer options for page printing, including shrinking to fit current printer paper sizes.

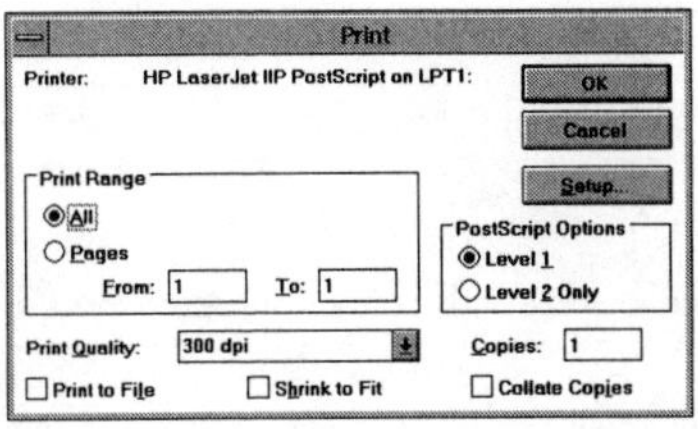

Figure 14.6.
The Print dialog box.

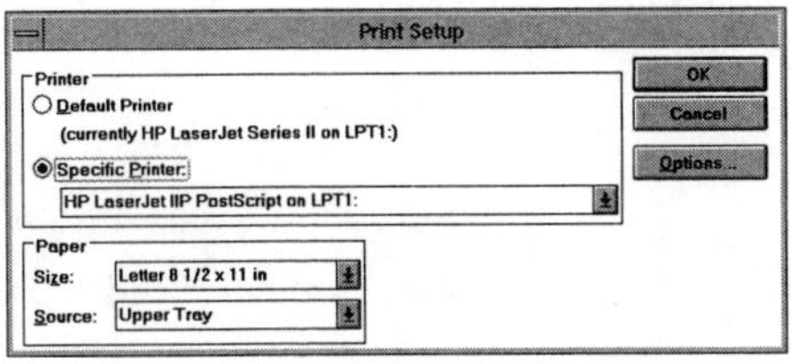

Figure 14.7.
The Print Setup dialog box.

Print Setup displays the standard system Print Setup dialog box that enables you to specify printer option control settings described in appropriate printer reference manuals.

1, **2**, **3**, or **4** opens or, if already open, selects the indicated document.

Exit (Alt+F4) closes all document windows, prompting you to save unsaved changes, and returns you to the operating system.

Edit Menu Commands

Figure 14.8 shows the Edit menu. Table 14.2 describes the Edit menu commands when a document window exists. In the Table, an asterisk (*) indicates an Acrobat Exchange-only command, and a plus sign (+) indicates an Acrobat Exchange-only Full Menu command. The **Exchange Reader program** provides those commands without a preceding asterisk or plus sign.

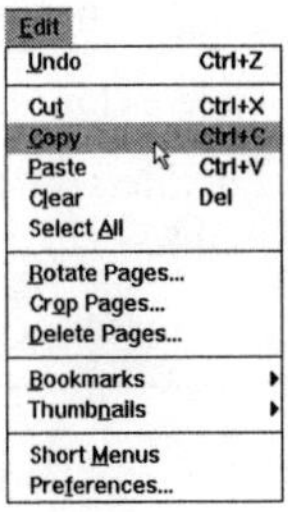

Figure 14.8.
The Edit Menu.

Table 14.2. The Edit menu commands.

Edit Menu Entry	*Shortcut*	*Description*
Undo	Ctrl+Z	Undo last operation (if possible)
*Cut	Ctrl+X	Remove selected text and place on Clipboard
Copy	Ctrl+C	Copy selected text to Clipboard
*Paste	Ctrl+V	Copy Clipboard text to target area
*Clear	Del	Remove selected text
Select All		Select all text (Macintosh only)
+Rotate Pages...		Rotate page range and erase thumbnails
+Crop Pages...		Crop page range and erase thumbnails
+Delete Pages...		Delete page range
+Bookmarks		
+New	Ctrl+B	Create new bookmark beneath selected bookmark
+Delete		Delete selected bookmark
+Set New Destination		Allow selected bookmark to move
+Move Up	Ctrl+Up	Move selected bookmark up
+Move Down	Ctrl+Down	Move selected bookmark down
+Move Left	Ctrl+Left	Move selected bookmark left
+Move Right	Ctrl+Right	Move selected bookmark right
+Thumbnails		
+Create All		Create missing thumbnails
+Delete All		Delete thumbnail set
*Short/Full Menus		Provide Full/Short menus and tool bar
Preferences...	Alt+F4	Set initialization preferences

Undo (Ctrl+Z) cancels the most recent text editing within an editable text field such as a note or bookmark name. Page rotations, insertions and deletions, bookmark reordering, and hypertext link modifications cannot be undone.

Cu**t** (Ctrl+X) moves selected text from a note or bookmark name to the Clipboard. This command only copies text to the Clipboard, not bitmapped graphics or images.

Copy (Ctrl+C) copies selected text within a document page, an active note, or a bookmark name, and places it on the Clipboard. This command only copies text to the Clipboard, not bitmapped graphics or images.

Paste (Ctrl+V) inserts text on the Clipboard into an active note or a bookmark name.

C**l**ear (Del) deletes selected iconized notes, Link buttons, or text within notes and bookmarks.

Select **A**ll (Ctrl+A—Macintosh Only) selects all text within an open note or a bookmark.

Rotate Pages displays the Rotate Pages dialog box (see Figure 14.9), which enables you to rotate one or more pages 90 degrees. Rotating a page right 90 degrees moves the top of the page clockwise so it becomes the right margin when displayed. Rotating a page left 90 degrees moves the top of the page counterclockwise so it becomes the left margin when displayed. Page inversion requires two rotations in the same direction. Rotation only applies to page display; when printing, Acrobat rotates pages to fit the paper as necessary.

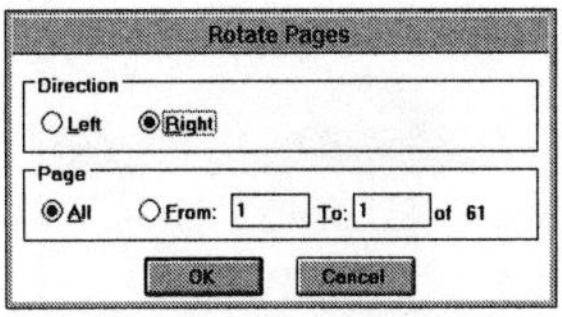

Figure 14.9. The Rotate Pages dialog box.

Cro**p** Pages displays the Crop Pages dialog box, which enables you to render page cropping for one or more pages. Cropped areas display as white space in the page view and print as white space. Cropping pages for the viewing window does not change printed page margins. The active page view previews the cropping values that take effect when you click OK (see Figures 14.10 and 14.11).

Figure 14.10. The Crop Pages dialog box and the active page view preview.

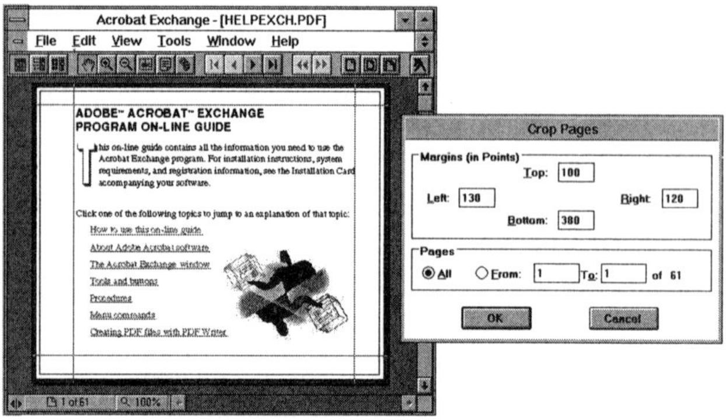

Figure 14.11. The cropped page.

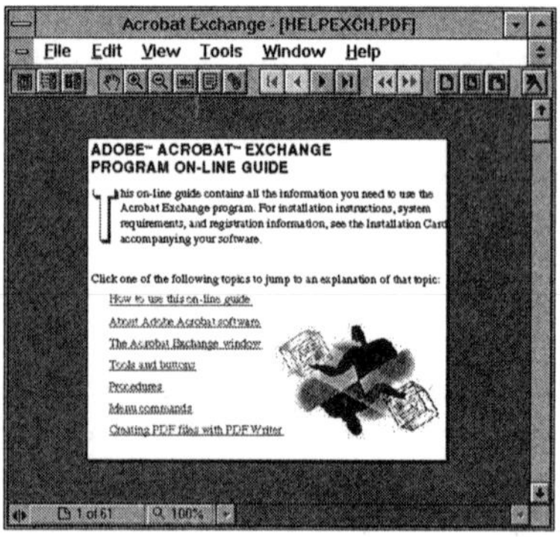

Delete Pages displays the Delete Pages dialog box (see Figure 14.12), which enables you to delete one or more pages.

Figure 14.12. The Delete Pages dialog box.

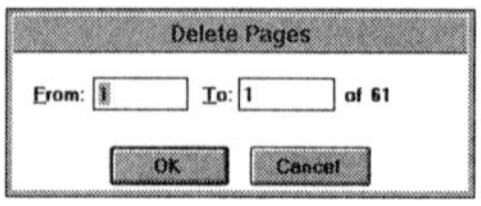

Bookmarks displays a submenu (see Figure 14.13) containing the following commands:

> **N**ew (Ctrl+B) adds an untitled bookmark to the bottom of the bookmark list, or beneath a selected bookmark at the selected bookmark's indentation level.
>
> **D**elete deletes selected bookmarks and all their subordinate bookmarks.

Set New Destination changes a selected bookmark's page view destination to the current page view. Only one bookmark can be selected for this option to appear.

Move Up (Ctrl+Up) moves selected bookmarks and their subordinate bookmarks up one level in a bookmark list.

Move Down (Ctrl+Down) moves selected bookmarks and their subordinate bookmarks down one level in a bookmark list.

Move Left (Ctrl+Left) un-indents selected bookmarks and their subordinate bookmarks left one indentation level in a bookmark list.

Move Right (Ctrl+Right) indents selected bookmarks and their subordinate bookmarks right one indentation level in a bookmark list.

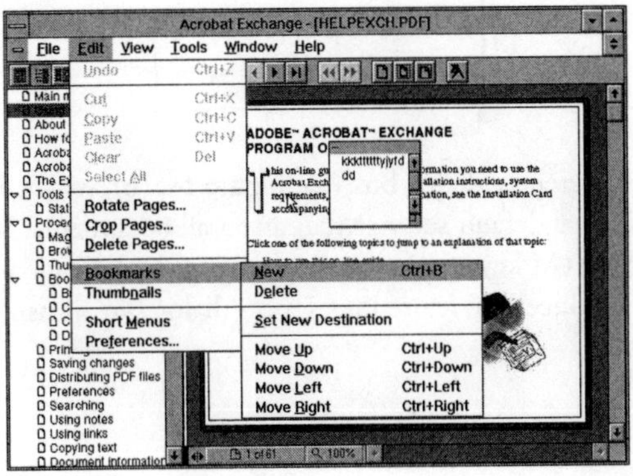

Figure 14.13. The Bookmarks submenu.

Thumbnails displays a submenu (see Figure 14.14) containing the following commands:

Create All... creates all missing thumbnail images in the active document. A dialog box opens and displays the progress of the thumbnail creation process (see Figure 14.15). Existing thumbnails are retained; they are not re-created.

Delete All deletes all thumbnail images in the active document.

Short/Full Menus (Alt+F4) toggles between Full and Short menus. The Insert, Rotate Pages, Crop Pages, Delete Pages, Bookmarks, Thumbnails, Note, and Link commands are available only with Full menus. Similarly, the Link and Note tools are available only with Full menus, although keystroke accelerators function whether Full or Short menus are in effect.

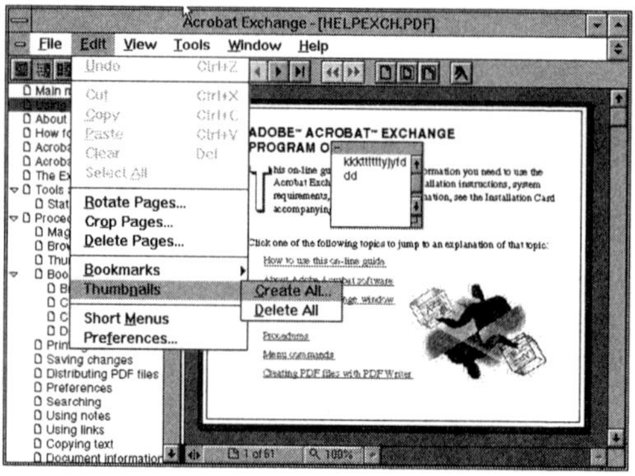

Figure 14.14. The Thumbnails submenu.

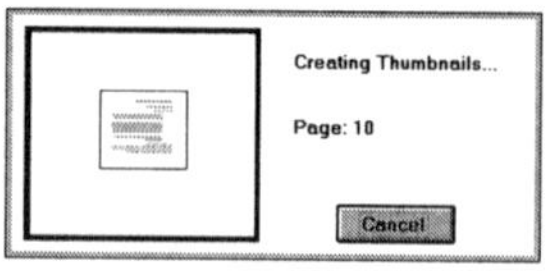

Figure 14.15. The Thumbnail Creation status box.

Preferences displays the Preferences dialog box (see Figure 14.16), which enables you to select the initial default settings that affect all documents. While holding down the Ctrl+Shift+M key combination, selecting the Edit menu's Preferences... command produces the More Preferences dialog box, if using Windows (see Figure 14.17).

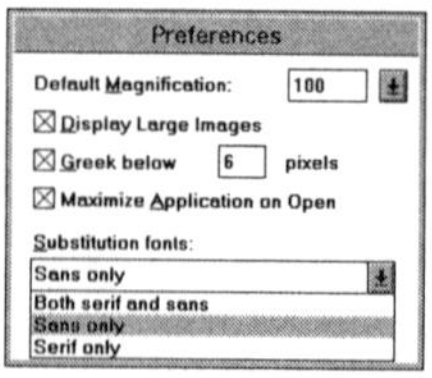

Figure 14.16. The Preferences dialog box.

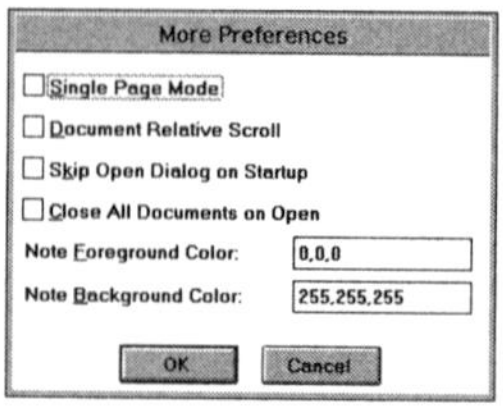

Figure 14.17. The More Preferences dialog box.

View Menu Commands

Figure 14.18 shows the View menu. Table 14.3 describes the View menu commands when a document window exists.

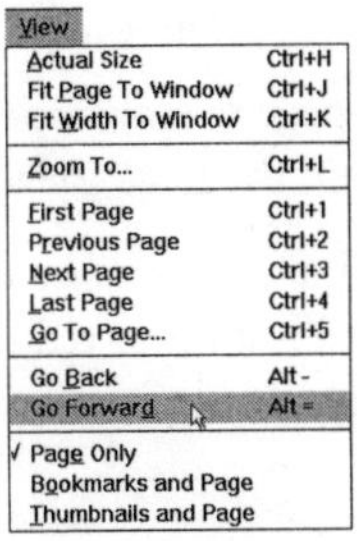

Figure 14.18. The View menu.

Table 14.3. The View menu commands.

View Menu Entry	*Shortcut*	*Description*
Actual Size	Ctrl+H	Set magnification to 100%
Fit **P**age To Width	Ctrl+J	Adjust magnification to fit entire page in Page View pane
Fit **W**idth To Window	Ctrl+K	Adjust magnification to fit page width to Page View pane
Zoom To...	Ctrl+L	Display the Magnification dialog box
First Page	Ctrl+1	Go to document's first page
P**r**evious Page	Ctrl+2	Go to previous document page
Next Page	Ctrl+3	Go to next document page
Last Page	Ctrl+4	Go to document's last page
Go To Page...	Ctrl+5	Display Go To Page dialog box
Go **B**ack	Alt+–	Navigate to previous page view
Go Forwar**d**	Alt+=	Navigate to next page view
Pag**e** Only		Close Overview pane
B**o**okmarks And Page		Display bookmarks in Overview pane
Thumbnails And Page		Display thumbnails in Overview pane

Actual Size (Ctrl+H) sets the page magnification level to 100 percent. Acrobat products assume screens have 72 dots per inch, so document size may vary for screens that have different dot resolutions.

Fit **P**age to Window (Ctrl+J) selects a page magnification level that allows the entire current page to fit within the Page View pane.

Fit **W**idth to Window (Ctrl+K) selects a page magnification level that allows the entire current page's width to fit within the Page View pane.

Zoom To... (Ctrl+L) displays a Zoom To dialog box (see Figure 14.19) in which you specify the percentage of magnification or reduction. You can reduce pages down to 12 percent of their normal size or expand pages up to 800 percent of their normal size.

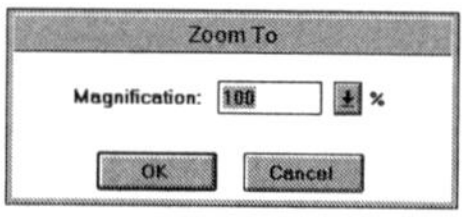

Figure 14.19. The Zoom To dialog box.

First Page (Ctrl+1) displays the active document's first page in the Page View pane at the current magnification level.

P**r**evious Page (Ctrl+2) displays the active document's previous page in the Page View pane at the current magnification level.

Next Page (Ctrl+3) displays the active document's next page in the Page View pane at the current magnification level.

Last Page (Ctrl+4) displays the active document's last page in the Page View pane at the current magnification level.

Go To Page (Ctrl+5) displays a Go To Page dialog box in which you specify the page you want to see (see Figure 14.20).

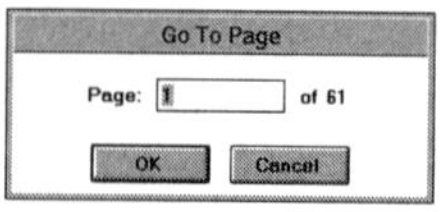

Figure 14.20. The Go To Page dialog box.

Go **B**ack (Alt+–) navigates the page view stack toward earlier document page views. You can redisplay 64 views.

Go Forwar**d** (Alt+=) navigates the page view stack toward later document page views, undoing the effect of previous Go Back operations.

Page Only closes the document window Overview pane.

Bookmarks and Page displays bookmarks in the active document window's Overview pane. Double-clicking a bookmark's page icon displays the bookmark's destination.

Thumbnails and Page displays thumbnail images of document pages in the active document window Overview area if thumbnails have been created for the document. Click a thumbnail to jump to its associated document page and display the click point at the current magnification level.

Tools Menu Commands

Figure 14.21 shows the Tools menu. Table 14.4 describes the Tools menu commands when a document window exists. In the Table, a plus sign (+) indicates an Acrobat Exchange-only Full Menu command. The Exchange Reader program provides those commands without a preceding plus sign.

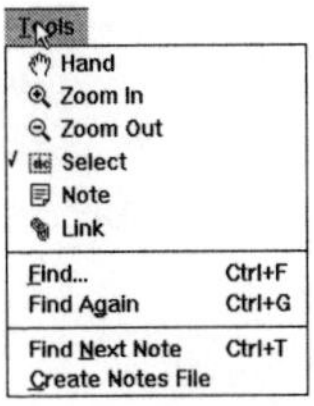

Figure 14.21.
The Tools menu.

Table 14.4. The Tools menu commands.

Tools Menu Entry	*Shortcut*	*Description*
Hand		Cursor becomes the Hand tool
Zoom In		Cursor becomes the Zoom In tool
Zoom Out		Cursor becomes the Zoom Out tool
Select		Cursor becomes the Text Selection tool
+Note		Cursor becomes the Note tool
+Link		Cursor becomes the Link tool
Find	Ctrl+F	Find search string
Find Again	Ctrl+G	Find another search string instance
Find Next Note	Ctrl+T	Find a following page with an appended note
Create Notes File		Collect all notes into a PDF file

The Hand transforms the mouse pointer into the Hand tool when it is over a document window. Holding down the mouse button and dragging the document window's active page view provides page view adjustments at the current magnification level.

Zoom In transforms the mouse pointer into the Zoom In tool when it is over the active document window's Page View pane. Click the tool over an active page view to double the view's magnification level, up to 800 percent, the maximum magnification level.

Zoom Out transforms the mouse pointer into the Zoom Out tool when it is over the active document window's Page View pane. Click the tool over an active page view to halve the view's magnification level, down to 12 percent, the minimum magnification level.

Select transforms the mouse pointer into the Text Selection tool when it is over the active document window's Page View pane. Holding down the mouse button and dragging it over an active page view selects text. Copy the text to the Clipboard using the Edit menu's Copy command.

Note transforms the mouse pointer into the Note tool when it is over the active document window's Page View pane. Holding down the mouse button and dragging it over an active page view draws a note window. Clicking over an active page view gives a default note.

Link turns the mouse pointer into the Link tool when it is over the active document window's Page View pane. Holding down the mouse button and dragging it over an active page view draws a Link button as in Figure 14.22. Clicking the mouse on the active page view produces a warning message (see Figure 14.23). After the Create Link dialog box appears (see Figure 14.24), generating a document page view and clicking OK associates a destination with the Link button. Clicking OK before producing a new page view produces the warning in Figure 14.25.

Figure 14.22.
Drawing a link.

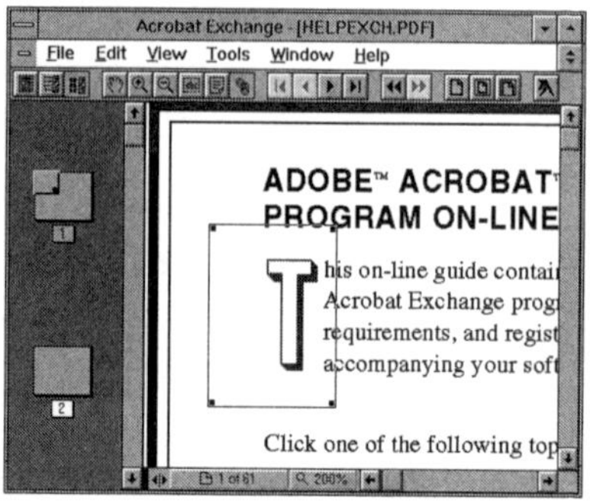

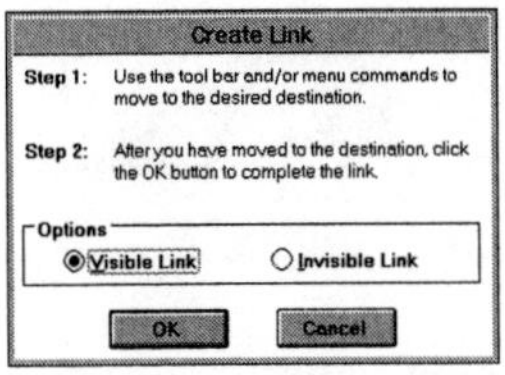

Figure 14.23. The Create Link dialog box.

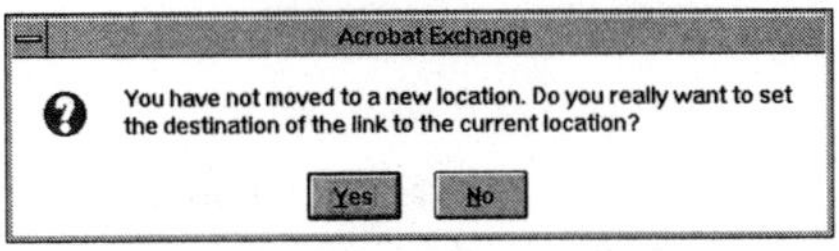

Figure 14.24. A Link Creation warning box.

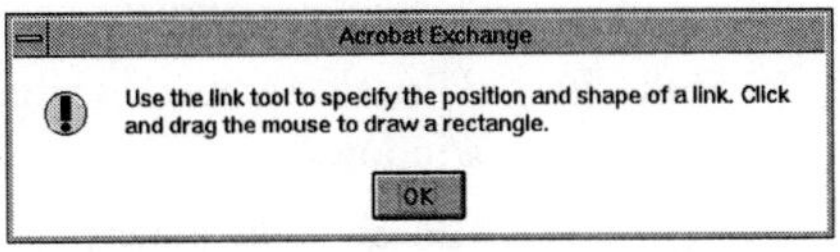

Figure 14.25. Another Link Creation warning box.

Find (Ctrl+F) displays the Find dialog box (see Figure 14.26), which enables you to search for a search string within the active document.

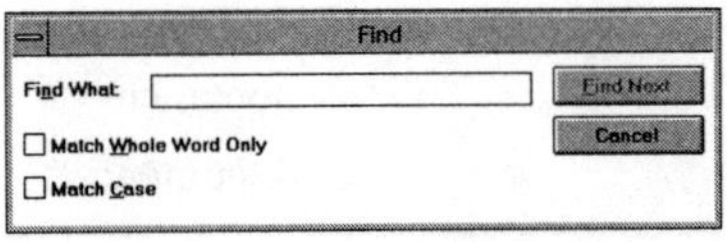

Figure 14.26. The Find dialog box.

Find **A**gain (Ctrl+G) performs the same operation as the Find dialog box's Find button: the search string's next occurrence displays.

Find **N**ext Note (Ctrl+T) moves to the next page containing one or more notes. Double-clicking closed notes opens and displays them.

Create Notes File converts all active document notes into a separate PDF file titled *Notes From XXXXXXXX*, where *XXXXXXXX* is the name of the document that contained the notes. Notes for a document's page appear within this file in creation order, not in the order found on the page. The File menu's Save **A**s... command saves the Notes from XXXXXXXX file.

Window Menu Commands

Figure 14.27 shows the Window menu. Table 14.5 describes the Window Menu commands when five document windows exist.

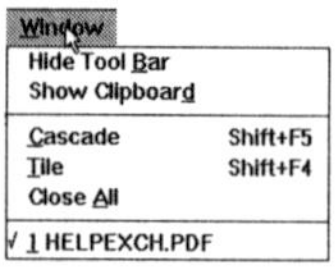

Figure 14.27.
The Window menu.

Table 14.5. The Window menu commands.

Window Menu Entry	*Shortcut*	*Description*
Show/Hide Tool **B**ar		Reveals/removes the tool bar
Show/Hide Clipboar**d**		Displays Clipboard contents
Cascade	Shift+F5	Cascades all Acrobat document windows
Tile	Shift+F4	Tiles all Acrobat document windows
Close **A**ll		Closes all document windows
C:\Kid$\Melissa.Pdf		Great document #1
C:\Kid$\Gregory.Pdf		Great document #2
D:\BowWow\Charlie.Pdf		Great document #3
D:\BowWow\Katie.Pdf		Great document #4
D:\Squeak\SweetHrt.Pdf		Great document #5

Show/Hide Tool **B**ar reveals or removes the tool bar.

Show/Hide Clipboar**d** opens the Clipboard's text display window, or closes the Clipboard if it is already visible. Clicking the window's upper-left corner close box closes it.

Cascade (Shift+F5) arranges open document windows as overlapping windows within the application window. The active document window has a scroll and title bar.

Tile (Shift+F4) arranges open document windows as non-overlapping windows within the application window. The active document window has a scroll and title bar.

Close **A**ll closes all open document windows, but leaves the application window open.

All open PDF filenames appear below the Close All command. A check mark precedes the active document window. To make another file's document window the active document window, select the file's name. When 10 documents are open, the tenth list entry is *More....* Click this entry to see a list containing all 10 open document names.

Help Menu Commands

Figure 14.28 shows the Help menu. Table 14.6 describes the Help menu commands when a document window exists.

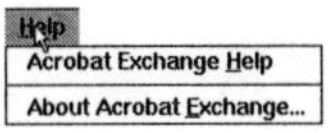

Figure 14.28.
The Help menu.

Table 14.6. The Help menu commands.

Help Menu Entry	*Description*
Acrobat Reader/Exchange **H**elp	Opens HelpExch.Pdf/ HelpRead.Pdf
About Acrobat **R**eader/**E**xcthange	Displays program information

Acrobat Reader/Exchange **H**elp makes the Reader or Exchange help file the active document.

About Acrobat **R**eader/**E**xchange displays program information. Click the logo for credits. Click the version number for the component versions. Click anywhere to make the screen disappear.

CHAPTER FIFTEEN

Troubleshooting

Just as the world isn't perfectly round, things don't always work out as intended. This chapter gives you an advantage in isolating and resolving Acrobat usage problems.

Launch Failure Numbered Error Messages

If you receive a numeric error message when launching Reader or Exchange, refer to Appendix G, "Reader and Exchange Launch Failure Numbered Error Messages."

PostScript Printing

For PostScript Level 1 or 2 printer problems, such as `VMerror` errors, the printer may not have enough memory. There are two potential solutions:

1. In the Preferences dialog box (select Preferences... from the Edit menu), choose either *Serif only* or *Sans only* for font substitution. This frees printer memory, increasing the chances for successful document printing.
2. Purchase more memory for your printer.

Acrobat Exchange cannot substitute fonts for Apple Personal LaserWriter NT printers that have not been upgraded to Personal LaserWriter NTR printers. Contact an Apple dealer for printer upgrade information.

Boosting Exchange and Reader Performance

Increasing the memory allocated to Adobe Type Manager's font cache usually improves the performance. Use the Main program group ATM Control Panel to increase ATM's Font Cache to 512KB or greater.

Miscellaneous

The following sections discuss problems that do not fit neatly into any of the preceding categories.

Cropping, Rotating, and Inserting Pages

Combining page cropping, rotation, and insertion sometimes produces unpredictable results. For complex documents with different page sizes and orientations, the most predictable results occur by first cropping the pages, then rotating them, and then inserting them.

Find

You may not be able to Find whole words adjacent to some special characters. Words adjacent to the bar (¦), apostrophe ('), quotation mark ("), period (.), opening or closing parentheses ((or)), question mark (?), hyphen (-), colon (:), and semicolon (;) characters *will* be found.

Notes File Page Size

In the Printers control panel, the system-wide page size setting that you select for the default printer driver determines the PDF file page size used for the Create Notes File command. Changing the page size from the File/Print Setup menu has no effect.

Patterns

Files produced by Distiller that contain fill patterns may display slowly and cause memory shortages.

Cropping and Rotating Pages

Cropping and rotating pages destroys the thumbnail images of the associated pages. You can regenerate new thumbnails by choosing the Create All command from the Thumbnails submenu of Exchange's Edit menu.

Rotated or Transformed TrueType Fonts

Displaying or printing rotated or otherwise transformed TrueType fonts may produce problems. For best results, use Adobe PostScript Type 1 document fonts.

Text Selection

Unexpected results may occur when using the Text Selection tool unless the text selection marquee rectangle intersects or bounds the desired text *only.*

Text Greeking

Type 3 fonts do not Greek.

PDF Writer Compatibility

The PDF Writer "advertises" itself to applications as a 300-dpi non-PostScript device. It expects to receive GDI document descriptions for Windows and QuickDraw document descriptions for Macintosh, which it translates into Portable Document Format (PDF) files. Applications that rely on PostScript, or any document containing Encapsulated PostScript (EPS) artwork or images, get poor results with PDF Writer. In most cases, the application sends PDF Writer a low-resolution preview page or EPS graphic image. In effect, PDF files look as if they were printed on a non-PostScript printer. In such cases, use the Acrobat Distiller to convert your document into a PDF file.

If software applications do not work well with PDF Writer, contact Adobe at 800-87-ADOBE to learn more about technical support options.

Application-Specific Issues

Table 15.1 details how to create PDF documents depending on the application or product you are using.

Table 15.1. Application-specific issues for PDF document creation.

Product	*PDF Document Creation*
Adobe Illustrator 4.X for Windows	Generate PostScript files and use Distiller to generate PDF files.
Aldus Freehand	Use the Acrobat Distiller.
Arts & Letters	Use the Distiller, or you may be unable to cancel the PDF Writer in a timely manner.
CorelDRAW	Use the Distiller.
Harvard Draw	Some minor problems may occur with text and white lines appearing between (or within) characters unless you use Distiller.
Harvard Graphics	Files take a long time to convert, display, and are large. Use the Distiller.
Lotus Freelance	PDF Writer returns control to applications other than the one from which you were printing. If Freelance uses any printer driver to print to a file, the same behavior occurs. This appears to be a Freelance bug.
Lotus Write	Rounded rectangles are not connected. This appears to be a Lotus Write bug.
MicroGraphix	Use the Distiller.
Type Align	Use the Distiller.

PART

III

Acrobat Distiller

- Distiller Preliminaries
- Operating Distiller
- Distiller Font Access
- Creating PDF Files with Distiller
- Distiller Troubleshooting

CHAPTER SIXTEEN

Distiller Preliminaries

Because the features of Personal Distiller are a subset of the features of Network Distiller, this chapter references Network Distiller features unless otherwise stated.

PDF File Creation Tips

Before creating PostScript file documents for Distiller, you need to recognize two limitations to the current version of Distiller.

One limitation is that Distiller *substitutes gray shades* for fill patterns that some drawing, painting, and charting applications use. This substitution often produces acceptable results, but when bar charts are filled with alternating diagonal stripes, Distiller fills the bars with the same gray shade. Filling shapes with varying gray shades instead of fill patterns avoids the problem.

The other limitation is that Distiller *does not process custom halftone functions*; it uses standard halftone functions instead. Usually, Distiller produces acceptable results. Complicated halftone functions, however, do not appear as the application prints them. No solution exists for this problem, except using standard halftone functions for PDF document images.

Creating Network Distiller Server Connections

Network Distillers monitor one or more subdirectories for submitted PostScript files to convert to PDF files. When network administrators specify directories for a Network Distiller to monitor, the Network Distiller creates two subdirectories within each specified directory. These subdirectories are named *In* and *Out*, and are a Distiller *In directory* and *Out directory*, respectively. When Network Distillers retrieve work from one In directory, it places its output in the source In directory's associated Out directory.

Suppose a Network Distiller monitors the SQUEAK directory on the MRCARROT server's MOUSE volume. The Network Distiller In directory pathname in this instance is `MRCARROT/MOUSE:SQUEAK\IN`.

To connect to a Network Distiller's In directory using Window's Network Connection dialog box, follow these steps:

1. Start the computer and connect to the server using standard network connection procedures. Network administrators can assist you in setting up an automatic server connection. Otherwise, contact the network software vendor.
2. Start Windows.
3. Double-click the Main program group's File Manager icon to start Windows File Manager.
4. When the File Manager window appears, select Network Connection from the Disk menu, and the Network Drive Connections dialog box appears.

NOTE

The next steps select Distiller's In directory network pathname, places it in the Path box, and maps a local drive letter to the directory using the Map button.

5. Select Browse for network servers activities. The Browse Connections dialog box appears. The Servers/Volumes box shows existing network connections.

6. Select Attach to attach a new network server connection.
7. When the Attach File Server dialog box appears, select the server name using the File Server list, enter a valid network user name and password, and click OK to return to the Browse Connections dialog box. The Server/Volumes list now displays all defined server volumes.
8. Select Distiller's In directory volume and the In directory from the Directories list.
9. When the Path box displays the full path of Distiller's In directory, click OK to return to the Network Drive Connections dialog box. The full pathname of Distiller's In directory now appears in the Path box.
10. Select the local drive letter to which to map Distiller's In directory and click Map. Distiller's In directory pathname displays as mapped to the selected local drive letter.

This maps network directories to local drive letters. The same method maps Distiller's Out directory to local drive letters. Selecting the Data Drives list's mapping entry and selecting the Permanent check box tells Windows automatically to map local drive letters to network directories.

Determining If Network Distiller Is Active

Network Distiller maintains a DTIME.TXT text file in every Out directory and writes a message to DTIME.TXT about once a minute. Checking DTIME.TXT's file time stamp indicates whether Distiller is actively monitoring its associated In directory. If the DTIME.TXT time stamp is recent or changes periodically, Distiller is watching its In directory for submitted PostScript conversion work. To check the DTIME.TXT time stamp, use the File Manager or the DOS `DIR` command.

NOTE

The DTIME.TXT time stamp value reflects the network file server's clock setting, which may not match other machine clock settings.

The DTIME.TXT File

Network Distiller maintains a DTIME.TXT text file in every Distiller Out directory. DTIME.TXT records the last time Distiller checked its In directory for input PostScript files, and lists current job settings. Because DTIME.TXT is a text document, Notepad, Write, or any word processor can open DTIME.TXT. DTIME.TXT lists the following Distiller setup options:

- *Watched Directory Frequency*—the interval in seconds Distiller waits before checking its In directory for new PostScript files.
- *After Distilling, PostScript Files = Deleted/Moved:*—whether Distiller deletes input PostScript files or moves them to its Out directory after distilling them.
- *Files deleted after = # days:*—the number of days files are left in the Out directory before Distiller automatically deletes them.
- *Text and Graphics LZW Compression = On/Off*—whether text and graphics are compressed.
- *Thumbnail Generation = On/Off:*—whether Distiller automatically generates PDF file page thumbnails.
- *Color* image compression option—described in Appendix D, "Acrobat Compression."
- *Grayscale* image compression option—described in Appendix D, "Acrobat Compression."
- *Monochrome* image compression option—described in Appendix D, "Acrobat Compression."

Listing 16.1 shows some typical DTIME.TXT output.

Listing 16.1. Annotated DTIME.TXT typical output.

```
Acrobat Network Distiller 1.0 for Windows ← Distiller version
Wednesday, June 9, 1993 at 7:02 AM ← Date and time Distiller
=====================================     last checked In directory
Watched Directory Frequency = 30 second(s)
After Distilling, PostScript Files = Deleted

Text and Graphics LZW Compression = ON
Thumbnail Generation = OFF

Color Image Downsampling = ON
Color Image Downsampling Resolution = 72
Color Image Compression = ON
Compression using = JPEG Medium

Grayscale Image Downsampling = ON
Grayscale Image Downsampling Resolution = 72
```

```
Grayscale Image Compression = ON
Compression using = JPEG Medium

Monochrome Image Downsampling = ON
Monochrome Image Downsampling Resolution = 300
Monochrome Image Compression = ON
Compression using = CCITT Group 4
```

Determining When PDF Files Are Ready

Network Distiller places PDF files in an Out directory when it finishes creating the files. As soon as the File Manager or the DOS `DIR` command displays an Out directory PDF file, users may copy it elsewhere if desired. Note that network administrators can configure Network Distiller to delete files automatically after they have remained in an Out directory for a specified number of days.

Distiller File Naming Conventions

Distiller uses input PostScript filenames to name PDF files it creates. By convention, PostScript filenames end with a *.ps* extension. When the PostScript filename has a filename extension such as .ps, Distiller substitutes .pdf for the filename extension. Otherwise, Distiller appends the .pdf file extension to the PostScript filename.

When Distiller processes two identically named PostScript files or versions of the same PostScript file over time, the second Distiller-created PDF file automatically replaces the first if it still exists in Network Distiller's Out directory. This means PostScript files should have unique names when many people share Network Distiller In directories.

Ensuring Distiller Has Font Access

When Distiller processes PostScript files, it needs document font access to create the PDF file. When Distiller can't find document fonts, it substitutes Courier for the missing fonts. Usually, PostScript files include document fonts or they are otherwise available to Distiller. But if Distiller substitutes Courier for another font, that means Distiller could not find the original font. Network administrators can set up Distiller to find fonts stored in any network directory. If Distiller cannot find a font, talk to a network administrator about placing the font in a directory where Distiller can find it.

CHAPTER

SEVENTEEN

Operating Distiller

Distiller is a complete PostScript processing engine that produces PDF files. Its simple interface belies its internal complexity.

Starting Distiller

Distiller starts like any other application program. Start Distiller by doing the following:

- Double-click the Adobe program group Distiller icon or Distiller's File Manager file list entry.
- Use the Windows Run command and specify input PostScript files.
- Drag one or more PostScript files onto Distiller's open application window.
- Drag one or more PostScript files onto Distiller's desktop icon, which starts Distiller and processes the PostScript files (see Figure 17.1).

Figure 17.1.
The Distiller screen.

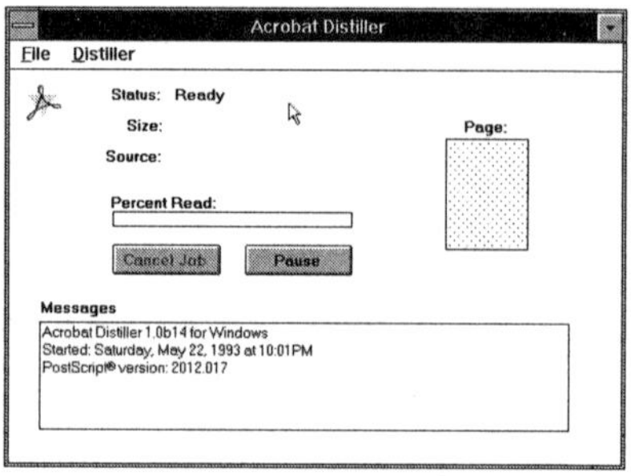

Using the Windows Run Command

The Windows version of Distiller starts by selecting the Program or File Manager File menu's Run command and entering `c:\anetdist\anetdist.exe` in the Run dialog box. (`c:\anetdist` is Distiller's default drive and directory. If Distiller installation defaults are different, use the drive and directory name you specified when Distiller installed.)

When you start Distiller with the Windows Run command, specify one or more PostScript files for Distiller to process. These files do not need to reside in Distiller's In directory. For example, the following Run command string specifies two PostScript files:

```
c:\anetdist\anetdist.exe D:\Kid$\kGregory.Ps, D:\Kid$\Melissa.Ps
```

As this example shows, the Windows Run command separates multiple PostScript filenames with commas.

The Startup Directory

The Distiller installation process creates a Distiller Startup directory in Distiller's application directory. When Distiller starts, it inspects its Startup directory for PostScript program text files. If the Startup directory contains one or more text files, Distiller assumes they are all PostScript programs and uses them to initialize its PostScript interpreter's virtual memory. The installation-created Startup directory contains an example file, example.ps, that illustrates startup file options.

Distiller Menus

Because Distiller performs a single function—PDF file production—it has a very simple menu set.

The File Menu

Figure 17.2 illustrates Distiller's File menu. Table 17.1 describes each of the File menu's commands.

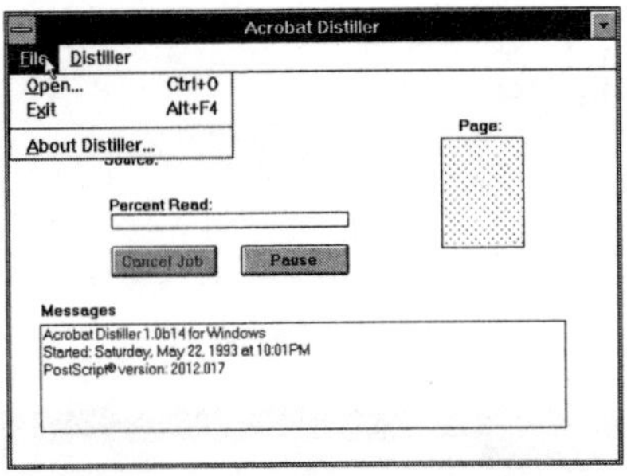

Figure 17.2. Distiller's File menu.

Table 17.1. Distiller's File menu commands.

File Menu Entry	*Shortcut*	*Description*
Open...	Ctrl+O	Opens a file to Distill
E**x**it	Alt+F4	Ends Distiller execution
About Distiller...		Displays the Distiller About box

Open (Ctrl+O) displays the standard system Open dialog box illustrated in Figure 17.3. The standard system Open dialog box also appears when the program begins. The List Files of Type box contains a default entry, PostScript Files (*.ps), that sets the filename value in the File Name box. This value limits the displayed drop-down file list to files having the *.ps* extension. There is also an option to choose EPS (*.eps) encapsulated PostScript files. Choosing the All files (*.*) entry displays all current directory files including, say, Macintosh PDF files without the *.ps* extension. Entering different values in the File Name box produces different file selection lists. Double-clicking entries inside the Directories box changes the current directory to the selected directory. Finally, clicking the Drives box and making the appropriate selection changes drives.

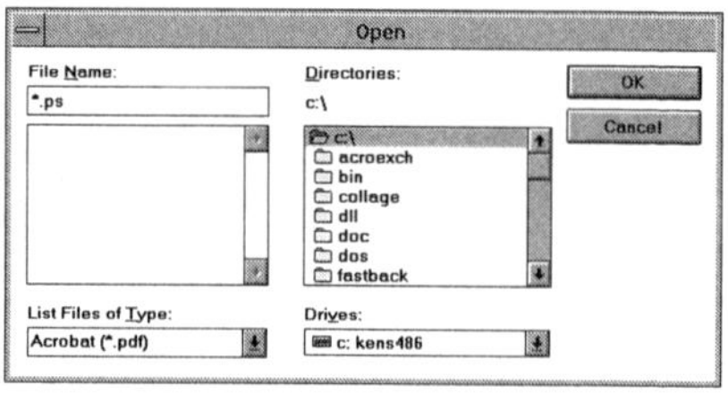

Figure 17.3.
The Open dialog box.

Exit (Alt+F4) exits Distiller after it asks whether the file it is currently distilling should complete before exiting.

About Distiller displays program information.

The Distiller Menu

Figure 17.4 illustrates Distiller's Distiller menu. Table 17.2 describes each of the Distiller menu's commands.

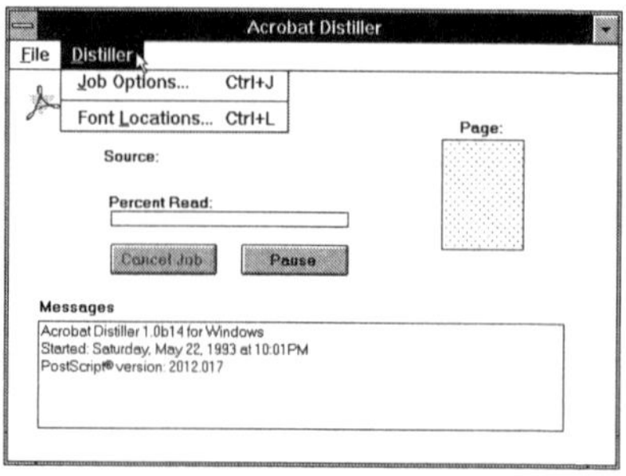

Figure 17.4.
Distiller's Distiller Menu.

Table 17.2. Distiller's Distiller menu commands.

Distiller Menu Entry	*Shortcut*	*Description*
Job Options...	Ctrl+J	Displays/sets options
Font **L**ocations...	Ctrl+L	Displays/modifies Font Search List
Watched **D**irectories...	Ctrl+D	Displays/sets Watched Directories

Job Options... (Ctrl+J) produces the Job Options dialog box (see Figure 17.5), which enables you to specify compression options and whether Distiller automatically generates PDF file thumbnails.

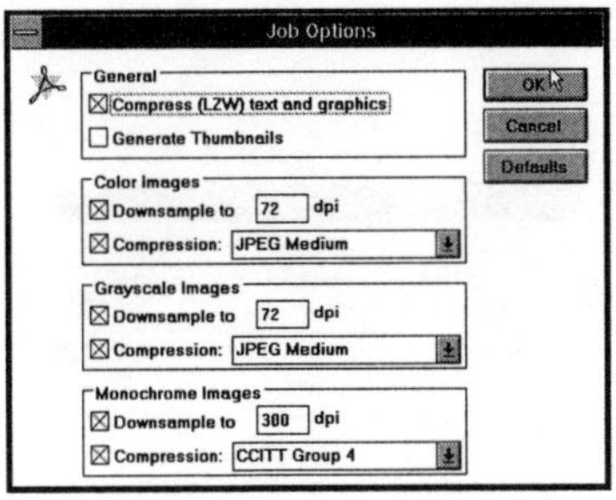

Figure 17.5. The Job Options dialog box.

Font **L**ocations... (Ctrl+L) produces the Font Locations dialog box (see Figure 17.6), which enables you to add directories with the Add Directory dialog box (see Figure 17.7) or remove directories from the Font Location search list. The Font Location search list lists the directories Distiller searches for fonts.

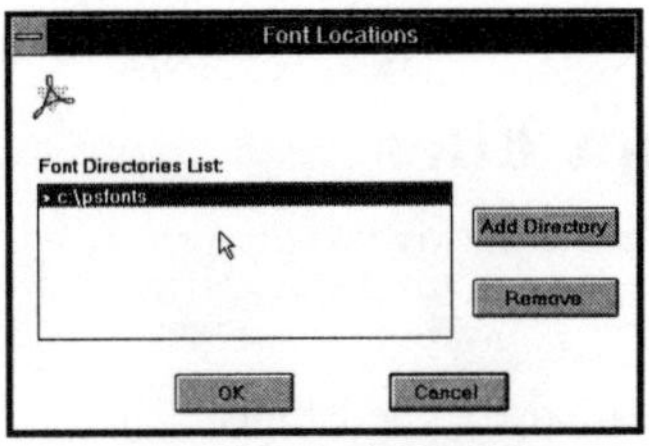

Figure 17.6. The Font Locations dialog box.

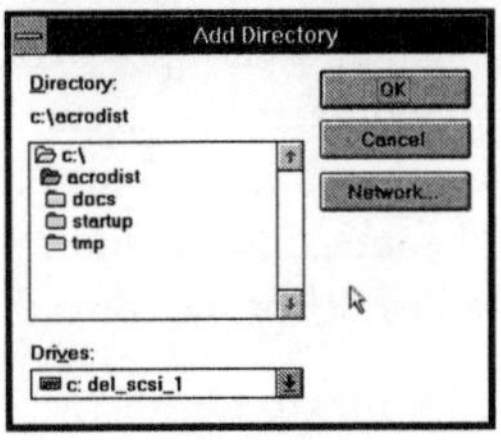

Figure 17.7. The Add Directory dialog box.

In the network version of Distiller, there is one additional menu item not available in the personal Distiller. **W**atched Directories... (Ctrl+W) produces the Watched Directories Options dialog box (see Figure 17.8), which enables you to specify the following:

- The periodic interval Distiller waits between In-directory search-list scans for input files
- Whether input files are deleted or moved to the Out directory with the corresponding PDF file after processing

- How long files can remain in the Out directory before automatic deletion

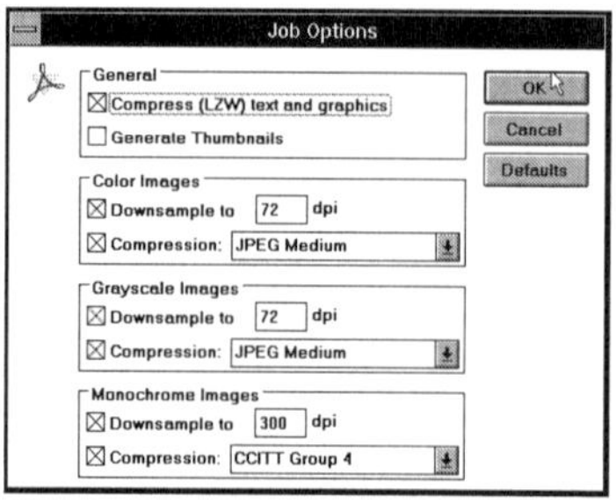

Figure 17.8. The Watched Directories Options dialog box.

Clicking Add Directory produces the Add Directory dialog box and enables you to add directories to the In directory search list.

Distilling PostScript Files

To create error-free PDF files, Distiller needs two things:

- Valid PostScript files
- Access to the document PostScript Type 1 fonts

Make sure documents print on PostScript printers before creating their PostScript files for Distiller. Documents that do not print correctly cannot distill correctly. Depending on a number of factors, a document's PostScript file might or might not include the necessary Type 1 fonts. When the PostScript file does not include Type 1 fonts, Distiller must find the Type 1 font in another location to process the PostScript file correctly.

Any of three methods supplies PostScript files to Distiller:

1. Start Distiller and use its File menu's Open command to open PostScript files for conversion. After selecting a PostScript file, Distiller asks for the PDF filename and location.
2. Drag one or more PostScript files onto the Distiller
    - application window,
    - program icon on the desktop while Distiller is running,
    - program name in the File Manager while Distiller is running,
    - program icon in a Program Manager group while Distiller is running.

3. The RunFile procedure allows Distiller to combine two or more PostScript files into a single PDF document with a single file open action.

Of course, Network Distiller users can process files simply by placing them in a Network Distiller's In directory.

Manually Opening PostScript Files

Using Distiller's File menu's **O**pen command selects input PostScript files. Opening PostScript files tells Distiller to create PDF files for them. By default, when Distiller opens a PostScript file, the Save As dialog box appears, which allows PDF file naming and location selection. Keyboard modifiers override the default behavior.

TIP

To bypass the Save As dialog box and save PDF files in the *same directory* as source PostScript files, hold down the Shift key when you click the Open dialog box's OK button. This gives PDF files the *same name* as source PostScript files with a *.pdf* file extension.

To save PDF files in the *same directory* as source PostScript files, but with a *different name*, hold down the Control key when you click the Open dialog box's OK button.

Drag-And-Drop Windows Distilling

The Windows version of Distiller enables you to drag-and-drop one or more PostScript files from the File Manager to Distiller's

- application window,
- program icon on the desktop while Distiller is running,
- program name in the File Manager while Distiller is running,
- program icon in a Program Manager group while Distiller is running.

You may also drag multiple files to the program name in the File Manager, but only the first file will be distilled due to an inconsistency in the Program Manager.

By default, the Save As dialog box does not display when using the drag-and-drop method. Instead, Distiller places PDF files in the same directory as the source PostScript files and appends a .pdf extension to the original filename. Distiller does display the Save As dialog box, however, if you press a modifier key while drag-and-dropping PostScript files.

TIP

To display the Save As dialog box with the *last directory* used as the default directory, hold down the Shift key while dragging the PostScript files.

To display the Save As dialog box with the *source directory* as the default directory, hold down the Control key while dragging PostScript files.

The RunFile Procedure

The PostScript RunFile procedure allows Distiller to include PostScript files in its current PostScript file processing. Distiller combines the separate PostScript files into a single PDF file.

Included PostScript files can exist in directories other than the one containing the source file Distiller is processing. This procedure can include PostScript headers from directories other than Distiller's Startup directory and distills PostScript files in directories other than those Network Distiller monitors.

For example, suppose the following text comprises a PostScript file called *SwtHeart.ps*:

```
%!
(D:\\Squeak\\TOC.ps)   RunFile
(D:\\Squeak\\Body.ps)  RunFile
(D:\\Squeak\\Index.ps) RunFile
%EOF
```

When Distiller processes SwtHeart.ps, it looks for each file the RunFile procedures reference (`D:\\Squeek\\TOC.ps`, `D:\\Squeek\\Body.ps`, and `D:\\Squeak\\Index.ps`) and, by default, creates a single PDF file named *SwtHeart.pdf* that combines all referenced files in the order listed.

How Network Distiller Prioritizes File Processing

Two or more Network Distillers can watch the same directory (or folder). In this instance, the first Network Distiller to open a PostScript file processes the file.

Individual Network Distillers watch up to 100 directories. While they process watched-directory PostScript files, Distiller's Open commands can select other PostScript files for processing. When more than one PostScript file waits for a Network Distiller's processing, a Network Distiller processes its files in the following order:

1. The Open command can open two or more files while the Distiller is processing another file. These new files process in the order they were opened.
2. Open-command files process before watched-directory files.
3. Watched directories are serviced in round-robin order: first one file from one directory, then one file from the next directory, and so on.
4. Within directories, file processing order is system dependent. If using Windows, files process in the order DOS `DIR` commands list them. Usually, older files process first. If using a Macintosh, files process in alphabetical name order.
5. If Distiller is processing a watched-directory file when the Open command opens another file, Distiller processes the opened file after completing the current file.

Distiller's Setup

When Distiller processes PostScript files, it creates PDF files according to its current setup. Distiller's setup options control the following:

- Color image compression
- Grayscale image compression
- Bilevel (monochrome or black-and-white) image compression
- PDF document page thumbnail creation

To change Distiller setup, select the Distiller menu Job Options command to display the Job Options dialog box (see Figure 17.5).

Appendix D, "Acrobat Compression," contains more information on Distiller compression options.

To list one or more directories containing Type 1 or Type 3 fonts Distiller may reference, select the Distiller menu Font Locations command. This displays the Font Locations dialog box, which enables you to specify desired directories.

Network Distiller also has the Distiller menu Watched Directories command. Selecting this command enables you to do the following:

- Set the directory watch interval, which is the maximum time Distiller waits before checking all In directories. Distiller accepts any value from 1 to 10,000 seconds. (10,000 seconds is about 2 hours and 45 minutes.)
- Create, delete, or modify existing watched-directory list entries.
- Indicate whether Distiller copies source PostScript files to Out directories with generated PDF files before deleting them from the In directory. The Macintosh version of Distiller copies PostScript files to Out directories even if the Delete PostScript Files option is chosen. The Windows version of Distiller copies PostScript files to Out directories only if the Move PostScript Files To The Out Directory option is chosen. Both versions delete In-directory PostScript files.
- Set the maximum number of days PDF and PostScript files can remain in the Out directory before Distiller purges them. This relieves network users of accumulated log, PDF, and PostScript file deletion responsibility. Users must retrieve files within the specified number of days, however, or they are lost.

Each Windows and Macintosh Network Distiller can monitor up to 100 directories or folders, and two or more Network Distillers can watch the same directory or folder. When adding watched directories, Distiller creates an In directory and an Out directory within the named watched directories. Thereafter, Distiller actually monitors the watched directories' In directory for input PostScript files. If it finds one, it processes the file, observing current job-setup options to create a PDF file. Distiller places the generated PDF file and, optionally, the source PostScript file, in the Out directory.

Windows and Macintosh System 7 support placing In directory and Out directory pairs in disk drive root directories. For example, selecting `E:\` as a watched directory creates an MS-DOS directory `E:\In` and `E:\Out` directory pair.

Security Issues

Network Distiller must have read, write, create, and delete access to every watched directory or folder. Therefore, Network Distiller machines must be trusted machines for all users or user groups requiring its services. Various approaches address obvious security issues.

Dedicating a Distiller to every network user or setting up guest access to every directory (or folder) a Network Distiller watches are extreme measures. With enough network administration and computer resources, it is always possible to set up Network Distillers to meet the established security policy and user needs. If network administration and computer resources are constrained, here are some suggestions to achieve maximum security with minimum resources:

> *Secure Network Distiller machines with either keyboard or software-locking mechanisms.* For example, some screen saver utilities can require users to enter passwords before relinquishing control of a computer monitor. (Screen savers slow Distiller operation, however.)

> *Create fictitious users for user groups that require private PostScript and PDF files.* Give each group member the user name and password for their group and restrict group access to In and Out directories to the fictitious user. This scheme maintains control of the fictitious user's password, allowing periodic changes or changes whenever a group member leaves.

Adding PDF File Thumbnails

Distiller can automatically create PDF file page thumbnails. *Thumbnails* are miniature document page images often helpful in browsing documents. Thumbnails are powerful browsing tools for documents containing illustrations and tables, such as software manuals, newsletters, and various textbooks. Thumbnails are less useful for documents containing few illustrations or tables, because all the thumbnails appear identical.

Acrobat Exchange users can create and delete thumbnails for individual PDF files. Because thumbnail creation increases Distiller processing time and the resulting PDF file sizes, tradeoffs exist between automatically generating thumbnails for all documents and generating them as needed with Acrobat Exchange.

To set up Distiller to create thumbnails:

1. Select the Distiller menu's **J**ob Options... command

2. When the Job Options dialog box appears, select the Generate Thumbnails option and click OK.

Status and Error Information

The Distiller window displays the following status and error information as it processes files (see Figure 17.9):

- The *Status* field displays current Distiller activity messages.
- The *Size* field displays the size of the PostScript file it is processing.
- The *Source* field indicates whether Distiller received the file from a manual user action, such as an Open command or a drag-and-drop action, or from an In directory retrieval operation.
- The *Percent Read* bar graph displays how much of the current PostScript file processing has completed.
- The *Message* text box displays PostScript processing status and error messages. Distiller writes all displayed messages to the Distiller application directory's *messages.log* file. Distiller also does the following:

    Writes any PostScript file error messages to a PostScript file log

    Gives the log file the PDF file's name but with a *.log* file extension

    Places the log file in the same directory as the PDF file

- The *Page* box at the right side of the window shows the current page's page number. The Page box also shows the current page's thumbnail image when creating thumbnails.

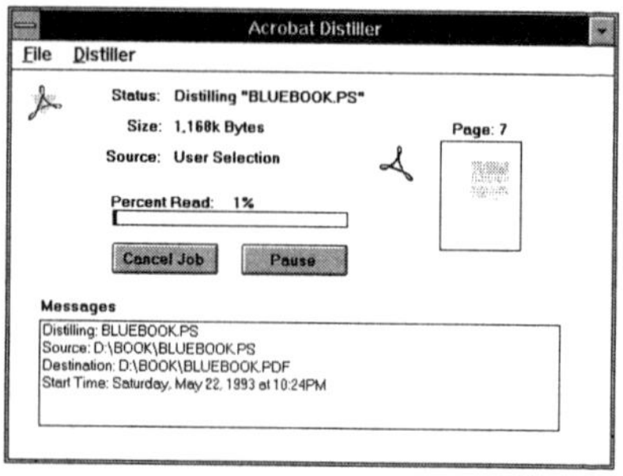

Figure 17.9. The Acrobat Distiller screen.

Status Field Messages

The Distiller window's Status field displays the following messages:

- `Starting Distiller` indicates Distiller is initializing.
- `Purging Out Directories` indicates Distiller is deleting files that have been left in Out directories longer than the maximum days specified in the Watched Directories dialog box.
- `Ready` indicates Distiller is idle, waiting to process submitted PostScript files.
- `Paused` indicates the Pause button was selected. Distiller remains paused until Resume is selected.
- `Distilling filename.ps` indicates Distiller is processing the specified file.
- `Relocating files` indicates Distiller is creating a PDF file or possibly moving a PostScript file from an In directory to its associated Out directory.
- `Building Font Table` (Windows only) indicates Distiller is building a PFM filename list for PostScript Type 1 fonts. This message displays when the Windows version of Distiller starts after the Font Locations dialog box adds font directories.

The *Pause* button tells Distiller to suspend processing after completing the current PostScript file.

The *Resume* button tells Distiller to continue processing PostScript files after a pause.

CHAPTER EIGHTEEN

Distiller Font Access

When Distiller processes PostScript files, it needs access to the document's fonts. When Distiller can't find document fonts, it substitutes Courier for fonts it can't find. Usually, the PostScript files include the fonts documents use or ATM can provide them. Distiller can find fonts stored in any system directory when it is correctly set up.

How PostScript Files Include Font Information

Distiller processes the PostScript files printer drivers create and generates PDF files. PostScript printer drivers include PostScript file font information using the following strategy:

- PostScript files include all of the Type 1 font names that a document uses. If a printer does not have a specific built-in font, the driver attempts to include the font outlines in the PostScript file.
- With Windows, depending on how the driver is set up, TrueType fonts may convert to Type 1 or Type 3 bitmap fonts, or Type 1 fonts may be substituted for TrueType fonts.

Distiller needs access to Type 1 font outlines when PostScript files do not include the font outlines. This occurs in the following instances:

- Windows PostScript drivers do not include Type 1 font outlines for fonts which are printer-resident in the printer's WIN.INI file entry. Usually, these fonts include built-in fonts and manually downloaded fonts.
- When a Type 1 font is removed from the system after a document is created, but before the PostScript file is created, the PostScript driver places only the font name, not the font outlines, in the PostScript file.
- If a PostScript file does not include a font, Distiller looks for the font on its local system and in locations specified in the Font Locations dialog box.

TrueType Fonts and Windows PostScript Driver

The Windows PostScript printer driver provides three TrueType font printing options:

- Substitute Type 1 fonts for TrueType fonts. With this option, the driver replaces the TrueType font characters with available Type 1 font characters. By default, the Windows PostScript printer driver substitutes Type 1 Helvetica fonts for TrueType Arial fonts. Users can override the defaults, specifying any Type 1 font as any TrueType substitute font.
- Create synthetic Type 1 fonts for TrueType fonts. With this option, the driver uses TrueType character outlines to create Type 1 TrueType font versions. Synthesized Type 1 fonts download to printers.
- Create Type 3 font bitmaps for TrueType fonts. With this option, the driver builds Type 3 bitmap fonts for TrueType fonts and downloads them to printers. Sending the characters to the printer just once instead of every time they appear in documents accelerates Type 3 bitmap printing over regular bitmap font printing.

Try to avoid using TrueType fonts in documents you Distill. TrueType font substitution is satisfactory, but when Type 1 or Type 3 fonts are loaded, they are given synthesized names and only the characters used by the document are sent to the printer. Consequently, the Distiller usually does not have enough font substitution information, and it must include a complete font representation in the PDF file.

Where Windows Distiller Searches for Fonts

When PostScript files reference but do not include Type 1 fonts, the Windows version of Distiller looks for the Type 1 fonts in these locations:

- If ATM is installed, in the directory ATM inspects for Type 1 fonts (usually `c:\psfonts`)
- Within the Distiller's application directory's fonts directory (usually `c:\anetdist`)
- In directories anywhere on the network specified using the Font Locations dialog box

When PostScript files reference but do not include Type 1 fonts, the Macintosh version of Distiller looks for the Type 1 fonts in these locations:

- When using System 6, in the System folder
- When using System 7, in the System folder, and in the System folder's Extensions and Fonts folders
- In the Distiller application folder's Fonts folder
- In directories anywhere on the network specified with the Font Locations dialog box.
- Font Folio or Type on Call devices if Distiller has access to these devices

Distiller uses Suitcase or similar programs to locate Type 1 font outlines in open suitcases. Finally, if missing fonts are Adobe fonts and Super ATM is installed, Super ATM creates substitute fonts for the missing fonts.

The Font Locations Dialog Box

Normally, ATM provides the Type 1 fonts documents use and automatically gives Distiller access to the fonts. To distill documents that use fonts unavailable from ATM, Distiller must find the fonts. Distiller can search for Type 1 fonts using a list with a maximum of 100 directory entries.

To add a font directory, follow these steps:

1. Select the Distiller menu's Font Locations command. The Font Locations dialog box (see Figure 18.1) displays a font subdirectory list which Distiller searches for fonts. Note that a Windows >> symbol or a Macintosh • symbol to the left of a directory name indicates the Distiller font directory is available. When no symbol appears, the directory's network connection has probably been lost.

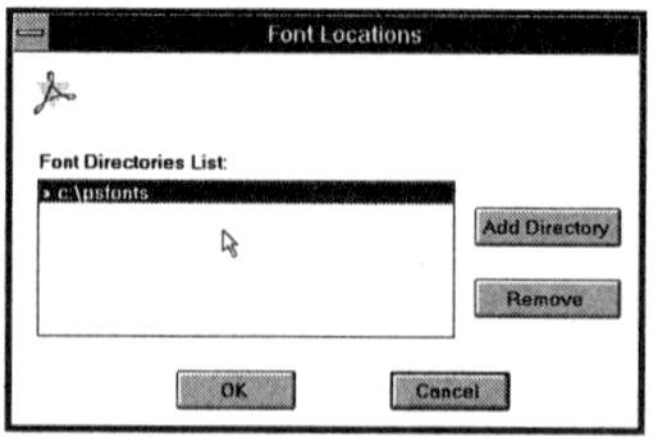

Figure 18.1.
The Font Locations dialog box.

2. Click theAdd Directory button and the Add Directory dialog box appears (see Figure 18.2).

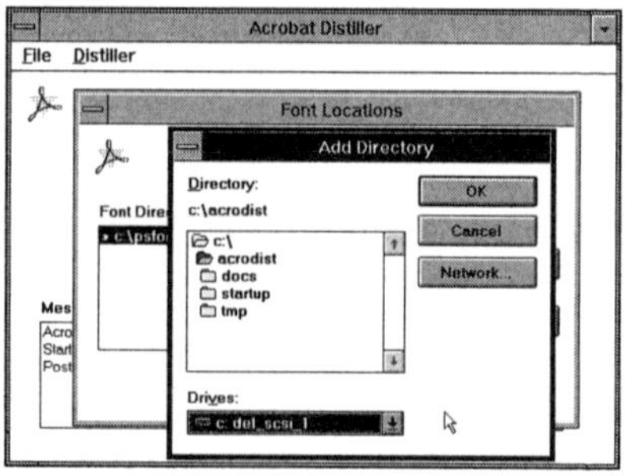

Figure 18.2.
Add Directory dialog box.

3. Select a new directory and open it so the directory name appears above the directory box. Click OK.
4. Add other font location directories using the same procedure.
5. When finished, click OK to close the Font Locations dialog box and return to Distiller's main window.

To remove font locations follow these steps:

1. Select the Distiller menu's Font Locations command. The Font Locations dialog box appears.
2. Select the font directory to remove, and click Remove. Click OK. The Font Locations dialog box closes, returning to Distiller's main window.

Initializing Distiller with PostScript Header Files

PostScript printer drivers use PostScript headers composed of document rendering procedure libraries. Distiller can initialize with predefined PostScript header files, so printer drivers can create PostScript files without headers. Because the typical size of PostScript header files is about 30 kilobytes, initializing Distiller with PostScript headers reduces each PostScript file's size. The reduced size decreases Network Distiller's network traffic.

To initialize Distiller with a PostScript header, copy the header file to Distiller's application directory's Startup directory. Any number of PostScript header files can exist in this directory. For example, both Windows and Macintosh System 6 standard headers can exist in Distiller's Startup directory when distilling both Windows and Macintosh application-created PostScript files.

The RunFile procedure can include PostScript header files from other directories. For example, creating a Startup directory text file containing the text line

```
(D:\Ps\Header\Win.Ps) RunFile
```

allows Distiller to initialize its PostScript interpreter using the header defined in Win.PS.

Macintosh Distiller program disks include standard System 6 PostScript headers. If this file initializes Distiller, Macintosh System 6 users can create PostScript files without the PostScript header. Unfortunately, if you are using System 7, you cannot create PostScript files without PostScript headers, but you can remove PostScript file headers using utility programs.

CHAPTER NINETEEN

Creating PDF Files with Distiller

Distiller provides the most complete PDF creation processing. This is important for Encapsulated PostScript processing and in instances where applications produce output that PDF Writer cannot correctly process.

General PDF File Creation Tips

Before Distilling document PostScript files, you need to recognize two limitations of the current version of Distiller:

- Distiller substitutes gray shades for fill patterns in some drawing, painting, and charting applications. This substitution often produces acceptable results. When bar chart bars are filled with alternating diagonal stripes, however, Distiller fills the bars with the same gray shade. Filling shapes with varying gray shades instead of fill patterns avoids the problem.
- Distiller does not process custom halftone functions; it uses standard halftone functions instead. Distiller usually produces acceptable results, but complicated halftone functions do not appear as the application prints them. No solution exists for this problem other than using standard halftone functions for PDF document images.

Distilling Adobe Illustrator EPS Files

When distilling Encapsulated PostScript (EPS) files, resulting PDF documents are 8½-by-11 inches, regardless of the artwork's dimensions. When using Adobe Illustrator to create nonstandard-dimensioned EPS files, use printer drivers to print intermediate PostScript files and distill them.

Macintosh Distiller running under System 7 enables you to drag icons of one or more PostScript files onto the Distiller icon (or a Distiller program alias). Drag-and-drop features do not work with System 6.

Distiller Window's Messages and Error Log Files

All the messages Distiller displays in its window's message text area, Distiller also writes to its application directory's Messages.log file. Messages.log, therefore, is Distiller's processing activity record. Because Distiller records both processing start and stop times, as well as PostScript file sizes, the Messages.log file helps record Distiller's performance behavior. Distiller limits the Messages.log file to 30K. When the file reaches 30K, Distiller deletes the file's first 10K and continues appending new messages to the end of the file.

Distiller also takes error messages produced during PostScript file processing and writes them to individual log files. Distiller gives log files the same name as their PDF files, but with a *.log* file extension, and places the log files in the same subdirectories as the PDF files. If PDF files have problems, first check the log file Distiller produced while processing the source PostScript file. Often log file error messages isolate the problem.

CHAPTER TWENTY

Distiller Troubleshooting

This chapter provides a comprehensive listing of error messages and their meanings. Where possible, the discussion provides suggestions to resolve the problem.

Launch Failure Numbered Error Messages

If you receive a numeric error message at Distiller program launch, refer to Appendix G, "Reader and Exchange Launch Failure Numbered Error Messages."

Distiller Initialization Failure

The Windows version of Distiller requires a numeric coprocessor or numeric coprocessor emulation program. Without either of these, Distiller fails after briefly displaying its window. See the Windows Distiller Installation Card for numeric coprocessor emulation installation instructions.

Distiller's In Directory Is Unavailable

When network connections to Network Distiller's In directory are lost, network access to Network Distiller's services are also lost. To remedy this situation, first attempt to reconnect to the server. If this is not possible, the following are possible causes of the problem:

- The network
- The user computer
- The physical network connection to the user computer

Report such problems to your network administrator.

Distiller Cannot Find Share.Exe

Share.Exe is a program with MS-DOS 5.0 or later versions that prevents two programs from simultaneously having the same file open. When the Network Distiller Windows version starts, it checks to see if Share is running. If it isn't, Network Distiller displays a warning message indicating it couldn't find Share.

When using MS-DOS 5, run the Share program. Some PostScript files are very large and take a long time to write to In directories. Running Share ensures that Distiller won't open PostScript files that are still being copied to the In directory. Share runs like any other MS-DOS program. Placing the Share command in AUTOEXEC.BAT files starts it automatically when computers switch on. To manually start Share, type `Share` and press Enter at the MS-DOS prompt.

Insufficient Memory to Run Distiller

To operate the Network Distiller Windows version requires 8MB of RAM. When starting Distiller with insufficient RAM, Distiller displays a message indicating it does not have enough memory to run. If this message appears while the Windows version of Network Distiller is starting, increase the size of Windows' available virtual memory using the 386 Enhanced Control Panel.

Poor Distiller Performance

Distiller's performance may suffer because of one or more of the following reasons:

- The network performance is poor.
- Distiller must compete with other applications for CPU time.
- Distiller is looking in too many directories for Type 1 fonts.

Deleting Distiller's Preferences file in Distiller's application directory and reconfiguring Distiller sometimes improves Distiller performance.

> **CAUTION**
>
> Stop Distiller before deleting the Preferences file.

findfont Errors

When Distiller cannot find the Type 1 fonts a PostScript file uses and it cannot use ATM to create a missing font substitute, it issues `findfont error` messages and substitutes Courier for missing fonts.

If Distiller can't find the Type 1 fonts because they are in a network server directory to which Distiller lost access, restore Distiller's server directory access and reprocess the PostScript file.

If Distiller can't find the font because it is not in a font directory identified with the Font Locations dialog box or installed on Distiller's system, place the font in a font directory listed in the Font Locations dialog box or install the font on Distiller's system.

Distiller Processes PostScript Files, but Does Not Produce PDF Files

Problems can arise with Distiller's PostScript file processing that prevent it from creating PDF files. When Distiller fails to create PDF files for PostScript files, it creates text log files in the directories where it would have created the PDF files. Any word processor can open the text log files that describe the specific problem.

The Windows version of Distiller derives log filenames from the original PostScript filenames. If the PostScript file extension is *.ps*, Distiller replaces *.ps* with a *.log* extension. Otherwise, Distiller appends *.log* to the PostScript file's name as the file extension. When Distiller fails to create a PDF file for a PostScript file, the PostScript file usually does not include a PostScript header and an alternate header is not available to Distiller. Either create PostScript files that include the PostScript header or report this problem to a network administrator who will make PostScript headers available to Distiller.

If a specific PostScript file containing a header repeatedly fails to print, the file may have been corrupted, or the error might be an application error. Make sure the document prints correctly on PostScript printers and then try making a new PostScript file.

PostScript Processing Is Not Prompt

Two problems prevent Distiller from processing PostScript files promptly:

- Distiller is not monitoring its In directory.
- Distiller is busy processing other PostScript files.

To tell whether Distiller is actively monitoring its In directory, check to see when it last modified the DTIME.TXT file in one of its Out directories. If Distiller has modified DTIME.TXT recently, Distiller is monitoring the In directory. If Distiller is not monitoring the In directory, either Distiller has stopped or has lost its network server connection for its In directory. In either case, report the problem to network administration. If Distiller is watching the In directory but has not yet processed a specific PostScript file, Distiller has been busy processing other files and will eventually process the file.

Courier Substitutes for Other Fonts

When Distiller cannot find PostScript file fonts, it substitutes Courier for the missing fonts. Two situations cause this problem:

- The font is not available to Distiller.
- Distiller lost a network connection to the directory that contains the font.

If Distiller apparently does not have font access, talk to a network administrator about providing Distiller to the fonts. Report lost network connections to network administrators, and copy the PostScript files to Distiller's In directory after the network connection is revived.

Photographic and Other Scanned Images Appear Unrefined

Photographic image files typically consume significant storage. To minimize PDF file sizes, Distiller uses various specified scanned image compression techniques that reduce scanned image detail and introduce processing artifacts. After compression, images may exhibit quilted looks and distort sharp lines. Reduce Distiller's compression amount and/or downsampling threshold if the quality of PDF file scanned images is unacceptable.

Fill Patterns Appear as Gray Shades

The current Distiller version substitutes gray shades for the fill patterns some graphics and charting programs use. There is no solution for this problem except to fill PDF document illustration shapes using varying gray shades.

Halftone Images Appear Incorrectly

PostScript printers support application-defined halftone functions. The current Distiller version processes halftone images with standard halftone functions. Distiller usually produces acceptable results, but complicated halftone functions, however, do not appear as the application prints them. No solution exists for this problem other than using standard halftone functions for PDF document images.

PART

IV

Acrobat Family Product Summary

- Acrobat Reader and Exchange Quick Reference Guide
- Acrobat Reader and Exchange Menu Summary
- Acrobat Reader and Exchange Keyboard Accelerators
- Acrobat Distiller Menu Summary

QUICK REFERENCE

1

Acrobat Reader and Exchange Quick Reference Guide

This section provides terse reference material for Acrobat products. This material is also available on the disk accompanying this book. An asterisk (*) before an entry in this quick reference indicates that the function exists only with Acrobat Exchange.

Document Browsing

Current Page Browsing: Drag the tool bar's Hand tool, the horizontal scroll bar, the vertical scroll bar, or the thumbnail's view box.

Preceding Page Top: Click the tool bar's Previous Page browse button, select the View menu's Previous Page command, or press the Up Arrow or Left Arrow key.

Following Page Top: Click the tool bar's Next Page browse button, select the View menu's Next Page command, or press the Down Arrow or Right Arrow key.

Page View Screens: Pressing the PageUp key moves one screen toward the top of the document. Pressing the PageDown key moves one screen toward the end of the document.

Specific Pages:

> **First Page:** Click the tool bar's First Page browse button, select the View menu's First Page command, or press the Home key.
> **Last Page:** Click the tool bar's Last Page browse button, select the View menu's Last Page command, or press the End key.
> **Vertical Scroll Bar:** The current page number appears while you drag the scroll bar.
> **Entering Page Number:** Click the status bar's Page Number box or select the View menu's Go To Page command and enter the page number in the Go To Page dialog box.
> **Bookmarks:** Double-click the bookmark's page icon.
> **Thumbnails:** Expose and click the page's thumbnail.

Navigation Stack Page View Retracing:

> **Backward:** Click the tool bar's Go Back navigation button, select the View menu's Go Back command, or press Alt+hyphen (Alt+–).
> **Forward:** Click the tool bar's Go Forward navigation button, select the View menu's Go Forward command, or press Alt+=.

Page View Magnification

Zoom Tools:

> **Global Page View Changes:** The Zoom In tool doubles magnification of the view to a maximum of 800 percent. The Zoom Out tool halves the magnification to a minimum of 12 percent. Click the desired Zoom tool; then click the desired page view.

Selected Page View Areas: Click the Zoom tool. Select a rectangle by dragging the tool. The Zoom In tool expands the rectangular area, filling the Page View pane. The Zoom Out tool shrinks the active page view to fit within the rectangular area.

Zoom-In/Zoom-Out Toggling: Hold down the Ctrl key with the selected Zoom tool over the active page view.

Status Bar Magnification Box:

Preselected Values: Click the magnification box while holding down the mouse button. Select a list entry.

Custom Values: Click the magnification box while holding down the mouse button and select Other. Alternatively, if Exchange or Reader is displayed as a full screen, quickly click the magnification box (Windows only). Enter the desired value in the dialog box.

Thumbnail View Box: Expose the thumbnails. Resize the view box by dragging the view box handle.

Tool Bar's *Actual Size, Fit Page to Window,* and *Fit Width to Window* Buttons:

Actual Size Button: Changes the magnification level to 100 percent.

Fit Page to Window Button: Changes the magnification level to display the entire page.

Fit Width to Window Button: Changes the magnification level to display the current page width.

Keyboard: Pressing the Ctrl+plus (Ctrl++) key combination (from the numeric keypad only) doubles the magnification to a maximum of 800 percent. Pressing the Ctrl+minus (Ctrl+–) key combination (from the numeric keypad only) halves the magnification to a minimum of 12 percent.

String Searching

Initial Occurrence: Click the tool bar's Find tool, select the Tools menu's Find command, or press Ctrl+F.

Search options include the following:

Match Whole Word Only: The strings will have identical lengths.

Match Case: The strings will have identical uppercase and lowercase letters (the search is case sensitive).

Enter the search string in the Find What text box. Click Find Next. The Find dialog box closes and page view highlights the word.

Subsequent Occurrence: Press Ctrl+G or reselect the Tools menu's Find command and click Find Next.

Notes

***Creating Multiple Notes:** Depress the Ctrl key when selecting the tool bar's Note tool or the Tools menu's Note command. Otherwise, the Note tool normally deselects after note creation. Clicking another tool deselects the Note tool.

***Creating Individual Notes:** Select Full Menus. Click the tool bar's Note tool or select the Tools menu's Note command. When over the Page View pane, the mouse pointer becomes a cross hair.

> **Default Note Window:** Click to indicate where to place the upper-left corner of the window (approximately 2" × 3" wide).
> **Custom Size Notes:** Drag the cross hair down and to the right to size the note (approximately 4" × 6" wide maximum).

Enter the note text optionally using Cut, Copy, Paste, Clear, and Undo. The text scrolls if the text cannot fit in the Note window.

Opening Notes: Double-click the note icon.

Closing Note Windows: Double-click the Note window's upper-left corner close box (single-click when on a Macintosh) to iconize the note. Note icons reside anywhere on the active page view and can remain open.

Resizing Notes: Select the note and drag the window handle to reflow the note text.

Deleting Notes: Close the note window. Click the note and it turns gray. Then press the Delete, Clear, or Backspace key.

Creating Note PDF Files

Select the Tools menu's Create Notes File command. You can only print the new file or copy its information to the Clipboard.

Printing

Select the Print Setup command print options. Select the File menu's Print command. The Print dialog box has the following options:

Shrink to Fit: Shrinks oversized pages to fit the printer's current paper size.

PostScript Options: Appears in the Print dialog box for only PostScript printers. The Adobe PSPrinter driver automatically selects the appropriate printer PostScript options. The Level 2 option accelerates printers capable of printing PostScript Level 2.

Bookmarks

Exposing: Click the tool bar's Bookmarks and Page button or select the View menu's Bookmarks and Page command.

Destination Viewing: Double-click the bookmark's page icon.

Expanding/Contracting Subordinate List: Click the bookmark triangle.

***Creating:** Select Full Menus. Generate the desired active page view. Expose the bookmarks. If the bookmark list exists, expand the list as necessary and click the bookmark under which to place the new bookmark. (The default list position is the bottom of the list.) Select Bookmarks from the Edit menu and New from the resulting submenu. Alternatively, press Ctrl+B in the Short Menus. A new, untitled bookmark entry appears. Enter the bookmark name or paste it from the Clipboard.

***Renaming:** Click the name and retype it or paste its name from the Clipboard.

***Simple Indenting to Right:** Select the intended bookmark by clicking the bookmark's page icon. Select Bookmarks from the Edit menu and Move Right from the resulting submenu, or press Ctrl+RightArrow.

***Bookmark List Reordering:** Select Full Menus. Select the intended bookmark by clicking the bookmark's page icon, holding down the Shift key while doing so to select two or more bookmarks. Select Bookmarks from the Edit menu and Move Left, Move Right, Move Up, or Move Down from the resulting submenu. Alternatively, use Ctrl+LeftArrow, Ctrl+RightArrow, Ctrl+UpArrow, or Ctrl+DownArrow key combinations, respectively.

***Changing Bookmark Destinations:** Select Full Menus. Generate the desired active page view. Select the intended bookmark by clicking the bookmark's page icon. Select Bookmarks from the Edit menu and Set New Destination from the resulting submenu.

***Delete Bookmarks and Subordinates:** Select Full Menus. Select the intended bookmark by clicking the bookmark's page icon. Hold down the Shift key while doing so to select two or more bookmarks. Select Bookmarks from the Edit menu and Delete from the resulting submenu.

Thumbnails

Exposing: Click the tool bar's Thumbnails and Page button or select the View menu's Thumbnails and Page command.

Page Jumps: Click the desired page's thumbnail. The point where you click will be the center of the page view, if possible.

Active Page View Adjustments: Drag the current page's thumbnail view box on the thumbnail, or click to relocate the center of the view box. Dragging the view box handle resizes the view box, adjusting the active page view magnification.

***Creation:** Select Full Menus. Select Thumbnails from the Edit menu and Create All from the resulting submenu.

***Deletion:** Select Full Menus. Select Thumbnails from the Edit menu and Delete All from the resulting submenu. Cropping and rotating deletes the associated thumbnails. Deleted thumbnails appear gray.

Hypertext Links

Using a Link: Click anywhere inside the Link button. The cursor becomes an arrow over Link buttons.

***Creating Multiple Links:** Hold down the Ctrl key when selecting the tool bar's Link tool or the Tools menu's Link command. Otherwise, the Link tool deselects after link creation. Clicking another tool deselects the Link tool.

***Creating Individual Links:** To create the Link button, select Full Menus. Generate the desired active page view for Link button placement. Click the tool bar's Link tool or select the Tools menu's Link command. The mouse pointer becomes a cross hair over the Page View pane. Draw the Link button by positioning the cross hair at the Link button's upper-left corner and dragging it down and to the right. Releasing the mouse button displays the Link button and displays the Make Link dialog box. For invisible links, select the Invisible Link option.

To associate the Link button with a destination, generate the desired active page view of the destination. Click OK to close the dialog box and redisplay the Link button's page view.

***Moving Link Buttons:** Click the tool bar's Link tool or select the Tools menu's Link command. The mouse pointer becomes a cross hair, displaying all active page view invisible Link buttons. To move a Link button, position the cursor inside the button and drag the button to a new location. The Link tool does not automatically deselect because a link was not created.

***Resizing Link Buttons:** Click the tool bar's Link tool or select the Tools menu's Link command. The mouse pointer becomes a cross hair over the Page View pane, displaying all active page view invisible Link buttons. To resize a Link button, select the button and drag its handles. The Link tool does not automatically deselect because a link was not created.

***Changing Link Button Destinations:** Click the tool bar's Link tool or select the Tools menu's Link command. The mouse pointer becomes a cross hair over the Page View pane, displaying all active page view invisible Link buttons. Double-click the intended Link button, revealing the Edit Link dialog box. Generate the desired active page view destination and click OK.

***Changing Link Button Visibility:** Click the tool bar's Link tool or select the Tools menu's Link command. The mouse pointer becomes a cross hair over the Page View pane, displaying all active page view invisible Link buttons. Double-click the intended Link button, revealing the Edit Link dialog box. Select either Visible Link or Invisible Link and click OK.

***Deleting Link Buttons:** Click the tool bar's Link tool or select the Tools menu's Link command. The mouse pointer becomes a cross hair over the Page View pane, displaying all active page view invisible Link buttons. Click the intended Link button and press the Backspace, Clear, or Delete key.

Copying Text to the Clipboard

Click the tool bar's Text Selection tool or select the Tools menu's Select Text command. The mouse pointer becomes a cross hair over the Page View pane. Dragging the tool over any part of a text line selects the enclosed area's text. Release the mouse button to highlight the selected text. To start over, click anywhere.

Choosing the Edit menu's Copy command copies selected text to the Clipboard. Select the Window menu's Show Clipboard command to view the selected text. Switch to other applications and paste the text elsewhere, or use it to paste into bookmark names.

*Deleting Document Pages

Select Full Menus. Select the Edit menu's Delete Pages command and the Delete Pages dialog box appears. Enter the page range to delete and click OK. Save the document.

*Inserting Document Pages

Select Full Menus. Select the File menu's Insert command and the Open dialog box appears. Enter the document to insert and click OK, and the Insert dialog box appears. By default, the file is inserted after the last page. Enter in the Page box the page number before or after which to insert the document. Select Before to insert the document before the specified page; select After to insert the document after the specified page. Click OK and the document is inserted at the specified location. Save the document file before attempting any other actions.

*Cropping Page Margins

Select Full Menus. Select the Edit menu's Crop Pages, and the Crop Pages dialog box appears. Previously defined page margin point values for the current document appear in the margin boxes (72 points equal one inch). Enter new Top, Bottom, Left, or Right margin point values. Lines appear in the Page View pane indicating the new margins when entering new margin values. Enter the page range to which the new margins apply or accept the default, All Pages. Click OK to close the Crop Pages dialog box. The selected document pages will display with new margins and deleted thumbnails.

*Rotating Pages

Select Full Menus. Select the Edit menu's Rotate Pages command. The Rotate Pages dialog box will appear. Select either Left (counterclockwise) or Right (clockwise) as the page rotation direction. Specify the page range or accept All Pages as the default. Click OK. The Rotate dialog box closes and the specified pages rotate, deleting their thumbnails.

*Saving Document Changes

***Incremental Save:** Select the File menu's Save command.

***New PDF File Save:** Select the File menu's Save **A**s... command.

Setting Preferences (Program Initialization Values)

Select the Edit menu's Preferences... command. Select the initial default page view magnification level, text Greek size, whether to display large images in the document, and whether to use both the Serif and Sans Serif fonts, only the Sans Serif, or only the Serif multimaster font for font substitution. Click OK.

Pressing Ctrl+Shift+M and selecting the Edit menu's Preferences... command displays the More Preferences dialog box.

Displaying Document Creation Information

Select the File menu's Document Info... command. Ctrl+Shift+click for font substitution information.

QUICK REFERENCE

2

Acrobat Reader and Exchange Menu Summary

This section provides a summary of Acrobat Reader and Exchange menu commands. An asterisk (*) indicates an Acrobat Exchange-only command. A plus sign (+) indicates an Acrobat Exchange-only Full Menu command.

File

	Open...	Ctrl+O	Open another document
	Close	Ctrl+W	Close current document
	Inser**t**...		Insert a PDF document in current document
*	**S**ave	Ctrl+S	Save current document
*	Save **A**s...		Save current document using a different name
	Document **I**nfo...	Ctrl+I	Display document's authoring information
	Print...	Ctrl+P	Print current document
	P**r**int Setup...		Set the printer up
	1 C:\Kid$\Melissa.Pdf		Great document #1
	2 C:\Kid$\Gregory.Pdf		Great document #2
	3 D:\BowWow\Charlie.Pdf		Great document #3
	4 D:\BowWow\Katie.Pdf		Great document #4
	E**x**it	Alt+F4	We're outta here!

Edit

	Undo	Ctrl+Z	Undo last operation (if possible)
*	Cu**t**	Ctrl+X	Remove selected text and place on Clipboard
	Copy	Ctrl+C	Copy selected text to Clipboard
*	**P**aste	Ctrl+V	Copy Clipboard text to target area
*	Cl**e**ar	Del	Remove selected text
	Select **A**ll		Select all text (Macintosh only)
+	**R**otate Pages...		Rotate page range and erase thumbnails
+	Cro**p** Pages...		Crop page range and erase thumbnails
+	**D**elete Pages...		Delete page range
+	**B**ookmarks		
	+ **N**ew	Ctrl+B	Create new bookmark beneath selected bookmark
	+ D**e**lete		Delete selected bookmark

+ **S**et New Destination		Allow selected bookmark to move
+ Move **U**p	Ctrl+Up	Move selected bookmark up
+ Move **D**own	Ctrl+Down	Move selected bookmark down
+ Move **L**eft	Ctrl+Left	Move selected bookmark left
+ Move **R**ight	Ctrl+Right	Move selected bookmark right
+ Thumb**n**ails		
+ **C**reate All		Create missing thumbnails
+ **D**elete All		Delete thumbnail set
* Short/Full **M**enus		Provide Full/Short Menus and tool bar
Pre**f**erences...	Alt+F4	Set initialization preferences

View

Actual Size	Ctrl+H	Set magnification to 100%
Fit **P**age To Width	Ctrl+J	Adjust magnification to fit entire page in Page View pane
Fit **W**idth To Window	Ctrl+K	Adjust magnification to fit page width to Page View pane
Zoom To...	Ctrl+L	Display the Zoom To dialog box
First Page	Ctrl+1	Go to document's first page
P**r**evious Page	Ctrl+2	Go to previous document page
Next Page	Ctrl+3	Go to next document page
Last Page	Ctrl+4	Go to document's last page
Go To Page...	Ctrl+5	Display Go To Page dialog box
Go **B**ack	Alt+–	Navigate to previous page view
Go Forwar**d**	Alt+=	Navigate to next page view
Pag**e** Only		Close Overview pane
B**o**okmarks And Page		Display bookmarks in Overview pane
Thumbnails And Page		Display thumbnails in Overview pane

Tools

	Hand		Cursor becomes the Hand tool
	Zoom In		Cursor becomes the Zoom In tool
	Zoom Out		Cursor becomes the Zoom Out tool
	Select		Cursor becomes the Text Selection tool
+	Note		Cursor becomes the Note tool
+	Link		Cursor becomes the Link tool
	Find	Ctrl+F	Find search string
	Find **A**gain	Ctrl+G	Find another search string instance
	Find **N**ext Note	Ctrl+T	Find a following page with an appended note
	Create Notes File		Collect all notes into a PDF file

Window

Show/Hide Tool **B**ar		Removes the tool bar
Show Clipboar**d**		Displays Clipboard contents
Cascade	Shift+F5	Cascades all Acrobat document windows
Tile	Shift+F4	Tiles all Acrobat document windows
Close **A**ll		Closes all document windows

Help

Acrobat Reader/Exchange **H**elp	Opens HelpExch.Pdf/ HelpRead.Pdf
About Acrobat **R**eader/**E**xchange	Displays program information

QUICK REFERENCE

3

Acrobat Reader and Exchange Keyboard Accelerators

This section provides a summary of the Windows keyboard accelerators. Most *Ctrl*+ key combinations are available on the Macintosh as *Command*+ key combinations.

Action or Operation	*Accelerator*
Stop active page view rendering	Esc
Find	Ctrl+F
Find again	Ctrl+G
Find next note	Ctrl+T
Fit page to window	Ctrl+J
Fit page width to window	Ctrl+K
Set magnification to 100%	Ctrl+H
Display the Magnification dialog box	Ctrl+L
Open document	Ctrl+O
Save current document	Ctrl+S
Print current document	Ctrl+P
Get current document's Document Info	Ctrl+I
Close current document	Ctrl+W or Ctrl+F4
Undo edit changes	Ctrl+Z or Alt+Backspace
Select all edit text	Ctrl+A (Macintosh only)
Clear selected edit text	Backspace or Del
Cut selected edit text	Ctrl+X or Shift+Del
Copy selected text	Ctrl+C or Ctrl+Insert
Paste Clipboard text into note or bookmark	Ctrl+V or Shift+Insert
Go to document's first page	Ctrl+1 or Home
Go to previous document page	Ctrl+2 or UpArrow or LeftArrow
Go to next document page	Ctrl+3 or DownArrow or RightArrow
Go to document's last page	Ctrl+4 or End
Display Go To Page dialog box	Ctrl+5
Create new bookmark	Ctrl+B
Move selected bookmark(s) up	Ctrl+UpArrow
Move selected bookmark(s) down	Ctrl+DownArrow
Move selected bookmark(s) left	Ctrl+LeftArrow
Move selected bookmark(s) right	Ctrl+RightArrow
Move one screen toward top of document	PageUp
Move one screen toward end of document	PageDown
Navigate to previous page view	Alt+–
Navigate to next page view	Alt+=
Zoom in	Ctrl++ (numeric keypad only)
Zoom out	Ctrl+– (numeric keypad only)

Action or Operation	*Accelerator*
Tile document windows	Shift+F4
Cascade document windows	Shift+F5
Display Help file	F1
Exit Acrobat	Alt+F4

QUICK REFERENCE

4

Acrobat Distiller Menu Summary

This section provides a summary of the Acrobat Distiller menu commands.

File

Open	Ctrl+O	Opens a file to distill
E**x**it	Alt+F4	Ends Distiller execution
About Distiller...		Displays the Distiller About box

Tools

Job Options...	Ctrl+J	Displays/sets options
Font **L**ocations...	Ctrl+L	Displays/modifies font search list
Watched **D**irectories...	Ctrl+D	Displays/sets watched directories

PART

V

Appendices

- Fonts, Fonts, and Fonts
- Creating PostScript Files for Distiller
- Distiller PostScript Parameters
- Acrobat Compression
- Reader and Exchange Error Codes
- Reader and Exchange INI File Settings
- Reader, Exchange, and Distiller Launch Failure Numbered Error Messages
- Reader and Exchange, Design Limits
- A Day in the Life of a Character
- Glossary

APPENDIX A

Fonts, Fonts, and Fonts

There are four font types:

- *Type 1*, such as basic Macintosh and Windows Helvetica, Times, and Courier
- *Type 3*, which are special PostScript language fonts
- *Bitmap*, such as Macintosh System 6 Chicago and Windows Modern and Roman
- *TrueType*, such as the Windows Arial, Times New Roman, and Courier New, as well as Macintosh System 7 Chicago, Courier, and New York

Type 1 Fonts

Type 1 fonts are actually PostScript language programs that comprised the first outline fonts. *Outline fonts* mathematically describe each character as collections of lines and curves forming the character's outline. When PostScript printers print Type 1 font characters, they scale character outlines to specified sizes and use the scaled outline to create the print bitmap.

Creating bitmaps for scaled outlines is called *font rasterizing* because raster devices—devices that create images one dot line at a time—render the bitmap. PostScript printer interpreters rasterize Type 1 font outlines to render printed characters on pages. The Adobe Type Manager (ATM) program rasterizes Type 1 font outlines to render displayed characters on monitors.

Every PostScript printer comes with a number of built-in Type 1 fonts. Virtually all PostScript printers have these 13 fonts:

- The Helvetica family (regular, bold, oblique, and bold-oblique)
- The Times family (regular, bold, italic, and bold-italic)
- The Courier family (regular, bold, italic, and bold-italic)
- Symbol, a Greek letter and mathematical symbol font

In addition to these 13 Type 1 fonts, many PostScript printers have these built-in fonts:

- The Avant Garde family
- The ITC Bookman family
- The Helvetica Narrow family
- The New Century Schoolbook family
- The Palatino family
- The ITC Zapf Chancery font (a cursive font)
- The ITC Zapf Dingbats font (a symbol font)

Adobe's Plus Pack font package for both Windows and Macintosh contains these fonts. Together with the base 13 Type 1 fonts, these fonts comprise the base 35 Type 1 fonts. Windows and Macintosh users can increase their Type 1 font sets by purchasing various vendor Type 1 font collections.

Downloadable Type 1 Fonts

Applications copy downloadable Type 1 fonts to PostScript printers at print time. Because downloadable fonts reside on user systems and are not built into printer hardware, these fonts are also called *soft fonts*. Users copy the downloadable Type 1 font outlines to their hard disk. When printing documents containing downloadable fonts, the printer driver sends the printer the font outlines. The PostScript interpreter rasterizes and prints characters using the outlines. For both Windows and Macintosh users, ATM uses installed

Type 1 outlines to rasterize characters for the monitor. If Windows does not have ATM, it substitutes available TrueType fonts. If a Macintosh does not have ATM, the Macintosh uses Type 1 font bitmap outlines for screen characters.

Type 3 Fonts

Type 3 fonts are special PostScript font types usually used for two purposes:

- Company logo fonts
- Bitmap fonts

For company logos, Type 3 fonts include just a few character outlines, which are usually logo character variations. Type 3 fonts are available on the Macintosh, which also contains bitmap fonts for screen display. Windows does not use Type 3 fonts for screen display.

Bitmap Fonts

Both Windows and Macintosh have system *bitmap fonts*. In contrast to outline fonts, bitmap fonts are already rasterized. This means bitmap fonts come in predetermined sizes, with larger sizes requiring significant storage. Basic Windows applications, such as NotePad and Terminal, use the System or Fixedsys bitmap font. Common Windows bitmap fonts include HP LaserJet and compatible printer HPPCL fonts. HPPCL bitmap fonts are either permanently installed in the printer with type cartridges or installed on system hard disks as soft fonts.

TrueType Fonts

Like Type 1 fonts, *TrueType fonts* are outline fonts because they mathematically describe each character as collections of lines and curves forming the character's outline. Both Macintosh System 7 and Windows have a basic TrueType font set and include TrueType software, which (like ATM) rasterizes character outlines creating display characters. The Windows and Macintosh System 7 TrueType software usually send rasterized character outline bitmaps to printers when printing documents containing TrueType fonts. Some newer printers, however, have built-in TrueType rasterizers. For these printers, printer drivers can print TrueType characters by sending TrueType outlines to the printer.

APPENDIX B

Creating PostScript Files for Distiller

Creating PostScript files is the first step in using Distiller to create PDF documents. To create PostScript files in many applications, select the application's Print dialog box's Print to File check box, select a PostScript printer, and click OK. Before creating the PostScript file, the Print to File dialog box requests the file's name. With applications that do not include a Print to File option, add a new PostScript printer entry that connects to `FILE:`. After creating PostScript files, restore the original printer setup to use it again.

NOTE

Before making any PostScript document file available to Distiller, the document must print correctly on PostScript printers.

Using Print to File

Follow these steps to create PostScript document files when application Print dialog boxes contain Print to File check boxes:

1. Start an application and open a document.
2. Use the File menu's Print Setup... command to select a PostScript printer as the printer.
3. Select the File menu's Print command.
4. When the Print dialog box appears, select the Print to File option and click OK.
5. When the Print to File dialog box appears, enter the PostScript file's filename, path, and click OK. The conventional PostScript filename extension is *.ps.* Saving PostScript files directly to Distiller In directories saves manually moving files to the directories.
6. After creating the PostScript file, the application resumes. Note that some applications preserve Print to File selections. In this instance, clear the Print to File check box to print to a printer.

Adding New PostScript Printer Entries

When application Print dialog boxes have no Print to File check box, add a new PostScript printer entry that creates PostScript files. To add a new PostScript printer entry:

1. Open the Program Manager Main program group's Control Panel.
2. Double-click the Printers icon or select the Settings menu's Printers command to open the Printers control panel.
3. When the Printers dialog box appears, select Add. The List of Printers drop-down list appears.
4. Select any suitable PostScript printer from the List of Printers, such as the QMS-PS 810, and click Install. The selected printer appears on the Installed Printers list and connects to an unused port such as *LPT2:* or *COM3:*.

5. Select the new PostScript printer entry and click Connect.
6. When the Connect dialog box appears, scroll the Ports list down until the FILE entry appears. Select FILE and click OK. In the Printers dialog box, the PostScript printer entry in the Installed Printers list shows the printer connects to FILE.
7. Clicking Close closes the Printers dialog box. Clicking the Settings menu's Exit command returns you to the Program Manager.

The PostScript printer's print driver can now create PostScript files when it is the selected printer in the Print dialog box.

To create PostScript files:

1. Start an application and open a document.
2. Select the File menu's Print command.
3. When the Print dialog box appears, select Setup.
4. When the Print Setup dialog box appears, select the PostScript printer connected to FILE from the Printer drop-down list and click OK.
5. Click OK to close the Print Setup dialog box.
6. When the Print dialog box reappears, click OK.
7. When the Print to File dialog box appears, enter the PostScript file's filename and path, and click OK. The conventional PostScript filename extension is *.ps.* Saving PostScript files directly to Distiller In directories saves manually moving files to the directories.
8. After creating the PostScript file, the application resumes. Note that some applications preserve Print to File selections. In this instance, clear the Print to File check box to print to a printer.

APPENDIX C

Distiller PostScript Parameters

Distiller's core is a PostScript interpreter that reads and evaluates the PostScript language programs. Normally, the current Distiller job settings determine the way the interpreter handles images and other conversion aspects. It is possible, however, to override current Distiller job settings by placing Distiller job-control operators in PostScript document files before submitting them to Distiller.

PostScript programmers can use this facility, for example, to specify different document image compression settings.

CAUTION

PostScript file modification requires good PostScript language understanding. Without it, it's easy to corrupt PostScript files, preventing successful PostScript interpreter processing.

Distiller Job-Control Operators

PostScript programmers insert the `currentdistillerparams dict` and `dict setdistillerparams` operators into PostScript files to modify Distiller job settings. Programmers use `currentdistillerparams dict` to determine current job settings. Programmers use `dict setdistillerparams` to change current job settings.

`currentdistillerparams dict` returns a dictionary containing all Distiller parameters keys and current values the implementation defines. Each `currentdistillerparams` execution allocates and returns a new dictionary. The dictionary is merely a container for key-value pairs.

`dict setdistillerparams` attempts to set one or more Distiller parameters using the `dict` operand containing keys and new values. `setdistillerparams` reads dictionary information but does not retain the dictionary itself. Distiller parameters included in `dict` remain unchanged. The dictionary is merely a container for key-value pairs.

Distiller Parameter Keys and Key Values

A *key*, which is always a name object, identifies each Distiller parameter. Implementations ignore nonexistent named Distiller parameters. If specified values are the correct type, but the implementation cannot achieve them, the nearest achievable values are substituted for the requested values without emitting errors. Wrong specified type values generate typecheck errors, leaving all keys unchanged.

Table C.1 lists the Distiller parameters.

Table C.1. Distiller parameters.

Parameter (type)	*Description*
CoreDistVersion (integer; read only)	The Distiller's (not the PostScript interpreter's) internal implementation version.
DoThumbnails (boolean)	Controls thumbnail rendering.
LZWEncodePages (boolean)	Controls text and graphics LZW encoding.
DownsampleColorImages (boolean)	Controls color image downsampling.
DownsampleGrayImages (boolean)	Controls grayscale image downsampling.
DownsampleMonoImages (boolean)	Controls monochrome image downsampling.
ColorImageResolution (integer)	Minimum color image downsample resolution.
GrayImageResolution (integer)	Minimum grayscale image downsample resolution.
MonoImageResolution (integer)	Minimum monochrome image downsample resolution.
EncodeColorImages (boolean)	Controls JPEG color image compression.
EncodeGrayImages (boolean)	Controls grayscale image compression.
EncodeMonoImages (boolean)	Controls monochrome image compression.
ColorImageFilter (name)	Specifies color image compression filter. Valid names: DCTEncode or LZWEncode.
GrayImageFilter (name; not validated)	Specifies grayscale image compression filter. Valid names: DCTEncode or LZWEncode.
MonoImageFilter (name; not validated)	Specifies monochrome image compression filter. Valid names: LZWEncode, RunLengthEncode, and CCITTFaxEncode.

continues

Table C.1. continued

Parameter (type)	*Description*
`ColorImageDict` (dictionary)	JPEG or LZW encoding option dictionary. See PostScript Reference Manual, Second Edition.
`GrayImageDict` (dictionary; optional)	JPEG or LZW encoding option dictionary. See PostScript Reference Manual, Second Edition.
`MonoImageDict` (dictionary; optional)	Dictionary that specifies options for the CCITTFaxEncode monochrome image filter. See PostScript Reference Manual, Second Edition.
`NeverEmbed` (array; optional)	Specifies an array of one or more Type 1 font names to never embed in PDF files.
`AlwaysEmbed` (array; optional)	Specifies an array of one or more Type 1 font names to always embed in PDF files.
`EmbedAllFonts` (boolean)	Specifies all fonts, other than `NeverEmbed` fonts, to embed.

Distiller Parameter Example

The following is a `setdistillerparams` usage example taken from Distiller's application directory's DParemEx.Ps file:

```
%!PS-Adobe-3.0
% ...
% Prolog and PostScript here...
% ...
% Temporarily change Distiller parameters for EPS image.
% LZW encode grayscale images and turn off downsampling.
 systemdict /setdistillerparams known
{ userdict /SaveDistParams currentdistillerparams put
  << /EncodeGrayImages true
  /GrayImageFilter /LZWEncode
  /DownsampleGrayImages false
 >> setdistillerparams} if
```

```
% ...
% EPS image here ...
% ...
% Reset Distiller parameters
systemdict /setdistillerparams known
{userdict /SaveDistParams get setdistillerparams} if
% ...
% Rest of PostScript here ...
% ...
%%EOF
```

APPENDIX D

Acrobat Compression

To minimize the size of PDF documents, Distiller provides different data-compression methods for its three information classes. Those information classes are text and graphics, color and grayscale images, and bi-level (monochrome black-and-white) images.

Distiller allows the color image compression method to differ from the grayscale compression method. PDF Writer forces color image compression to use the same compression method as grayscale compression.

Selecting Job Options from the Distiller menu presents the Job Options dialog box (see Figure D.1), from which you can change the compression options.

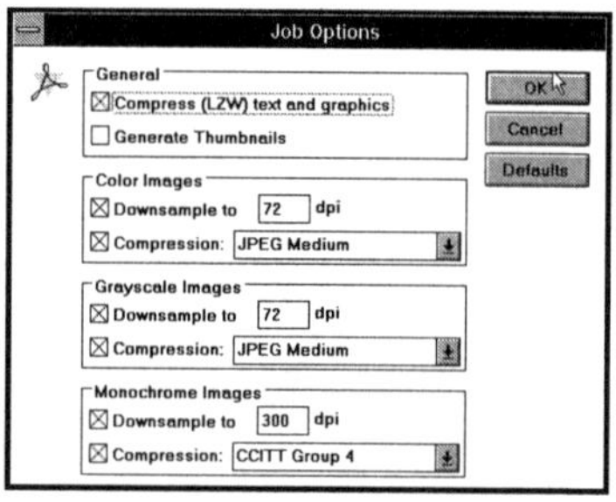

Figure D.1. Distiller's Job Options dialog box.

Compress (LZW) Text and Graphics

Other than scanned images or illustrations created from a paint or photo program, Acrobat classifies all document information as text and graphics. Acrobat text and graphics includes everything but bitmaps. The Compress (LZW) Text and Graphics option is the only available text and graphics compression option Acrobat supports. This option uses the industry standard: LZW (Lempel-Ziv-Welch) compression. LZW compression is lossless; no information is lost when the data is decompressed. Compressed text and graphics take slightly longer to display, but LZW compression typically reduces PDF file sizes significantly.

Network administrators can set up Distiller to compress text and graphics using the LZW (Lempel-Ziv-Welch) data-compression method. The LZW compression method is also an option for color and grayscale images.

Compressing Color and Grayscale Images

Color and grayscale images include scanned photographic images, scanned hand-drawn art images, and bitmap images created from screen captures, paint programs, and photo programs. Two, four, eight, 16, or 24 information bits may represent each color or grayscale image pixel. Creating a full-page color photograph's 24-bit image at 300 dpi requires more than 25MB of storage, so it is important to reduce image sizes where possible.

Distiller reduces color and grayscale image file sizes with two options (see Figures D.2, D.3, and D.4). Either or both options can be used for color images and either or both options can be used for grayscale images. The options are the following:

- *Sample to*—reduces the dots-per-inch (dpi) resolution as much as possible, but not below the specified dpi.
- *Compression*—uses either JPEG or LZW compression for 16-bit and 24-bit color images and for 8-bit grayscale images. (LZW compresses color and grayscale images with fewer bits per dot.)

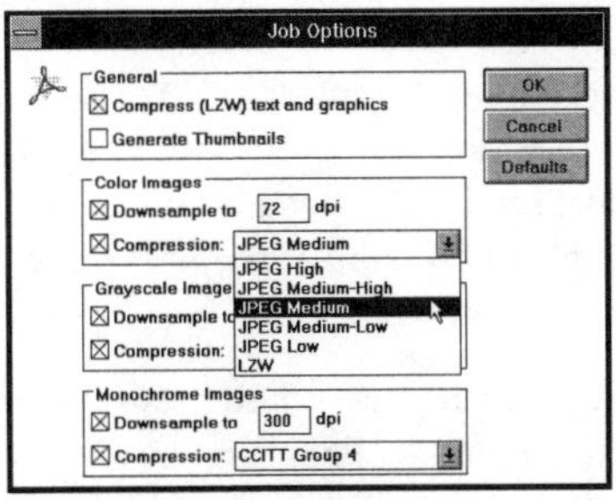

Figure D.2. Distiller Color Image options.

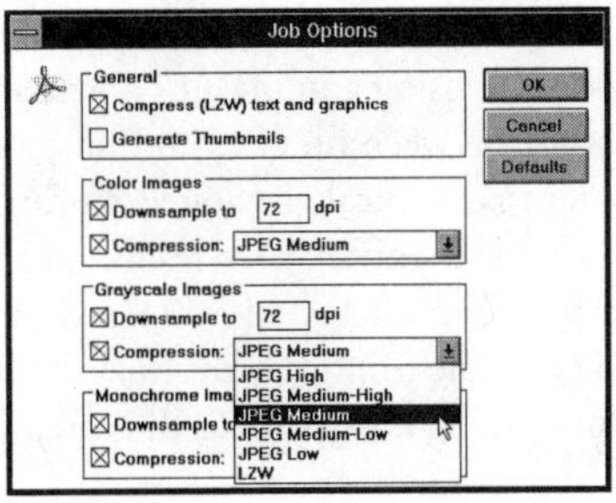

Figure D.3. Distiller Grayscale Image options.

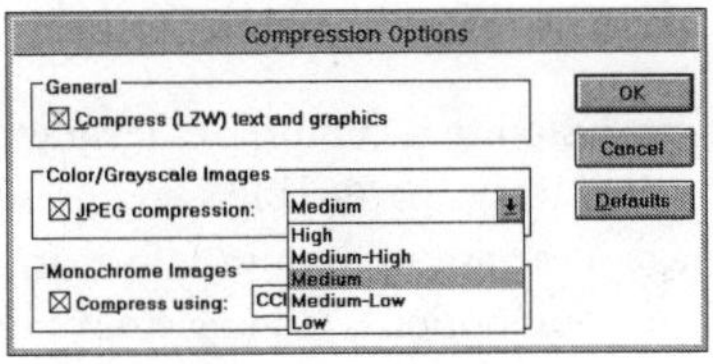

Figure D.4. PDF Writer Color/ Grayscale options.

Downsampling

Downsampling combines several image bitmap pixels to make a single larger pixel, producing smaller bitmap file sizes. Downsampling reduces image sizes with detail loss. The following list shows how images at two different resolutions downsample.

Value	150 dpi	100 dpi
2	150/2 = 75 dpi	200/2 = 100 dpi
3	150/3 = 50 dpi	200/3 = 67 dpi
4	150/4 = 37 dpi	200/4 = 50 dpi

Minimum downsampled image resolution restricts the downsampling process. Given a minimum resolution, images downsample as much as possible in whole number divisions of original resolution. For a minimum resolution of 72 dpi, 200 dpi images downsample to 100 dpi; 150 dpi images downsample to 75 dpi.

When an image cannot downsample to any resolution greater than the specified minimum, it does not downsample. For example, given a minimum resolution of 72 dpi, images at 140 dpi do not downsample.

Network administrators control downsampling by specifying the minimum resolution of downsampled images. Choosing a minimum downsampled-image resolution offers a compromise between file sizes and image quality. Preserving image resolutions greater than typical viewing and printing device resolutions is usually unnecessary. Most monitors have resolutions less than 100 dpi, and most office printers have a resolution of 300 dpi or less. For example, most 300 dpi color and grayscale printers print images at 60 lines per inch. For such printers, downsampling images to 72 dpi often produces excellent results.

JPEG Compression

JPEG compression is a lossey compression that compresses less-detailed image parts more than it compresses detailed image parts. JPEG compression attempts to reduce the size of image files with minimum information loss. Distiller provides five JPEG compression options, ranging from High (maximum compression) to Low (minimum compression). The detail loss with the Low and Medium-Low compression options is so minimal, most people cannot differentiate between the compressed images and the original. Higher compression settings give images blocky, quilted looks. A compression level applies to all document images.

Suitable JPEG compression settings depend on the image types that documents contain and the image quality they require. When you are unsure which JPEG option to select, try various compression levels. Distiller only uses JPEG compression for 8-bit grayscale images and for 16-bit and 24-bit color images. Even when JPEG is available, Distiller LZW compresses all other images.

TIP

JPEG decompression code resides in internal Reader and Exchange routines, as well as in a separate 32-bit code Dynamic Link Load module named AAJPEG.DLL. If sufficient, nonfragmented memory exists at launch, and if Windows is running in Enhanced mode, AAJPEG.DLL loads for high-performance JPEG decompression. Otherwise, the contingent internal 16-bit code performs JPEG decompression. This code provides approximately half the performance as AAJPEG.DLL. You can detect which code performs the JPEG decompression by repeatedly clicking the About dialog box's version number with the right mouse button until the JPEG information appears.

Compressing Bi-level (Monochrome Black-and-White) Images

Bi-level images include most black-and-white illustrations made by paint programs and images scanned with an image depth of 1 bit. A single bit value represents each monochrome image pixel. In addition to the bi-level image downsample option, Distiller provides four additional lossless compression options (see Figure D.5).

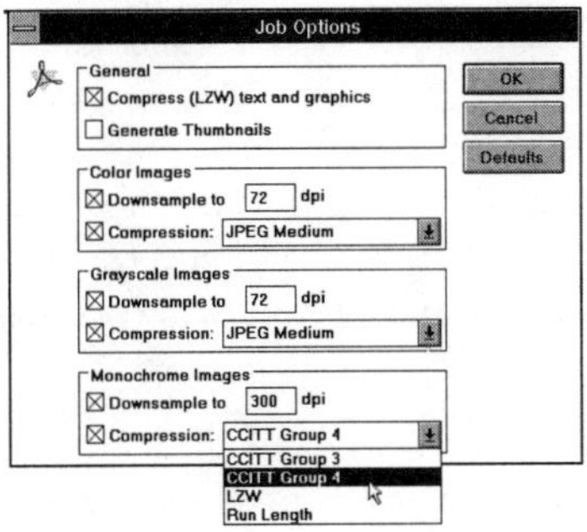

Figure D.5. Monochrome Image Compression options.

Distiller's four additional lossless compression options are the following:

CCITT Group 3—used by most FAX machines, this method compresses monochrome bitmaps one row at a time.
CCITT Group 4—a general-purpose method that produces good compression for most types of monochrome images.
LZW—produces the best compression for images that contain repeating patterns.
Run Length—produces the best results for images that contain large areas of solid white or black.

APPENDIX E

Reader and Exchange Error Codes

Two general error message types occur during Acrobat use that display an error number. The first type is general errors; the second type is for PDF document file syntax errors. The following sections list error message numbers and their meaning. Most error messages are useful only to PDF document software developers.

General Errors

Number	*Meaning*
8	The file contains a string that does not specify a length.
9	The file contains a filtered string that does not specify a decoded length.
10	The file contains a string that is shorter than its specified length.
11	The file contains data that is too complex. The resulting data structure would overflow.
12	A number is out of range.
13	A file string specifies an unknown filter.
14	This document contains an ensemble that is not supported in this version.
15	A dictionary object was expected and not found.
16	An array object was expected and not found.
17	A number object was expected and not found.
18	A boolean object was expected and not found.
19	A name object was expected and not found.
20	A string object was expected and not found.
21	A stream object was expected and not found.
22	An array was out-of-bounds.
23	A dictionary key must be a name object.
24	An error occurred in the JPEG data filter.
25	An error occurred in the CCITT fax data filter.
26	An error occurred in the LZW data filter.

Syntax Errors

Number	*Meaning*
101	The file does not begin with `%PDF-1.0`.
102	The file is missing `%%EOF`.
103	Acrobat was not able to find the `startxref` address.
104	The value of the `startxref` address is not an integer.
105	The file is missing the `xref`.
106	The `xref` header should be two integers.
107	Error reading `xref` entry.
108	Trailer dictionary start missing <<.
109	Object label badly formatted.
110	Unrecognized object name.
111	Unrecognized token type.
112	Missing endstream.
113	Unexpected endstream.
114	Unterminated string.
115	String too long.
116	Token too long.
117	Non-hex character in a hex string.
118	Unexpected token type.
119	End of image not found.
120	Unexpected end of dictionary.
121	Unexpected end of array.
122	Error reading dictionary.
123	Error reading object.
124	Expected dictionary or array.
125	Bad foreign object reference.
126	Parse stack underflow while reading object.

APPENDIX F

Reader and Exchange INI File Settings

The Windows ACROEXCH.INI file (for Acrobat Exchange) and ACROEXCH.INI file (for Acrobat Reader) are located in the windows directory. They are text files that contain associated program settings. Each file contains several sections that begin with a single line contained in brackets.

For example, the three lines of text displayed in the About Box are in a section marked `[Oem]`. Each section contains one or more lines and is separated from the next with a blank line (mainly for readability). Each line begins with a tag and an equal sign followed by Acrobat data. For example, in the `[AdobeViewer]` section, the line that specifies the startup magnification is `DefaultMag=`. The following is an annotated list that identifies each of these entries and then gives a sample of an ACROEXCH.INI file.

Section *[Oem]*

`OEM1=`	First line of text in About Acrobat Box
`OEM2=`	Second line of text in About Acrobat Box
`OEM3=`	Third line of text in About Acrobat Box

Section *[AdobeViewer]*

`IS8514`	(See the note at the end of this appendix.)
`DefaultMag=`	Default magnification. Range is 12% to 800% (do not use the "%" character).
`ShowLargeDIBS=`	Display large images or display a gray box for the image: 1 = Display image—slower display. 0 = Just display a gray box—faster display.
`GreekThreshold=`	For text that is displayed smaller than this value in pixels, just display a gray box. 0 = Never Greek text. 1.99 = Greek below this value.
`MaxApp=`	Maximize the application when first launched: 1 = Maximize application on launch. 0 = Use default size and position on launch.
`ShortMenu=`	Specifies initial menu configuration: 1 = Use Short menus. 0 = Use Full menus.
`User=`	Specifies the name to place in the Author field of PDF documents created by PDF Writer.
`PrintDriver=`	The driver of the currently selected printer for Acrobat Exchange or Reader (DO NOT CHANGE).
`PrintDevice=`	The name of the currently selected printer for Acrobat Exchange or Reader (DO NOT CHANGE).
`PrintOutput=`	The connection of the currently selected printer for Acrobat Exchange or Reader (DO NOT CHANGE).

`Chameleons=`	Specifies which font substitution is to be used: 0 = Use both serif and sans. 1 = Use sans only. 2 = Use serif only. Adobe Exchange and Reader ship with AdobeSerifMM for serif, and AdobeSansXMM for sans serif.
`SinglePage`	Single Page Mode: 1 = Scroll bar indicates position in current page. 0 = Scroll bar indicates position in document.
`ScrollDocRelative=`	Document Relative Scroll: 1 = Scroll bar moves evenly throughout document. 0 = Scroll bar moves only between top of pages.
`SkipOpenDialog=`	Specifies Open dialog at launch: 0 = Show Open dialog at launch. 1 = Skip Open dialog at launch.
`CloseAllOnOpen=`	Specifies disposition of all open files when a new open is specified: 0 = Leave open files open on new open request. 1 = Close all open files when a new open request is received.

Section *[RecentFiles]*

`File-1=`	Full path to the most-recently opened file.
`File-2=`	Full path to the next-most-recently opened file.
`File-3=`	Full path to the third-most-recently opened file.
`File-4=`	Full path to the least-recently opened file.

Section *[TextAnoColor]*

`Bkgd=`	Specifies the color of the Note background. Format is Red,Green,Blue with values between zero and 255 for each color.
`Frgd=`	Specifies the color of the Note text. Format is Red,Green,Blue with values between zero and 255 for each color.

Sample ACROEXCH.INI File

The following is an example of a valid ACROEXCH.INI file:

```
[Oem]
OEM1=Please see the file Support.pdf in the Exchange
OEM2=directory to learn about Technical Support
OEM3=options, or call 1-800-87-ADOBE.

[AdobeViewer]
IS8514=5
DefaultMag=100
ShowLargeDIBS=1
GreekThreshold=6
MaxApp=1
ShortMenu=0
User=Kenneth D Grant
PrintDriver=pscript
PrintDevice=HP LaserJet IIP PostScript
PrintOutput=LPT1:
Chameleons=0
SinglePage=1
SkipOpenDialog=1
ScrollDocRelative=1
CloseAllOnOpen=1

[RecentFiles]
File-1=C:\ACROEXCH\HELPEXCH.PDF
File-2=C:\ACROEXCH\SUPPORT.PDF
File-3=A:\TOUREXCH.PDF
File-4=A:\HLPEXCHM.PDF

[TextAnoColor]
Bkgd=255,255,255
Frgd=0,0,0
```

NOTE

The `IS8514` entry is a flag used to correct problems displaying text color on some 8514 and other display adapters. Acrobat Exchange and Reader normally test for and set this switch on launch. However, some system and display adapter combinations cannot be detected. If some color text apparently displays incorrectly, try setting this value to 105.

APPENDIX G

Reader, Exchange, and Distiller Launch Failure Numbered Error Messages

During Reader and Exchange initialization, certain errors can occur that terminate program execution before text error messages can appear. Until a language library loads, no text message can display. If errors occur before loading a language library, only a number displays.

Reader and Exchange

Exchange's ACROEXCH.EXE and Reader's ACROREAD.EXE share a common architecture. Both invoke ACROVUE.DLL, which contains the rasterizer, and AAJPEG.DLL, which contains the JPEG code for 32-bit use.

All these components are identical, regardless of the national language Acrobat uses. The only difference between, for example, German and English versions, is Exchange's AAXLIB.DLL and Reader's AARLIB.DLL language library. These country-specific libraries contain all Exchange and Reader language-dependent components, such as dialog boxes, error messages, and so on.

The following list describes these messages:

`**0001**`	Can't load language library. Perhaps the library AAXLIB.DLL or AARLIB.DLL is missing or not in the Acrobat's directory (i.e., ACROEXCH or ACROREAD).
`**0002**`	Can't initialize Acrobat file system, such as AAJPEG.DLL.
`**0003**`	Wrong language library version. Has a partial Acrobat update occurred?
`**0006**`	Not enough memory or resources (Acrobat requires 2.6MB of RAM and 30% of the available GDI resources.

PDF Writer

PDF Writer also exhibits Reader's and Exchange's modular design. The PDF Writer logic component, PDFWRITR.DRV, is language independent and loads its resource language library, PDFWLIB.DLL, before it can display any error messages in a national language.

Two messages can appear when users print to *PDF Writer on File*:

`PDF Writer 0001`	PDF Writer cannot allocate memory for data storage or cannot initialize its allocated memory. This is probably a low-memory condition indication. Close other applications, increase the Windows swap file size, or increase your workstation's RAM amount.
`PDF Writer 0002`	Cannot find or load the language library DLL. This is probably due to PDFWLIB.DLL being misplaced, missing, or damaged. Re-install PDF Writer.

Distiller

Distiller uses different failure approaches before and after loading its language library DLL. When Distiller fails to load its language DLL, DISTRES.DLL, it resorts to English messages and continues loading. While this precludes missing or miss-matched language library launch failures, subsequently displayed messages and dialog boxes are in English, not in host languages. While this is useful in averting a launch failure, users may have comprehension problems with subsequent menus, settings, and error messages.

APPENDIX H

Reader and Exchange Design Limits

Due to constraints of the host system on which Acrobat Exchange and Reader operate (such as RAM memory or available disk space), some system limits may be reached before the values shown in the following list. These values are shown only to document the limits that are imposed by the design in version 1.0.

Maximum pages per document	32,000 pages
Smallest page size	1 inch by 1 inch
Largest page size	45 inches by 45 inches
Maximum bookmarks per document	2,000 total bookmarks expanded at any time
Maximum bookmark levels	20
Maximum bookmarks selected	100
Maximum links on a page	500
Maximum notes on a page	100
Maximum open notes on a page	10
Maximum total notes open in Acrobat at one time	50
Largest content of note	4,999 characters
Largest content of bookmark	127 characters
Maximum Type 1 fonts per document	Approximately 1,000 (limited in practice by memory)
Maximum Type 3 fonts per document	Approximately 180 (limited in practice by memory)
Maximum zoom-in factor	800% (×8 scale)
Maximum zoom-out factor	12.5% (1/8 scale)
Maximum history	64 positions
Smallest horizontal size of a note	1 inch at screen resolution
Largest horizontal size of a note	6 inches at screen resolution
Default horizontal size	3 inches at screen resolution
Largest vertical size	4 inches at screen resolution
Maximum documents open at one time	10 in addition to the Help file

APPENDIX I

A Day in the Life of a Character

The path of a character from producer to PDF view is complex. Figure I.1 is meant to take some of the mystery out of the trip for the reader and font producers. The truly important point is that fonts that are supposed to be in the ISOLatin1 character set can be mistaken for decorative or symbol fonts, because the font vendors have not properly marked the font in its internal data structure. During development of Acrobat, many fonts were found marked as `FF_DONTCARE` instead of `FF_ROMAN` or `FF_DECORATIVE`. Because there is little that can be done to identify the character as belonging to the ISOLatin1 character set from the metrics of the font other than what the vendor has marked it, these fonts risk losing their "text attribute."

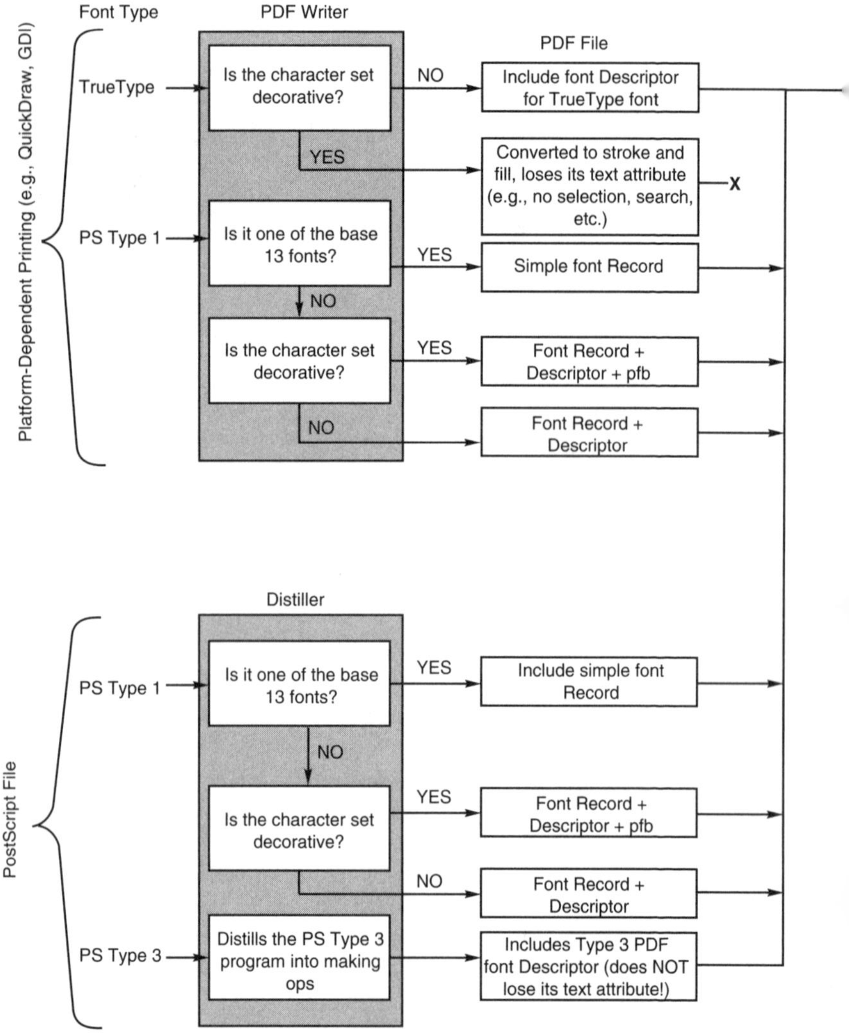

Figure I.1a.
A day in the life of a character.

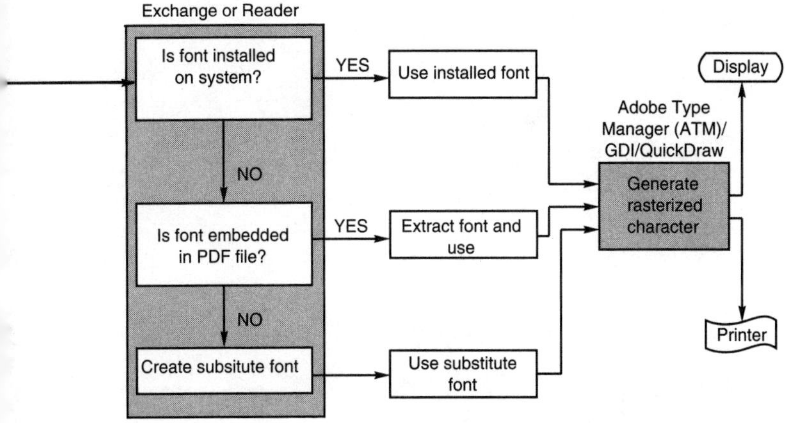

Figure I.1b.
A day in the life of a character (continued).

In the case of the PDF Writer, some additional logic was added to partially overcome this problem. In the case of a TrueType font, it is determined to be a decorative font if any of the following are true:

- The character set is not ANSI.
- The character set is ANSI, but is marked as `FF_DECORATIVE`.
- The character set is ANSI, is marked as `FF_DONTCARE`, and is on a list of known decoratives such as Zinbats, Dingbats2, Barcodes, and so on.

To repeat: Font venders *must properly mark their fonts* if they want them properly handled in Acrobat.

GLOSSARY

Achromatic Image See *Grayscale Image.*

Active Document The document in the currently selected document window.

Active Note The currently selected note. A selected closed note is a gray icon; a selected open note displays title and vertical scroll bars. A deselected closed note is a yellow icon; a deselected open note appears opaque on the document.

Active Page View The exposed portion of a PDF document page visible within an Acrobat Reader or Exchange Page View pane. Also see *Page View.*

Annotation Acrobat Reader and Exchange 1.0 have two annotation types: hypertext links and text notes.

Artifacts Visually distracting phenomena that appear in digitally reproduced images. Artifacts may appear in isolation or as repeating instances caused by collective interactions of other patterns.

Bi-level Image An image that consists of all black and white dots (or some other constant dot color pair), as opposed to colored or grayscale (achromatic) images. Also referred to as *line art* or *monochrome images.* Also see *Grayscale Image* and *Color Image.*

Black-and-White Image See *Bi-level Image.*

Bookmark A name of a destination PDF document appearing in Acrobat Reader and Exchange bookmark wind ows. Bookmarks enable you to display page view destinations by clicking a page icon to the left of the bookmark name. Bookmarks may appear in any bookmark list position, independent of their associated document destinations. Using optional indentation, a document's bookmark list can collectively be a hierarchical outline of the document's content. A bookmark may be subordinate to other bookmarks and have subordinate entries to itself. Also see *Destination.*

Bookmark Window A window contained within its document window that displays its document's bookmarks. Also see *Document Window.*

Browse Buttons The four Browse buttons reside in the tool bar. Clicking the respective buttons enables Acrobat Reader and Exchange users to go to the top of the first document page, the top of the previous document page, top of the next document page, and to the top of the last document page.

Button A tool bar icon that users click to produce a specific document window effect. Also see *Tool, Tool Bar,* and *Tool Icon.*

CCITT An abbreviation for the International Coordinating Committee for Telephony and Telegraphy standards body.

CCITT Group 3 A lossless CCITT compression standard used in facsimile and other image compression applications where the image consists of black and white dots (bilevel image). CCITT Group 3 compression compresses individual image scan lines independently of any other image scan line. A special End Of Line (EOL) bit pattern follows each compressed scan line to assist image corruption recovery. Acrobat Distiller products and PDF Writer optionally use CCITT Group 3 Compression to compress bilevel images for PDF file inclusion.

CCITT Group 4 A lossless CCITT compression standard used in facsimile and other image compression applications where the image consists of black and white dots (bilevel image). CCITT Group 4 compression compresses groups of image scan lines. A group's first scan line compresses using CCITT Group 3 compression. Successive group scan lines are compressed as differences to the previous scan line. A special End Of Line (EOL) bit pattern follows each compressed scan line group to assist image corruption recovery. CCITT Group 4 compression often achieves greater compression than CCITT Group 3 compression. Acrobat Distiller products and PDF Writer optionally use CCITT Group 4 Compression to compress bilevel images for PDF file inclusion.

Clear Removing text from a source without copying it to the Clipboard.

Clipboard A system resource that holds cut or copied objects from application windows. Clipboard objects are pasted into other application windows.

Color Image Color televisions and photographs typically display color images. Color images consist of dots described as having hue (a base pure color such as from a rainbow), saturation (the amount of pure white color necessary to dilute the hue to form a derivative pastel matching the dot's color tint), and intensity (gives viewers a dot brightness sensation). Acrobat represents colors as combinations of red, green, and blue, or as combinations of cyan, magenta, yellow, and black. Also, see *Bi-level Image* and *Grayscale Image.*

Completion Meter An informational windoid that temporarily overlays the pane Number box and Magnification box during potentially extended operations such as creating note files, rotating pages, cropping pages, and saving files. The windoid displays a horizontal white bar which increases in length to indicate the completed activity percentage.

Copying Copying text from a source to the Clipboard.

Cropping A user-controlled process to facilitate page viewing by inhibiting Acrobat Reader and Exchange from displaying unnecessary top, bottom, and side document margins in the Page View pane. The individually set margin croppings apply to user-selected page ranges within individual PDF documents. PDF files contain the viewing crop specifications. Original page margins still appear on printed pages, but information within the cropped areas does not print.

Current Document The document in the currently selected window.

Current Page View See *Active Page View.*

Cutting Removing text from a source and copying it to the Clipboard.

Death March A sustained endeavor, such as marathon programming or writing, popular in an increasing number of professional circles. In Silicon Valley, death marches have recently achieved newly dimensioned artistic levels. Also, see *Ides.*

Destination A Link button's or bookmark's associated page view. PDF destination specifications indicate whether Acrobat should do any of the following:

1. Display a specified page point in the Page View pane's upper-left corner at a specified magnification level
2. Fit the entire destination page to the Page View pane at whatever magnification is required to achieve the fit
3. Fit the page width to the Page View pane starting at a specified point from the page top at whatever magnification is required to achieve the fit
4. Fit the height of the page to the Page View pane at whatever magnification is required to achieve the fit
5. Fit a rectangle to the Page View pane at whatever magnification is required to achieve the fit

A displayed destination's magnification level may be different than the destination's specified magnification level following Page View pane resizing. Acrobat Exchange 1.0 only creates the fifth type of destination specification. Acrobat Reader and Exchange 1.0 support all types of destination specification for Page Viewing. Also see *Page View.*

Device Space The Cartesian coordinate system Adobe products use to represent the display device dot space for devices such as monitors and printers. A device space is device dependent. Also see *User Space.*

Document Pane See *Page View Pane*, *Document View*, and *Active Page View.*

Document Window The Acrobat Reader and Exchange programs create a document window for every open PDF document. The document window contains other windows, windoids, and two panes: an Overview pane and a Page View pane. An Overview pane exposes either a bookmark or thumbnail window. A Page View pane exposes a Page View window. The document window's Width Control position determines the Overview and Page View pane horizontal size within the document window.

Downsample A technique that reduces image resolution before image compression commences to reduce compressed image sizes. As an example, one technique collectively replaces a group of dot values with its average. Dots averaged together reside in non-overlapping squares. A single averaged value replaces the collectively averaged dot values, reducing image dot counts, resolution, and PDF compressed image sizes. A downsample factor of 2 reduces both horizontal and vertical image resolutions by a factor of 4, replacing four dot values in all 2-dot-by-2-dot image areas with their area's average dot value. Similarly, a downsample factor of 3 reduces both horizontal and vertical image resolutions by a factor of 9, replacing nine dot values in all 3-dot-by-3-dot image areas with their area's average value. Downsampling typically forfeits image detail, but yields significantly smaller compressed images. Acrobat Distiller products enable you to specify the minimum image resolution acceptable and use the maximum downsample factor that does not violate your selected minimum resolution specification or exceed your selected downsample integer value specification.

Downsampling The process of reducing image size using a downsample technique. Also, see *Downsample.*

Full Menus Acrobat Exchange menus that provide various functions unavailable from the Short menus. Full menus also provide the tool bar with the Note and Link tools. Also see *Short Menus.*

Grayscale Image Black-and-white televisions and photographs typically display grayscale images. Grayscale images consist of black dots, white dots, and gray dots varying in shade between black and white. Grayscale images—also called *achromatic images* because they lack color—differ from bilevel images that consist of individual dots that are either black or white (or some other dot color pair), but not gray. Also see *Bi-level Image* and *Color Image.*

Greek Level The Greek level specifies the pixel height text characters must have for Acrobat Reader or Exchange to render them as characters. Otherwise, Acrobat Reader or Exchange displays the text as gray lines. Users typically set the Greek level to the point value (72 points equals one inch) at which text becomes illegible on their screen. Greeking accelerates rendering activities. Because Acrobat products assume a screen has 72 dots per inch, users actually set how high characters need to be (in pixels) to escape render-oblivion. Type 3 fonts do not Greek.

Greeking Applying a Greek level to accelerate rendering activities.

HPPCL Hewlett-Packard Printer Control Language.

Hypertext Link See *Link.*

Ides Et tu Brute? Also, see *Death March.*

Image Resolution The number of dots per inch (dpi) in an image. Typical dpi values are 300, 200, 150, 100, and 75. An image's individual dots all have the same format, which varies from image to image.

Incremental Save An Acrobat Exchange technique that records PDF file change activity such as bookmark changes, hypertext link changes, croppings, page rotations, page additions, page deletions, and so on, in PDF files. Acrobat Exchange flags existing PDF page specifications as changed and appends updated information to PDF file ends. This minimizes save activity duration, permitting changed PDF file save durations to reflect change extents rather than PDF file sizes. It also preserves previous information, potentially permitting future extensions to perform subsequent undo operations if necessary.

In-Place PDF Save See *Incremental Save.*

Invisible Link Button A hypertext Link button that is not visible unless Acrobat Exchange users click the Link tool.

JPEG An abbreviation for the Joint Photographic Experts Group. This association creates image compression standards.

JPEG Compression The Joint Photographic Expert Group creates JPEG compression standards. Depending on the specific method used, JPEG compression may be lossless or lossey. Lossey techniques can vary in their decompressed image fidelity, depending on the source image content.

Large Image An imbedded document image requiring considerable memory and computational resources for Acrobat Reader and Exchange to display. Also see *Preferences.*

Line Art Image See *Bi-level Image.*

Link An association between a user-specified document page rectangular area (Link button) and an associated destination. Clicking a Link button produces the associated page view in the Page View pane. Also see *Link Button* and *Destination.*

Link Button A rectangular area on a document page that you can click to produce an associated page view.

Link Tool A tool on the Acrobat Exchange tool bar that permits PDF hypertext link creation or editing. The Link tool does not appear unless Full Menus are available.

Locked File A Macintosh file that cannot be erased or modified until it is unlocked.

Lossless Compression Compression that allows decompression without data loss. The decompressed data is identical to the original data.

Lossey Compression Compression that allows data loss to achieve increased compression. Decompressing the compressed data produces data that approximates the original data and is still presumably useful, although it is not identical to the original data.

LZW Compression A widely used lossless compression technique named after Abraham Lempel, Jacob Ziv, and Terry Welch. United States patent 4,558,302 assigns LZW compression rights to the UNISYS Corporation.

Magnification Box An Acrobat Reader and Exchange status bar windoid that indicates the active page view's magnification factor. Clicking the Magnification box and holding down the mouse button produces a predefined magnification level menu. Quickly clicking the Magnification box and releasing the mouse button produces a dialog box that enables you to enter a new Page View pane magnification level.

Magnification Level A specification designating how much a page view expands or contracts line segments. Acrobat products assume a 72 dpi screen resolution. A 200 percent magnification level means line segments are twice as long as they would be at a 100 percent magnification level. Square areas are therefore four times bigger at a 200 percent magnification level. The magnification must be greater than or equal to 12 percent (100 percent divided by 8 and discarding the decimal) and be less than or equal to 800 percent (100 percent multiplied by 8). Also see *Greek Level.*

Monochrome Image See *Black-and-White Image, Bi-level Image,* and *Grayscale Image.*

Navigate Acrobat Reader and Exchange have a navigation stack that records up to 100 sequential active page views. The Navigation buttons enable you to navigate (redisplay) these views sequentially.

Navigation Buttons The Navigation buttons reside in the Acrobat Reader and Exchange tool bar. Clicking the respective buttons enables Acrobat Reader and Exchange users to display previous page views in the Page View pane or to return to subsequent views that appeared in the Page View pane before backstepping one or more page views using a Navigation button.

Navigation Stack An Acrobat Reader and Exchange feature that records up to 100 active page views. You may sequentially navigate backward or forward in the stack to review earlier user-generated active page views.

Note A PDF document text annotation created by an Acrobat Exchange user. The note can be iconized or left expanded, in which case it overlays the PDF document as an opaque text annotation similar to a sticky note. The

Acrobat Reader and Exchange Find Next Note function enables you to jump to pages containing notes. The Acrobat Reader and Exchange Create Note File function transforms a document's notes into a single PDF file for copying and printing activities.

Overview Pane The area within an Acrobat Reader or Exchange document window that reveals a portion of either the thumbnail window or bookmark window. Also see *Document Window.*

Page A single document page.

Page Number Box An Acrobat Reader and Exchange status bar windoid that indicates the active page view's page number. Clicking the Page Number box produces a dialog box that enables you to enter a new page number.

Page Number Windoid A small windoid that appears in the Page View pane and displays a page number while the vertical scroll bar is dragged.

Page View A PDF document page portion that can appear within an Acrobat Reader or Exchange Page View pane. A page view's specification comprises a document page, page location, and magnification level. The magnification level may not be achievable, depending on whether you resized the Page View pane using the Pane Width control. Also see *Destination.*

Page View Pane The area within an Acrobat Reader or Exchange document window that displays page views. Also see *Document Window.*

Pane Acrobat Reader and Exchange document windows contain two panes: the Overview pane and the Page View pane. The Pane Width control enables you to resize the two panes within the document window. Also see *Document Window.*

Pane Width Control An Acrobat Reader and Exchange windoid you can drag to resize Overview and Page View panes within the document window. Also see *Document Window.*

Paste The act of copying Clipboard objects into application windows.

PDF An abbreviation for Portable Document Format. PDF is the Acrobat Product family native file format and extends Adobe's PostScript technology. Addison-Wesley's Portable Document Reference Manual (ISBN 0-201-62628-8) documents the PDF file format.

PFM PostScript Font Metrics.

Point A typography distance measure. There are 72 points per inch. Acrobat products assume a 72 dpi screen resolution.

Preferences Acrobat Reader and Exchange users can specify a default magnification level, a text Greek level, whether to display large (complex) images, and whether to maximize the Acrobat Reader and Exchange application window at application initialization. The preference settings apply to all subsequently viewed documents until changed.

Read-Only File A PC file whose directory attribute does not allow the file's erasure or modification.

Resolution The number of dots per inch (dpi). Also see *Image Resolution.*

Run Length Compression A general compression technique that compresses repeated instances of identical data elements, such as individual characters, as a data element repeat count followed by the element. Acrobat Distiller products and PDF Writer optionally use a Run Length Compression implementation to compress bilevel images for PDF file inclusion. Adobe documents its specific Run Length Compression algorithm in Addison-Wesley's Portable Document Reference Manual (ISBN 0-201-62628-8).

Sans Serif Literally, without a serif.

Serif Small decorative character flourishes extending out from main character strokes.

Short Menus Acrobat Exchange menus that do not provide various functions available from the Full Menus and do not provide the tool bar with the Note and Link tools. Also see *Full Menus.*

Status Bar The Acrobat Reader and Exchange status bar contains the Pane Width control, Page Number box, and Magnification box.

String In Acrobat string searching, a consecutive text character sequence without imbedded spaces.

Text Greek Level See *Greek Level.*

Text String See *String.*

Thumbnail A miniature graphical representation of a document page. The thumbnail for the active document visible in the Page View pane also has a view box that you can resize and drag to other positions on the same page by using the Hand tool. To move the view box to another thumbnail, simply click the desired page's thumbnail and the view box moves to the thumbnail, appearing centered over the click point if possible. To resize a view box, drag the view box's resizing handle to a different location. When a thumbnail is completely gray, the thumbnail does not exist.

Tool A transformed mouse pointer that provides you with application capabilities. You can transform the mouse pointer into a tool by clicking the tool's icon in the tool bar. The transformed icon allows specific manipulations of, or operations on, the active page view. Also see *Button*, *Tool Bar*, and *Tool Icon.*

Tool Bar A collection of Tool and Button icons Acrobat Reader and Exchange users may optionally display in their application window. In Acrobat Exchange, the number of tool bar icons depends on whether Full or Short Menus are available. Also see *Button*, *Tool*, and *Tool Icon.*

Tool Icon A tool bar icon that you can click to produce a dialog box or transform the pointer into a tool shape when the pointer moves over a document window. Also see *Button*, *Tool*, and *Tool Icon.*

User Space The Cartesian coordinate system Adobe products use internally to device-independently represent document pages. By default, the origin is at a page's lower-left corner and coordinate values are expressed as point values, where 72 points equal one inch. Adobe products present page images by transforming user-space renderings to device-space renderings. Also see *Device Space.*

View Box A rectangular outline superimposed on the thumbnail for the page visible in the Page View pane. The view box has the same rectangular proportions as the Page View pane and outlines what page portion is visible in the Page View pane. View box resizings typically result in document magnification level changes, but preserve the Page View pane's rectangular proportions. Clicking another thumbnail moves the view box to the new thumbnail and the corresponding view box page area appears in the Page View pane.

View Box Sizing Handle View boxes have a sizing handle in their lower-right corner. You can drag the sizing handle to display the page at different magnification levels. View box resizings preserve the Page View pane's rectangular proportions.

View Stack See *Navigation Stack.*

Visible Link Button A Link button that is always visible to Acrobat Reader and Exchange users. Also see *Link Button.*

Windoid A small informational window. Some windoids are selectable and provide menus, dialog boxes, or other functions.

Zoom Tools Two tool bar tools that enable you to change the current magnification level. Also see *Zoom In Tool* and *Zoom Out Tool.*

Zoom In Tool A tool bar tool that enables Acrobat Reader and Exchange users to increase the Page View's magnification level by a factor of 2, up to 800 percent. Also see *Zoom Out Tool.*

Zoom Out Tool A tool bar tool that enables Acrobat Reader and Exchange users to decrease the Page View's magnification level by a factor of 2, down to 12 percent. Also see *Zoom In Tool.*

INDEX

E

R

T

U–V

W

X–Z

Book ISBN 0-672-30393-0

Installing the Floppy Disk

The companion disk contains sample exercise files, a help file, and other documents for Adobe Acrobat. Additionally, two chapters from this book have been distilled and placed on the disk. To install the software to your hard drive, follow these steps:

1. From Windows File Manager or Program Manager, choose **F**ile **R**un from the menu.
2. Type *<drive>*INSTALL and press Enter. *<drive>* is the letter of the drive that contains the installation disk. For example, if the disk is in drive B:, type B:INSTALL and press Enter.

Follow the on-screen instructions in the installation program. The files will be installed in a directory named \AAH unless you change this name during the installation program.